A Nuclear-Weapon-Free Zone in the Middle East

A Nuclear-Weapon-Free Zone in the Middle East

PROBLEMS AND PROSPECTS

Mahmoud Karem

Contributions in Military Studies, Number 65

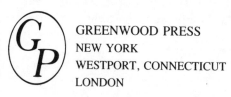

GREENWOOD PRESS
NEW YORK
WESTPORT, CONNECTICUT
LONDON

Library of Congress Cataloging-in-Publication Data

Karem, Mahmoud, 1949–
  A nuclear-weapon-free zone in the Middle East.

  (Contributions in military studies, ISSN 0883–6884 ;
no. 65)
  Bibliography: p.
  Includes index.
  1. Nuclear-weapon-free zones—Middle East.
I. Title. II. Series.
JX1974.M627K37   1988   327.1'74'0956   87–8531
  ISBN 0–313–25628–4 (lib. bdg. : alk. paper)

British Library Cataloguing in Publication Data is available.

Library of Congress Catalog Card Number: 87–8531
ISBN: 0–313–25628–4
ISSN: 0883–6884

First published in 1988

Greenwood Press, Inc.
88 Post Road West, Westport, Connecticut 06881

Printed in the United States of America

The paper used in this book complies with the
Permanent Paper Standard issued by the National
Information Standards Organization (Z39.48–1984).

10 9 8 7 6 5 4 3 2 1

For Yasmina, Myral, and Reem

CONTENTS

TABLES AND FIGURES

TABLES

FIGURES

PREFACE

Can the proliferation of nuclear weapons in the Middle East be prevented? How might a nuclear-weapon-free zone (NWFZ) regime for the Middle East be created? To address these questions, this study offers a viable alternative towards the prevention of nuclear weapons proliferation into the Middle East by implementing United Nations' resolutions (1974–1985) on the establishment of a NWFZ in the Middle East. It is a salient fact for students of this region that the Middle East is indeed one of the most sensitive regions, witnessing almost continuous military conflict and political upheaval. This study demonstrates that the explicit integration of nuclear weapons into the overall military capabilities and national security policies of the countries within this region could lead to devastating international effects. It offers the NWFZ approach as a viable solution as well as showing how it could be implemented and how to overcome diplomatic obstacles facing this proposal.

In chapter 2 a historical preview and examination of previous international NWFZ initiatives are presented in order to identify applicable patterns useful for the establishment of a ŃWFZ in the Middle East. Four military denuclearization treaties including Tlatelolco are thus carefully considered. Chapter 3 discusses all NWFZ proposals that have not culminated in a treaty. In both

chapters an analytic study is presented of why and how these treaties and initiatives have unfolded or failed. The positions of the United States and the Soviet
Union for instance are examined. This study then makes the task carried out in
the last chapter instructive, since it denotes an important margin of success
already working in favor of a NWFZ in the Middle East.

Chapter 4 explores the complications that arise in the Middle East as a result
of the dangers of nuclear weapon proliferation. It presents the reader with a
survey of Israel's nuclear capabilities, which is basic to an understanding of the
current policy predicaments and prospects for a NWFZ. It offers ten basic reasons
for Israel's categorization as the dominant nuclear threshold country in the Middle
East.

Chapter 5 traces historically and chronologically the United Nations' resolutions on the establishment of a NWFZ in the Middle East from 1974 until 1985.
It attempts to answer questions such as the following: What prompted Egypt and
Iran to propose a NWFZ in the Middle East in 1974 and why? Why did Israel
join the consensus in 1980 on the Egyptian draft in the General Assembly? How
did Anwar Sadat's trip to Jerusalem in 1977 and the Iranian revolution in 1979
affect this NWFZ proposal?

Finally, policy prescriptions, recommendations, and options on how to invigorate the proposal are presented in the last chapter. This chapter extracts useful
lessons from other NWFZ proposals and tailors them to the Middle East NWFZ
case. It also recommends what should not be emulated and why, using action-
oriented policy language.

The methodology used throughout relies on content analysis by studying UN
documentary evidence from 1974 until today. This study also relies on elite and
specialized interviewing in presenting the case under study. It offers various
tables describing nuclear- and conventional-weapon status in Europe and signatory status of states in the Middle East vis-à-vis nuclear prevention treaties.

ACKNOWLEDGMENTS

At the outset I would like to present my special gratitude to Dr. James B. Holderman, President of the University of South Carolina, to whom I owe an enormous debt. Dr. Holderman's infinite wisdom, sterling leadership, and cherished friendship have guided me and this enterprise from its preliminary form to its final stage. Caroline Holderman deserves my family's heartfelt thanks for making our sojourn in South Carolina a memorable one. And a thank-you to Robert Woody for a lifetime of friendship.

In 1981 Dr. Holderman offered me the prestigious Fellowship of the Byrnes International Center. Since then I have proudly become a member of the South Carolina community. Many people have helped in this respect, and I owe them all a special thanks. These include Chris and Mary Vlahoplus, Frank and Kay Borkowski, Saadallah Hallaba, my dear friend Steven Beckham, Mac Bennett, Mike Genau, Carol Danner, Mac Rood, Paul Kattenburg, Don Puchala, Lee J. Hevener, Mark Cichock, and the entire staff of the Byrnes International Center.

I will forever be grateful to those who helped in my difficult transition from the world of policy-making to that of academia. I emerge from this rich experience with a better understanding and analytic conceptualization of the world in which we live. Dr. James Kuhlman has been throughout my mentor and friend. His genuine assistance and infinite expertise will be always valued. I am especially grateful to Dr. Charles Kegley for his impeccable help. He has inspired me with stimulating and valuable reviews. My thanks also go to Dr. Roger Coate and Dr. Ken Stein, Director of the Carter Center in Atlanta, Georgia.

I especially want to thank Marsha Curles for her invaluable and patient assistance in diligently typing and retyping numerous versions. My gratitude also goes to Sandra Hall, Sallie Buice, Patti Concklin, Ann Lesch, and Professor J. Myerson of the Department of English.

In my own Foreign Service I wish to acknowledge Deputy Prime Minister and Minister of Foreign Affairs of Egypt Dr. Ahmed Esmat Abdel Meguid, a salient figure viewed with distinction in international diplomatic circles. I proudly consider myself his student. My thanks also go to Dr. Boutros Ghali, Minister of State for Foreign Affairs. My special gratitude is extended to Ambassador Dr. Ashraf Ghorbal, who assisted me throughout with his profound knowledge, experience, and search for excellence. I owe a special gratitude to Ambassador Dr. Nabil Elaraby for inspiring the topic. The genesis of this proposal has been spurred by his boundless enthusiasm and energy. I deeply thank Ambassador Saad El Farrargy in Geneva for having relentlessly opened doors for me since 1973. I am also indebted to Ambassador Dr. Mohamed Shaker in Vienna for his professional and academic advice. My gratitude goes to Ambassadors Omran El Shafei, Dr. Ahmed Osman, Abdel Haleem Badawi, Amre Moussa, and Hussein Mesharrafa for their endless support. For his support I wish also to acknowledge Dr. Osama El Baz, Director of the Political Bureau for the President of Egypt. Counsellor Gehad Madi and Guigno Pulcini (Bob), document officer in the Mission of Egypt to the United Nations in New York, deserve my special gratitude for their efficient and diligent help.

I wish also to pay tribute to the memory of Minister Mohamed Riad.

Finally, I wish to recognize my parents and sister. Needless to state, ultimate responsibility for the content of this study remains my own; the content does not necessarily represent the opinion of the above mentioned or any other institution with which this author is affiliated.

A Nuclear-Weapon-Free Zone in the Middle East

1

INTRODUCTION

Nuclear weapons pose the greatest danger to mankind and to the survival
of civilization. It is essential to halt and reverse the nuclear arms race in
all its aspects in order to avert the danger of war involving nuclear weapons. The ultimate goal in this context is the complete elimination of nuclear
weapons.

Program of Action, Final Document of the Tenth Special Session of the
United Nations' General Assembly Devoted to Disarmament, 1978

STATEMENT OF THE PROBLEM

The convictions underlying this goal are compelling. Since the nuclear catastrophe of Hiroshima and Nagasaki in 1945, the international community has understandably channeled its efforts to reduce the dangers posed by such lethal
devices to the very survival of mankind. However, strategies for reducing the
danger of nuclear catastrophe invite a plethora of approaches. Regional measures
designed to halt and reverse the proliferation of nuclear weapons to specific-

regions such as the establishment of nuclear-weapon-free zones (NWFZs) have been one of the most salient and practical of such alternatives. The concept of NWFZs has been, over the years, repeatedly emphasized by the United Nations.

Suffice it to quote here some of these examples of support. On December 11, 1975, the General Assembly of the United Nations, during its thirtieth session, adopted resolution 3472B, which stated, ''Nuclear weapon free zones constitute one of the most effective means for preventing the proliferation, both horizontal and vertical, of nuclear weapons and for contributing to the elimination of the danger of a nuclear holocaust.'' Year after year the United Nations continued to approve a wealth of resolutions on the subject of NWFZs, as they related to different regional and geographic zones. In 1975, for example, the United Nations invited twenty-one governmental experts to conduct what was called a Comprehensive Study on the Question of NWFZs in All Its Aspects (Resolution 3261F, December 9, 1974). Seven years later the General Assembly decided to review and supplement the 1975 study (Resolution 37/99F of December 13, 1982). These efforts are ongoing. An important event took place in 1978 when the General Assembly adopted by consensus a document following the first-ever United Nations Special Session devoted to disarmament. This document stressed the significance of NWFZs as a disarmament measure and proclaimed that the ''process of establishing such zones in different parts of the world should be encouraged with the ultimate objective of achieving a world entirely free of nuclear weapons'' (Resolution S-10/2). Principal proposals have sought to cover Latin America, Africa, South Asia, the Pacific, the Indian Ocean, Central Europe, the Balkans, the Adriatic, the Mediterranean, Northern Europe, and the Middle East. The most recent proposals include a Soviet initiative to establish a nuclear-weapon-free zone, or corridor, covering no less than 311 square miles wide astride the borders of Eastern and Western Europe, including large areas of West and East Germany and Czechoslovakia.

In the wake of the European disarmament conference convened in Stockholm in January 1984, the *Washington Post* (December 31, 1983) reported that West Germany's iconoclastic Green Party along with the Social Democrats and the West German public at large have shown growing support for such a NWFZ. Additionally, the late Swedish Prime Minister Olof Palme launched a similar initiative to create a NWFZ in Central Europe that would ultimately ''free Europe from tactical nuclear weapons'' (Power, 1983a). On the other hand, two NATO allies, Greece and Turkey, have agreed to conduct regional discussions with nonaligned Yugoslavia and two Warsaw Pact members, Bulgaria and Romania, to explore the possibilities of establishing a NWFZ in the Balkans (*Washington Post,* December 31, 1983).

Varied recommendations have also been put forward by spokespeople representing a variety of political perspectives; different peace movements, leftist socialist Western parties, and noted international figures such as George Kennan (1982) are all included among the diverse advocates of this approach to the control of nuclear weapons. Now the support for a NWFZ in Europe stems from different national organizations such as the British Campaign for Nuclear Disarmament, Green Peace, the Greater London Council with its policy to "Make London Nuclear Free," the Norweigan *Nei til Atomvapen* (No to Nuclear Weapons), with similar affiliates in Denmark, Belgium, Netherland, and France's Le Comité pour le Désarmament Nucléaire en France (CODENE).

In the United States, on the other hand, the Committee for a Sane Nuclear Policy (SANE), Ground Zero, the Freeze campaign (Nuclear Weapon Freeze Campaign Clearinghouse) and the National Conference of Catholic Bishops are all examples of growing support for the concept of establishing NWFZs around the world (Stockholm International Peace Research Institute, 1983:108–25). Sydney Bailey (United Nations, 1983c:8–18), a former member of the working party that prepared the Church of England's statement of position with regard to nuclear weapons, entitled *The Church and the Bomb,* explained how the Church supported the concept of establishing NWFZs around the globe:

> The Treaty of Tlatelolco for keeping Latin America free of nuclear weapons gave a fillip to efforts for creating zones free of nuclear testing, nuclear weapons and the disposal of nuclear waste. The Pacific Conference of Churches, for example, condemned the use of the Pacific for "the testing, storage, and transportation of nuclear weapons and weapons delivery systems." The Catholic Justice and Peace of Hiroshima Conference and the Japan Catholic Justice and Peace Commission began collecting signatures for a petition against the dumping of nuclear waste in the Pacific. The National Christian Council of Japan protested when the United States battleship New Jersey, reportedly carrying nuclear missiles, entered Japanese ports. The All-African Conference of Churches supported the idea that the Indian Ocean should be declared a zone of peace, and the Christian Conference of Asia urged the UN to declare the Indian and the Pacific Oceans as nuclear-free zones. (9)

Sentiments of support for the concept of NWFZs have also been expressed within the Soviet Union and among different East European member countries. A noted Soviet scholar explains:

> The establishment of NWFZs is one of the measures promoting detente, disarmament, non-proliferation of nuclear weapons, and peaceful utilization of nuclear energy. The enhancement of regional security being the initial goal of NWFZs, they nonetheless should be regarded as an element of the general efforts being made to curb the arms race and to strengthen international security. This is the primary reason why the Soviet Union has always come out in support of nuclear free zones. (Shchyolokova, 1981:104)

These previous international initiatives have been directed mainly towards two types of intraregional and extraregional dangers. First, intraregionally, a number of states in different regions of the world have or could have the ability to develop a nuclear weapon within a relatively short period. Should this occur, new threats could be posed to the security of states that at present remain free from nuclear weapons. The threat emerging from such a development could easily escalate into a perilous nuclear arms race, adding new sources for the outbreak of a nuclear war to the existing dangers inherent in prevailing volatile international situations.

On the other hand, extraregional nuclear powers may decide to include certain members from different regions in their overall security schemes, targeting actors outside their own immediate locale and thereby expanding the number of potential victims for a subsequent nuclear attack. Within a nuclear weapons context this could mean either the use or threat of use of nuclear weapons against certain states in a noncontiguous region, or the deployment of nuclear weapons in the territories of states in such regions. Both these intra- and/or extraregional measures could lead to increasing superpower rivalry, political polarization, and instability. However one assesses such a development, it is difficult to accept the view that worldwide security can be enhanced by increasing the number of actors targeted by nuclear weapons or by increasing the number of hands with the capacity to initiate a nuclear strike.

This study, accordingly, proceeds from the premise that today's world is governed increasingly by the emergence of conditions of complex interdependence, in which relations among nations have grown denser and have become more closely entwined. Our present-day world security is symbiotically related to, if not totally dependent on, regional security. Sporadic regional disputes, under such conditions, can more readily spill over to and incorporate those nuclear powers external to the region, culminating in a catastrophic nuclear confrontation. International security is therefore interrelated with, if not dependent on, regional security. Thus, the establishment of nuclear-weapon-free zones is assured of making a positive contribution to the nonproliferation of nuclear weapons and to the limitation of the nuclear arms race. Although the primary purpose of a nuclear-weapon-free zone is to ''enhance national and regional security, it should also be seen as a part of the process of averting nuclear weapon proliferation, of arresting the nuclear arms race, and of diminishing the danger of nuclear war. Thus with this process the interests of all states are involved'' (United Nations, 1976b:31).

It is for such reasons that regional initiatives such as the establishment of NWFZs have gained increasing international recognition. Some may view such regional initiatives within the framework of disarmament measures proper. Others may see it as complementary machinery to other collateral measures of disarmament, such as the nonproliferation of nuclear weapons, confidence building measures, and the development of peaceful uses of nuclear energy. Whatever our net assessment the concept of nuclear-weapon-free zones provides a potentially useful instrument for reducing the possibilities of a nuclear war, diminishing the risks of a nuclear arms race, and consolidating universal efforts to strengthen international peace and security in an interdependent but precarious global environment.

DEFINITION OF TERMS

A definition of a NWFZ is generally considered minimally to contain reference to a prohibition of the importation, deployment, or development of any nuclear weapons by all members inside the zone (Clarke and Grieco, 1976:161).

A UN resolution (3472 of the thirtieth General Assembly, adopted on January 21, 1976) adopted the following definition of the concept of a NWFZ:

> A NWFZ shall, as a general rule, be deemed to be any zone, recognized as such by the General Assembly of the United Nations, which any group of states, in the free exercise of their sovereignty, has established by virtue of a treaty or convention whereby:
>
> (a) The statute of total absence of nuclear weapons to which the zone shall be subject, including the procedure for the delimitation of the zone is defined;
>
> (b) An international system of verification and control is established to guarantee compliance with the obligations deriving from that statute. (Also see Special Report of the Conference of the Committee of Disarmament CCD/476 of August 28, 1975.)

The term *nuclear-weapon-free zones,* however, is used here instead of other widely circulated terms, including *nuclear-free zones.* The reasons are twofold. First the objective of this study centers on the dangers of the proliferation of nuclear weapons and the risks of destruction associated with them. The emphasis, then, should be on the term *nuclear weapons,* and this study highlights the means towards averting its catastrophic dangers. That is precisely why this study differentiates between two distinct approaches, namely, the establishment of NWFZs versus the concept of zones of peace. While the emphasis in the former is on the word *weapons, zone of peace,* at present implies only a nuclear-weapon-free status. A United Nations study asserts:

> In the present context reference may be made to the concept of zones of peace. In proposals put forward up to now for countries of the zone . . . the case of zone encompassing a part of the high seas raises difficult problems beyond those of naval and air presence in the narrow sense, notably the question of transit and the presence of nuclear-missile carrying submarines which, while not primarily related to the regional situation, may all the same be perceived as affecting it. (United Nations, 1981c:46)

William Epstein makes a similar distinction. He defines peace zones as considerably broader than NWFZs but includes the latter concept. In an attempt to clarify this difference between a NWFZ and the call for establishing a zone of peace in the Indian Ocean, Epstein (1975b:25–35) explains:

> It should be noted that a peace zone does not seek to establish a NWFZ in the territories of the littoral states of the Indian Ocean but rather is aimed at the

denuclearization and further demilitarization of the Indian Ocean itself and of naval bases in the ocean. Therefore it differs fundamentally from other NWFZ proposals in that it is intended to apply to the high seas rather than to bordering states. (35)

As we note the difference, reference must be made to the fact that both disarmament measures are conducive to the realization of the objectives of general and complete disarmament and in this sense are complementary.

Second, there is a great deal of ambiguity associated with the concept nuclear-free zones. Related to this issue is the fact that many states are presently aspiring to the peaceful use of nuclear energy. Hence, while these states exert efforts to prevent the proliferation of nuclear weapons into their territories, they do not seek to inhibit utilization of nuclear energy for peaceful purposes. Therefore, the use of the phrase nuclear-weapon-free zone is more in tune with the objectives of this study. The distinction between peaceful and nonpeaceful nuclear power is entirely at the heart of the proliferation question. A growing number of developing countries argue in favor of the beneficial potentialities and the desirability of promoting the peaceful application of nuclear energy. On the other hand, there are those who caution against weapons-proliferation risks posed by the diffusion of nuclear technology, in particular with respect to the enrichment of uranium in the isotope 235 and the reprocessing of irradiated fuel that may be used to bring about a nuclear explosion. Charles Kegley and Eugene Wittkopf (1981:293–94) have observed that "at current and projected rates of production the amount of such material created will eventually make available enough weapons grade material to place within reach the construction of tens of thousands of nuclear weapons every year."

These fears concerning the dissemination of nuclear know-how has prompted the international community to initiate measures to preclude such developments. As a result the Non-Proliferation Treaty was signed in 1968. Concomitantly the role of the International Atomic Energy Agency (IAEA) was enhanced, particularly in the field of safeguard applications to all nuclear materials, equipment, and facilities. On the national level additional measures were taken to reduce the risk of nuclear weapon proliferation. In the United States the Ford and Carter administrations, for instance, placed a moratorium on the development of the breeder reactor. In an article published in 1979 in *Foreign Policy,* Lewis Dunn (quoted in Kegley and Wittkopf, 1981:293) demonstrated how the Carter administration called for an international treaty "to defer all commercial reprocessing of spent fuel, to renounce the recycling of plutonium as fuel, and to slow commercialization of the fast breeder reactor." Anxieties of this sort spurred the conduction of an international study, launched by the United States in 1977, and called the International Nuclear Fuel Cycle Evaluation (INFCE), to study the margin of energy security and proliferation dangers associated with nuclear decision-making.

LIMITATIONS

We must be guarded and cautious with our expectations. The concept of NWFZs is only a means towards an ultimate end. A noted Norwegian scholar states:

> A NWFZ constitutes no panacea. It cannot substitute for a national security policy, nor can it remove the threat of nuclear war. It is primarily a confidence building measure which needs to be tailored to the specific circumstances of the region in question and to the links which exist between that region and broader systems of international order. It is a possible instrument in support of broader purposes. (Johan J. Holst, 1983:5)

This present study does not, therefore, portray the concept of NWFZs as the sole method to eliminate nuclear weapons. What it does attempt is to show how NWFZs can help in controlling them. The issue of control versus elimination is indeed cardinal, since a great number of policymakers and scholars believe in the viability of a world stabilized by the deterrence of nuclear weapons. In a book published by Harvard five noted professors and a doctoral candidate associated with Harvard—Albert Carnesale, Paul Doty, Stanley Hoffman, Samuel P. Huntington, Joseph S. Nye, Jr., and Scott Sagan—concluded that a world without nuclear weapons is "a fictional utopia" and that living with nuclear weapons "is our only hope" (The Harvard Study Group, 1983).

However, we should not despair. Jonathan Schell (1984) in a follow-up article from his latest book, *The Fate of the Earth*, responded by stating that these weapons are built for war "but their significance greatly transcends war and all its causes and outcomes. They grew out of history yet they threaten to end history. They were made by men, yet they threaten to annihilate man" (3). Some analysts view NWFZs as creating an unstable and dangerous situation by rendering the region victim of its own power distribution, especially when some members enjoy superiority in the conventional field. NWFZs, they argue, could render some states helpless before an overwhelming conventional use of force (The Round Table, 1981:302). In a study entitled *No Substitute for Peace* (1983:24), published by the Centre for Conflict Studies of the University of New Brunswick, Canada, ten international scholars cautioned against the value of the NWFZ approach. Such an approach could be a tactic of political warfare. These scholars, including a dissident Soviet professor, warned against Project Ploughshares aimed at declaring Canada a NWFZ. They stated: "For Canada's NWFZ status would not in the end provide any guarantee that her cities would escape attack. By tilting the strategic balance sharply in favor of the USSR, a Canada that declared itself a NWFZ on these terms would destabilize the situation and make war far more likely."

Abba Eban (1983), Israel's former Minister of Foreign Affairs, delivers a similar assertion:

A region declaring itself "nuclear-free" is very similar to a nation declaring itself "neutral." If some neutral countries have not been invaded, such as Switzerland in the two world wars, it would be hard to prove that this was because of their declared neutrality. It was either because there was no stategic necessity for a belligerent to violate their frontiers, or because the neutrality was useful to the belligerents or because they had prudently modelled themselves on the example of the porcupine; bristly animals are not a tempting target for a wrestling match. Nuclear-free zones, like neutrality, are a unilateral hope, not a prescription for safety. (321)

Despite these criticisms[1] the concept of NWFZs should be enhanced, since it offers together with other arms control and disarmament initiatives the foundation for avoiding the dangers of nuclear war, nuclear weapon proliferation and the threat to world peace and security. NWFZs present an incremental but important achievement towards international stability. If the realization today of the goals of general and complete disarmament seems unattainable in a world governed by political tension, mistrust, and lack of negotiations on fundamental arms control and arms reduction measures, NWFZs can lay the groundwork by increasing confidence for a better future.

It is these beliefs and propositions that motivate the present study and that serve to rationalize its execution. However, rather than attempting to put these propositions themselves to a direct empirical test, this investigation will seek instead to probe their applicability to one of the most turbulent and troubled regions in the world, the Middle East. This is justifiable because these propositions are not amenable to direct testing, inasmuch as they entail predictions that only time can verify or falsify. They are nonetheless supported by a substantial body of deductive theory and have gained the stature of conventional wisdom. Few scholars or statesmen question the belief that the creation of nuclear-weapon-free zones can contribute meaningfully to the prospects for arms control and international security.

A NWFZ IN THE MIDDLE EAST: A RATIONALE

The objective of this investigation is to explore the means through which the Middle East might be freed from the use, development, introduction, proliferation, and stationing of nuclear weapons within its regional territory. It is a salient fact for students of this region of the world that the Middle East is indeed one of the most sensitive regions, witnessing almost continuous military conflict and political upheaval. The Middle East today, as ever, is exposed to the pressures exerted by strong political commitments, geographic proximity between bloc territories, the concentration of forces, and superpower involvement—all of which create a setting conducive to a large-scale military confrontation. A deeply rooted conflict of historical claims and national interests between the Arabs and the Israelis renders the Middle East acutely contentious. At the core of that conflict a host of critical issues remain unresolved. These include, *inter alia,*

Israel's occupation of Arab territories, the building of Israeli settlements, the Arab quest for the realization of a homeland for the Palestinian people, Israel's invasion of Lebanon, and the final status of the holy city of Jerusalem. On the other hand, Israel's quest for security and recognition remains unresolved. Indeed, the Middle East suffers from rising tensions, the absence of direct channels of communication (Holsti, 1972) between the Arabs and the Israelis, strong perceptions and misperceptions, defiant and erratic leaderships, and vacillating and seemingly irrepressible religious feuds.

The explicit integration of nuclear weapons into the overall military capabilities and national security policies of the countries within this region could therefore lead to devastating international effects. This gives credence to the hypothesis that asserts that the more the Middle East swings towards a nuclear arms race, the less are the chances of regional and international security. It is indisputable that the introduction of nuclear weapons in this tense and unstable setting could add a new element of danger and fear into the already volatile configurations of the Arab-Israeli conflict and would, as such, be detrimental to both Arab and Israeli national interests in the long run. Thus, the possibilities of drawing both superpowers into a course of direct confrontation could become exceedingly high. The Middle East, accordingly, is appropriately considered by both superpowers a high-stakes region, where peace and security are already in jeopardy. This serves to underscore the cardinal topicality of the establishment of a NWFZ in the Middle East in order to prevent such detrimental international repercussions.

The establishment of a NWFZ in the Middle East should also serve to protect the indigenous populations from the scourge of a financially costly nuclear arms race. Such a measure could add one very important safeguard against the advent of escalated tensions resulting from the stationing of nuclear weapons by any third party into such a proposed denuclearized zone. This could enhance the possibility of zonal states remaining outside the immediate dangers of a nuclear weapons exchange, as well as protecting them from a policy of nuclear blackmail by such powers.

A NWFZ in the Middle East could eventually assist in the process of establishing a new environment of confidence building between the countries of the Middle East. With the reduction of nuclear ambiguity and the removal of the necessity of forging a strategy for unilateral deterrence, the foundation could be created for the establishment of legal commitments to maintain the Middle East free of nuclear weapons. The proposed letter and spirit of confidence that would emerge between and among states of the region could possibly spill over to other fields and eventually help in restoring political tranquility.

Within this new environment the prospects for bringing the conventional arms race under control, possibly accompanied by a reversal would be enhanced. The expenditures released as a result of this process could be reallocated and directed towards social, economic, and cultural development of the peoples of this region. The zone might also pave the way for an incentive, within a regional framework, for enhanced international cooperation in the field of peaceful uses of nuclear energy, with added dividends for regional welfare.

GOAL CLARIFICATION

One of the primary purposes of the present analysis, therefore, will be to explore the preconditions necessary for the establishment of a zone free of nuclear weapons in the Middle East. In so doing it will be appropriate to identify, list, and examine previous other initiatives to establish similar NWFZs that have taken place elsewhere. This historical preview (chapters 2 and 3) will help, first, to underscore the importance of this disarmament initiative and second, to identify possible patterns applicable to the Middle East. A comparative review of past efforts can reveal the different characteristics of each region that should be taken into consideration before an effort is made to generalize these lessons to the Middle East setting.

This assumes that the conditions under which NWFZs might be viable and could strengthen international security are bound to differ from one geographic region to another (United Nations, 1976b:31). For example, while the Treaty for the Prohibition of Nuclear Weapons in Latin America (Treaty of Tlatelolco) offers valuable insights, it cannot be transplanted in its entirety to the Middle East because of functional and regional differences. However, by exploring this Latin American NWFZ initiative, lessons may be drawn and useful patterns can be identified. In this way, the obstacles and facilitative factors involved in the creation of NWFZs can be detected, and these in turn can then be employed to inform the discussion about the establishment of a NWFZ in the Middle East. We can, in short, be instructed by previous successes—and failures. Otherwise, we're left with approaching the problem without the benefit of previous experience. Alternately stated, in order to discover the best route to reach our goal— the creation of a nuclear-weapons-free zone in the Middle East—we can profit by discovering where others have already been and what characterized their development in other regional contexts. (Chapters 2 and 3 will elucidate the comparative case-study approach that will be utilized for this purpose.)

Hence, in order to achieve a conceptual apparatus for the dangers of nuclear weapons proliferation in the Middle East, the possibilities of transforming the Arab-Israeli conventional-weapons arms race into the nuclear stage need to be explored (Rosen, 1975:157). An overview will be given of Israel as a nuclear threshold country or "pariah state" (Harkavy, 1981:135) in the Middle East. Israel is focused on in chapter 4 because of its advanced nuclear program, and because most international observers and experts believe that Israel "is apt to remain for some time the dominant military and nuclear state in the Middle East" (Power, 1983a:269).

The study of Israel's nuclear capabilities serves as a reminder to all interested parties that the dangers of nuclear proliferation in the Middle East has already begun. This gives credence to the purpose of this study insofar as it attempts to rally international efforts to implement, without any delay, the United Nations' resolution on establishing a NWFZ in the Middle East.

Having done the groundwork by exploring the necessary preconditions that should make a proposal for a NWFZ in the Middle East urgently needed and warranted, an attempt will be made to discuss in historical detail the origins of this initiative. In so doing, both the genesis of this 1974 UN proposal to establish a NWFZ in the Middle East and its evolution in international diplomatic circles will be explored (chapter 5). This entails a historical analysis of the Arab and Israeli positions as they have unfolded to the present. Critical emphasis will also be placed on the roles played by the United States and the Soviet Union throughout the process of deliberating on and negotiating the text of this General Assembly resolution.

Finally, in the conclusion, policy recommendations will be put forth by discussing the modalities and procedures for the establishment of such a zone. Useful lessons learned from other NWFZ proposals will be emulated in the Middle East case.

In sum, what this project seeks to accomplish is threefold: first, to highlight the dangers posed by the proliferation of nuclear weapons in the Middle East and the possible linkage of such proliferation to the volatile configurations of the Arab-Israeli conflict; second, to demonstrate the necessity of implementing a denuclearized Middle East; and finally, to advance policy recommendations on how to achieve this objective.

The hope is that the reader will emerge with a better understanding of the exigency of the study under consideration. Today in the Middle East, time is running short and patience is wearing thin. Academics, policymakers, and members of the international community must uphold their obligation to warn in advance and prevent the Middle East and the world from sinking into an apocalyptic demise. Any effort, collective or unilateral, incremental or abrupt, should be exerted in order to prevent the dangers of nuclear weapon proliferation from spreading into the region and to dismiss the possibilities of the transformation of conventional disputes in the Middle East into an annihilative nuclear exchange.

NOTE

1. In a research study conducted by the Proliferation Reform Project of Cambridge, Massachusetts, opposition to the NWFZ approach was found to be based mainly on two assumptions: first, that NWFZs do not mean anything if a nuclear war breaks out and second, that a NWFZ may grant the potential adversary "comparative advantages in the over-all power equation." For further details see Reino Paasilinna, "Why We Should Advocate Nuclear Free Zones As Part of a Non-Proliferation Regime," *Perspectives on Proliferation*, vol. 1 (August 1985), p. 13.

2

NWFZs: A HISTORICAL COMPARATIVE SURVEY

This and the following chapter intend to survey, historically, previous international initiatives to establish NWFZs around the globe. The rationale for this survey is to draw lessons, to identify applicable patterns for the Middle East, and to effectuate a comparative synopsis. Since the primary purpose of this study centers on a NWFZ in the Middle East, chapters 2 and 3 intend to present only a brief summary of other proposals dealing with establishing NWFZs in other parts of the world, so as to inform the treatment that follows. In chapter 2 we will study only NWFZs that already have been established by international treaties. These constitute the following: (1) Antarctica, outer space, and the sea bed; (2) the model of the Treaty for the Prohibition of Nuclear Weapons in Latin America (Tlatelolco), which could be emulated in the Middle East as the sole existing, legally binding international instrument establishing a NWFZ in a densely populated region.[1]

The difference, among other differences, between both categories lies in their concept of applicability. While the first applies to noninhabited regions, the second is the only one applicable, as of yet, to a densely populated region; namely, the Latin American continent.

The purpose of this chapter is to present a descriptive and analytical overview of those NWFZ proposals in order to identify lessons that could inform the discussion of the modalities of establishing a Middle East NWFZ. The task, then, in the final chapter would be to segregate those elements embodied in these NWFZ proposals that are applicable to the Middle East setting from those that are not suitable. Let us consider each category of initiative in succession.

MILITARY DENUCLEARIZATION TREATIES: THE ZONAL APPROACH

Since the advent of the nuclear age, three international treaties have been signed and ratified prohibiting the introduction or stationing of nuclear weapons in uninhabited zones. They are the Antarctic Treaty, the Outer Space Treaty, and the Seabed Treaty. Each of these agreements will be examined in turn.

The Antarctic Treaty

Signed on December 1, 1959, by twelve states[2] the Antarctic Treaty provides in Article 1 that Antarctica shall be used exclusively for peaceful purposes. This led to the internationalization and demilitarization of the continent. Thus, conflicting claims of sovereignty were replaced by a common approach of cooperative exploration. The treaty helped in the avoidance of future conflicts over the possible discovery of exploitable economic resources such as oil and in the avoidance of penetration by any one state for military purposes.

The significant achievement of the treaty is in its elevation of the concept of multilateral scientific quest through cooperation, which would precede any military aspirations by any party. In 1958, a joint scientific effort by twelve states to conduct studies of the earth and its cosmic environment led to the International Geophysical year. On May of the same year the United States proposed to convene a special conference to discuss the future of the Antarctic continent. The conference was convened and culminated in the 1959 treaty signed by all twelve sponsoring nations.

The treaty stipulated in Article 1 that Antarctica was to be free of military bases, fortifications, military maneuvers, as well as the testing of any type of weapon. Article 5 prohibited nuclear explosions and any type of radioactive waste disposal in Antarctica.

The treaty also emphasized the right of the contracting parties for the conduction of scientific research. Article 9, in fact, carried this norm a step further by calling for multilateral cooperation among the parties to exchange scientific information and to consult on matters of common interest pertaining to Antarctica. The parties, according to the treaty, have the right to designate observers to conduct inspection measures in Antarctica, including stations, equipment, and ships and aircraft at discharge or embarkation stations. The treaty gave its members the right to carry out aerial inspections.

In 1964, for example, the United States invoked this right of inspection, which involved six stations operated by Argentina, Chile, France, New Zealand, the United Kingdom, and the USSR. Similar inspections took place in 1971, 1975, 1977, and in 1980. All American inspection visits included Soviet stations (Arms Control and Disarmament Agency, 1982:21). These inspections teams were able to verify compliance on each occasion. Each report rendered similar findings: "No military activities, armaments, or prohibited nuclear activities were observed, and all scientific programs were in accord with previously published plans. The observed activities at each station were in compliance with the provisions and spirit of the Antarctic treaty" (Arms Control and Disarmament Agency, 1982:21).

Hence, what the treaty established was a successful and enforceable multilateral verification mechanism. Two ingredients contributed to the success of this zone: first, the fact that the region was not previously occupied and hence no alterations of military balance structures were voiced and secondly, the consent of both superpowers yielding to on-site inspections.

It is important to mention some ongoing efforts exerted mainly by Malaysia and aimed mainly at reviewing the Antarctic Treaty. During the Thirty-ninth General Assembly (1985) Malaysia introduced an item on the agenda entitled the "Question of Antarctica." Malaysia requested a United Nations' administration of the zone, since the future of Antarctica was decided on by only a limited number of contracting parties. The treaty, according to Malaysia, lacked universality and was allowing a limited number of nations, with certain technical capabilities, to reach Antarctica and exploit its mineral wealth.

Others believed that such requests were invalid, since the treaty realized the objectives of the United Nations' Charter and maintained the zone free of nuclear weapons and military rivalry. Whatever our net assessment is, it remains true that the Antarctic Treaty established a successful regime and was the first treaty ever to militarily denuclearize a zone.

The Treaty on Principles Governing the Activities of States in the Exploration and Use of Outer Space, Including the Moon and Other Celestial Bodies

Modeled after the Antarctic Treaty, this treaty entered into force on October 10, 1967. In 1982 the total number of signatory states was ninety-one, while the total number of states depositing instruments of ratification reached sixty-one (United Nations, 1983b:37–44).[3] Like its predecessor, the agreement and cooperation of both superpowers was vital to its conclusion. The phases of negotiations demonstrated how an amelioration in their positions was cardinal for the successful conclusion of that treaty.

For example, on September 22, 1960, when U.S. President Dwight D. Eisenhower proposed to the UN General Assembly the application of the principles of the Antarctic Treaty to outer space including celestial bodies, the Soviet position then was to link any such initiatives to the dismantling of U.S. military bases and the withdrawal of medium- and short-range nuclear missiles from Europe. This was rejected by the Western powers on the grounds that such Soviet "linkage" policy "would upset the military balance and weaken the security of the West." The Soviets dropped their demand at the conclusion of the Partial Test Ban Treaty in 1963 (Arms Control and Disarmament Agency, 1982:48).

During the early phases of the UN's eighteenth General Assembly on September 19, 1963, the Soviet Foreign Minister, Andrei Gromyko, called for the necessity of preventing the proliferation of the nuclear arms race into outer space and suggested reaching an agreement between both superpowers to ban the placement in orbit of any "objects equipped with nuclear weapons or other weapons of mass destruction" (United Nations, 1976a:176). On September 20, 1963, U.S. President John F. Kennedy took the same podium to welcome this Soviet proposal and to call for detailed negotiations (Arms Control and Disarmament Agency, 1982:49). These forthcoming Soviet and American positions were conducive to the General Assembly's approval by acclamation of resolution 1884 (18th, 1963), which offered the genesis of the treaty.

Later two draft proposals were presented by the United States and the Soviet Union in June 1966. By September of the same year all differences were resolved, and a unified text of the treaty was agreed upon. On December 19, 1966, the UN General Assembly approved by acclamation a General Assembly resolution commending the treaty (Arms Control and Disarmament Agency, 1982:49).

Two lessons may be drawn from the discussion thus far. First, the successful coordination and high-level cooperation between the governments of the United States and the Soviet Union remained a crucial prerequisite for the successful conclusion of this disarmament treaty, which led to space exploration in cooperative spirit (as shown by the United States and USSR's jointly planned and manned space enterprises). Second, the successful use of the United Nations' negotiation forum and channels of communications should be noted. Undoubtedly the United Nations facilitated the implementation of the agreement and helped give it the momentum necessary to propel it to a successful conclusion (that is, the interests and pressures of nonaffected nations played an important positive role).

As far as the relevant provisions of this treaty that are applicable to the concept of NWFZs, two articles apply. Article 4 of the treaty restricts militarily affiliated measures in two respects. First, the treaty prohibits the placement of nuclear weapons or any other weapons of mass destruction in orbit around the earth, on the moon or any other celestial body, or in outer space (United Nations, 1983b:32). Second, it limits the use of the moon and other celestial bodies to exclusively peaceful purposes. This article in fact prohibited the "establishment of military bases, installations and fortifications, the testing of any type of weapons and the conduct of military maneuvers on celestial bodies" (United Nations, 1983b:32).

The provision in Article 12 stipulates that "All stations, equipments and space vehicles on the moon and other celestial bodies shall be open to representatives of other states parties to the treaty on the basis of reciprocity.'' This provision is an important measure of verification in order to check adherence to the letter of the treaty. Even though few states possess the technology to reach the moon and outer space, the fact remains that both superpowers have respectively agreed to yield to inspection measures conducted on their stations by the other party. This in itself is a significant step forward, broadening considerably the jurisdictional boundaries of the regime that was established to allow yet new states to enter into the constraints it imposes.

As such, it can be hypothesized that the involvement of "outside" parties, and the support by them of negotiations between the superpowers, is fundamental to the prospects for the eventual broadening of the regime to regulate the conduct of additional states. It should also be noted, as an additional hypothesis, that the fact that this "zone" in space had not yet been decisively exploited by one state to the disadvantage of the rest was a significant factor in its formalization.

But the verdict on this—or any disarmament treaty—is never conclusive. Threats to the continuation of a regime always exist. *U.S. News and World Report* (January 16, 1984:16) reported that one of the areas targeted for an increase in the 1985 U.S. military budget is outer space. The main new items include a permanent space station—with possible military use—initially costing $200 million, with an eventual price tag of $8 billion. Testifying before the U.S. Congress on March 1, 1984, Under Secretary of Defense Richard D. DeLaner observed that such space-age defense mechanisms may cost at least $26 billion through 1989, and that the shield employing laser or particle beams may be used to destroy intercontinental nuclear missiles targeted against U.S. territories (*The State*, March 2, 1984). On the other hand, a group of American scientists, members of the Union of Concerned Scientists, issued a report (published by United Press International, March 22, 1984) on the subject in which they criticized these plans as costing too much and upsetting arms control with the Soviet Union. A different group of scientists, however, known as the Federation of American Scientists has contended that the Soviets were building a "high power radar installation" in central Siberia intended for use with an "advanced Soviet satellite-Killer system" (*The State*, March 12, 1984).

Recently on December 15, 1983, the UN General Assembly, in an effort to curb the process of escalation, adopted resolution 38/70, which reiterated its request for the establishment of a working group in the Geneva-based Committee on Disarmament in order to discuss a Soviet draft Treaty on the Prohibition of the Use of Force in Outer Space and from Space against the Earth. The United States, however, voted against that proposal. Noteworthy of mention at this juncture is the work conducted by the UN Conferences on the Exploration and Peaceful Uses of Outer Space. However, most of these proposals remain in the deliberative form. The only tangible accomplishment in this field remains embodied in the 1967 Outer Space Treaty.

The Treaty on the Prohibition of the Emplacement of Nuclear Weapons and Other Weapons of Mass Destruction on the Seabed, the Ocean Floor, and in the Subsoil Thereof

Like the two previous treaties, the Seabed Treaty extended the concept of nuclear-weapon-free zones to incorporate the seabed, ocean floor, and the subsoil thereof underlying the high seas beyond the limits of national jurisdiction, thereby preserving all of them exclusively for peaceful purposes. The treaty thus prohibited the extension of technological and oceanographic strife, especially among the most advanced maritime powers, to the seabed where valuable untapped resources remain on the ocean floor.

Throughout the course of negotiations both the United States and the Soviet Union presented draft proposals.[4] Even though both drafts differed on crucial items, these differences were resolved through private U.S.-USSR consultations following deliberations of the United States with its allies (Arms Control and Disarmament Agency, 1982:100; United Nations, 1976b:18). The United Nations' Eighteen National Disarmament Committee (ENDC) based in Geneva played a cardinal role in facilitating the achievement of this agreement. The lessons to be learned here are threefold: First, it is important to create a worldwide climate of reduced military tension in order to enhance the prospects of international arms control and disarmament agreements; linkage, therefore, between arms control negotiations and a stable international climate appears crucial. Conversely stated, periods of high international tension are not conducive to the achievement of agreements to control the level of armaments. For example, U.S. President Ronald Reagan stated in 1980 that sitting down with the Soviets to negotiate arms limitation measures alone is not sufficient: "You discuss the whole attitude as to whether we're going to have a world at peace or whether we're simply going to talk about weaponry and not bring up these other subjects" (cited in Kegley and Wittkopf, 1981:414). Henry A. Kissinger articulated the same ideas, contending that

> an unconstrained arms race in the strategic field will, over any period of time, be inconsistent with improved political relationships. Sustaining the build-up requires exhortations by both sides that in time may prove incompatible with restrained international conduct. The very fact of a strategic arms race has a high potential for feeding attitudes of hostility and suspicion on both sides, transforming the fears of those who demand more weapons into self-fulfilling prophecies. (Cited in Kegley and Wittkopf, 1981:415)

This linkage, however, need not operate as a rigid prerequisite for conducting arms reduction talks, since the dangers inherent in this reasoning could incite states into obstinacy and thereby increase national military buildups, which could eventually escalate into still further arms buildups. This vicious circle, as argued by a noted group known as the Independent Commission on Disarmament and Security Issues, must be broken. They stated:

It is important not to construct, as a matter of deliberate policy, linkages between particular negotiations to limit specific aspects of the arms race and international behavior in general. The task of diplomacy is to split and subdivide conflicts rather than generalize and aggregate them. Linking them into broader issues tends to limit rather than broaden the scope for diplomatic manoeuvre. (United Nations, 1983a:140)

Hence, the wedding of arms reduction, arms limitations, or disarmaments negotiations to the existence of constructive political will and broader political accommodations may facilitate progress. The two appear to interact and symbiotically move together. To this effect the same independent Commission asserted that both components

> can aid one another in facilitating progress, but neither can proceed very far without progress in the other. Just as arms negotiations would fail in the absence of political accommodations, so too would movements toward more cooperative political and economic relations come to an end without concurrent progress towards stabilization and reduction in the size of armed forces. (United Nations, 1983a:10)

Second, cooperation and agreement of both superpowers appear to be vital. And third, the United Nations system of deliberations and negotiations again appeared to present a viable forum for concluding such an international agreement. Apart from its traditional goal as a peacemaker, the United Nations assumed the role of peacekeeper by entrusting the Security Council according to Article 3 section 4 of the treaty to act as a mechanism for dispute settlement, a forum to whom state parties may refer for "negotiations, enquiry, mediation, conciliation, arbitration, judicial settlement, or other peaceful means of their own choice," in accordance with Article 33, Chapter 6 of the Charter of the United Nations. To illustrate the points just raised, it is useful to briefly trace one of the most controversial items of the treaty as it has unfolded, namely, the principle of verification.

The Soviet Union, for example, using the provisions for verification incorporated in the Outer Space Treaty (Article 12), proposed that all installations and structures be open to inspection, provided that reciprocal rights were granted (Arms Control and Disarmament Agency, 1982:100). The United States rejected this provision on the grounds that within the Outer Space Treaty, claims to the national jurisdiction of the moon were absent. The United States contended that "provision suitable for the moon would not be adequate for the seabed, where many claims of national jurisdiction already existed and many kinds of activities were in progress or possible" (Arms Control and Disarmament Agency, 1982:100). Additional intractable problems arose with regard to the definition of territorial waters. Some countries, as is known, presented claims of up to 200 miles. On the other hand, coastal states were concerned about protecting their legal rights of jurisdiction. Smaller parties expressed their doubt, based on their lack of ownership of advanced verification means. Violations, they contended, would pass unnoticed. Hence, these parties called for a broader role of the United Nations (United Nations, 1976a:179–87).

Nevertheless, through "constructive ambiguity" an agreement was reached. The treaty adopted the 12–mile limit to define the seabed area and called on smaller states to ask for the assistance of any other states in case of an alleged violation (Articles 2 and 3 section 5). Article 2 provided that the "seabed zone" was to be determined by the provisions of the 1958 Convention on the Territorial Sea and the Contiguous Zone was balanced by Article 4 to become, in reality, a disclaimer that none of the treaty's provisions would be interpreted as supporting or prejudicing national positions vis-à-vis law-of-the-sea issues (Arms Control and Disarmament Agency, 1982:101). The treaty thus demonstrated how agreement coupled with political will could enhance international cooperation.

One other principal provision of this treaty related to the concept of NWFZs is contained in Article 1, which stipulates that parties to the Treaty have pledged not

> to emplant or emplace on the seabed and the ocean floor and in the subsoil thereof ... any nuclear weapons or any other types of weapons of mass destruction, as well as structures, launching installations or any other facilities specifically designed for storing, testing or using such weapons.

The treaty entered into force on May 18, 1972, and at present is signed by eighty-eight states and ratified by seventy members (United Nations, 1983b:170–76).

These existing treaties denuclearizing Antarctica, outer space, and the seabed hold promise for the future of agreements to limit the spread of nuclear weapons and point to how such achievements might be realized. They also reflect the emergence of international security regimes that until today and despite various challenges, have proved successful. Political scientist Susan Strange (1984:306–13) argued that such regimes rested not on the observance of provisions of the UN Charter but rather on the balance of power between the superpowers. She added, "In order to maintain that balance, each has engaged in a continuing and escalating accumulation of weapons and has found it necessary periodically to assert its dominance in particular frontier areas" (309).

It is important to observe at this juncture that despite these challenges the regimes[5] of Antarctica, outer space, and the seabed have survived and are still upheld by both superpowers. Even when American-Soviet relations are governed by contestation rather than by detente (Kegley and Wittkopf, 1982:64–69), the respect for those regimes was and still is evident. At present no attempt has been reported on either the American or Soviet's part to place nuclear weapons in Antarctica, outer space, or on the seabed. This is a manifestation of success direly needed in a world governed by crisis and tension.

This study will now turn to the examination of the Latin American NWFZ, which represents the only application of the NWFZ approach to a densely populated region. The historical and textual analysis of Tlatelolco is warranted, since it offers valuable lessons and ideas that could be transferred to the Middle East. It must always be remembered that Israel, for instance, has insisted repeatedly on applying the Tlatelolco model to the Middle East NWFZ.

THE TREATY FOR THE PROHIBITION OF NUCLEAR WEAPONS IN LATIN AMERICA (TLATELOLCO)

Unlike some of the examples previously mentioned, the Tlatelolco Treaty marked the first—and heretofore the only—application of the principle of establishing a NWFZ in a densely inhabited region. Tlatelolco elevated some of the principles enshrined in a General Assembly resolution (1911–18 of November 27, 1963) and translated them in an internationally legally binding instrument, (that is, *pacta sunt servanda*). This achievement provides an example and a classic model of how a UN resolution can pave the way for the realization of such a political accomplishment through the international treaty process.

The provisions of Tlatelolco also marked the first agreement to establish a system of international control under the auspices of a permanent supervisory organ (the Agency for the Prohibition of Nuclear Weapons in Latin America, or OPANAL) coupled with a system of inspection to deal with alleged violations. No other region has yet devised such an effective system of control and verification, under a permanent and supervisory organ. This system also incorporated full application of safeguards by the International Atomic Energy Agency (Statement released by the Secretary General of the United Nations, SG/SM/661 of February 13, 1967).

A UN study on "All Aspects of Regional Disarmament" describes the regional and global purposes of the treaty:

> On the one hand, the treaty was designed to strengthen peace and security in the region, to avert the possibility of a regional nuclear weapons race, and to protect the parties against possible nuclear attacks. At the same time, it was conceived as a significant contribution towards preventing the proliferation of nuclear weapons and as an important factor for general and complete disarmament. (United Nations, 1981c:6)

As a result of the Cuban missile crisis of 1962, it became evident to Latin American countries how easily their own part of the globe could be drawn into the complexities of the ongoing nuclear arms race between the two superpowers and into the heat of the cold war. Following the Cuban missile crisis in April 1963, the presidents of five Latin American countries—Bolivia, Brazil, Chile, Ecuador, and Mexico—announced their readiness to sign a multilateral agreement that would establish a NWFZ. In 1963 this declaration received the support of the UN General Assembly, and under the leadership of Mexico the Latin American countries decided to establish the Preparatory Commission for the Denuclearization of Latin America (COPREDAL) with the specific task of preparing a draft treaty. On February 16, 1967, the treaty was finalized and signed at Tlatelolco, a borough of Mexico City.

The text of the treaty comprises a preamble, thirty-one articles, and two additional protocols. The treaty signed by twenty-five countries is in effect for twenty-two alone.[6] Cuba and Guyana along with several newly independent Caribbean states have not yet signed (Power, 1983a:6). Cuba, for instance, has asserted that it could not accept Tlatelolco, since it could not "provide the necessary elements of security" for Cuba (United Nations, 1976a:336). Cuba argued in the mid-1970s that until the United States gave assurances regarding the denuclearization of Puerto Rico, the Panama Canal Zone, and the Virgin Islands and withdrew military forces from all military bases in the region including Guantanamo Naval Base in Cuba, supporting Tlatelolco would be impossible. As a result Cuba has consistently abstained on all resolutions related to Tlatelolco. The United States, however, after a decision taken by U.S. President James E. Carter in 1977, decided to include the Virgin Islands and Puerto Rico in the zone and subsequently signed Protocol 1. The issue of the Panama Canal also was resolved, following the signature of the Panama Canal Treaty between the United States and Panama in September 1977. The Panama Canal Treaty, for its part, established a mandatory military denuclearization of the canal zone (Arms Control and Disarmament Agency, 1982:61; Shaker, 1980:914).

Protocol 1 of Tlatelolco has been signed and ratified by all the concerned parties outside the region: the Netherlands, the United Kingdom, and the United States (United Nations, 1983b:63; Arms Control and Disarmament Agency, 1982:80–81). France has signed but has not ratified. This prompted the UN General Assembly in December 1983 to adopt a resolution deploring France's procrastination in signing Additional Protocol 1. The Assembly also urged France not to "delay any further ratification, which has been requested so many times" (Resolution 38/61 of December 15, 1983). When France ratifies this protocol, Guadeloupe, Martinique, and French Guyana will all fall within the context of militarily denuclearized areas.

Additional Protocol 2 was signed and ratified (completed) by all the parties concerned: China, France, the Soviet Union, the United Kingdom, and the United States (United Nations, 1983b:63).

TLATELOLCO: A TEXTUAL SUMMARY

In Article 1 of Tlatelolco the contracting parties undertook to use exclusively for peaceful purposes the nuclear material and facilities under their jurisdiction and to prohibit and prevent in their respective territories:

(a) The testing, use, manufacture, production or acquisition by any means whatsoever of any nuclear weapons, by the parties themselves directly or indirectly, on behalf of anyone else, or in any other way;

(b) The receipt, storage, installation, deployment and any form of possession of any nuclear weapons, directly or indirectly, by the parties themselves, by anyone on their behalf, or in any other way. They also undertook to refrain from engaging in, encouraging, or authorizing, directly or indirectly or in any way participating in the testing, use, manufacture, production, possession or control of any nuclear weapon.

Article 5 of the treaty defined a nuclear weapon as

any device which is capable of releasing nuclear energy in an uncontrolled manner and which has a group of characteristics that are appropriate for use for warlike purposes. An instrument that may be used for the transport or propulsion of the device is not included in this definition, if it is separable from the device and not an indivisible part thereof.

Article 17 reaffirmed the right of the contracting parties to use nuclear energy for peaceful purposes, to facilitate economic and social—but not military—development. Article 18 highlighted the right of the contracting parties to carry out nuclear explosions for peaceful purposes, including explosions that involve devices similar to those used in nuclear weapons, or to collaborate with third parties for the same purpose, provided that those explosions are carried out in accordance with the treaty and in particular with Articles 1 and 5.

Specific measures for the control of nuclear explosions for peaceful purposes are provided in paragraphs 2 and 3 of Article 18, according to which the states or parties undertake to notify OPANAL and the IAEA,

as far in advance as the circumstances require, the date of the intended explosion; the nature of the nuclear device and the source from which it would be obtained; the place and purpose of the planned explosion; the proposed procedures for observation by OPANAL and IAEA; the expected force of the device and the fullest possible information on any radio-active fall-out that may result from the explosion as well as other measures to be taken to avoid danger to the population, flora, fauna and territories to any other party or parties.

Additionally, the Secretary-General of OPANAL and the technical personnel designated by the council of OPANAL and IAEA have an unrestricted access to any area in the vicinity of the site of the explosion, in order to ascertain whether the device and the procedures followed during the explosion are in conformity with the information supplied and the provisions of the treaty (United Nations, 1976b:14).

Article 28 stipulated the rules for the treaty's entry into force: Paragraph 1 of Article 28 requires adherence to the treaty by all the states included in the zone, and to the protocols by all the states. The article also called for the conclusion of safeguard agreements with the IAEA. However, since these requirements might have considerably delayed the creation of the zone, paragraph 2 of Article 28 permitted the signatory states to waive them, wholly or in part.

Annexed to the treaty are two additional protocols which together with the treaty itself establish a system of mutual rights and obligations engaging three categories of states: the states of the region, extraregional states having responsibility for territories within the region, and the nuclear-weapon states, "present and future." A UN study posits that upon the accession of all these states to the treaty and appropriate protocols, the treaty's zone of application shall extend to include a precisely defined maritime area surrounding South and Central America as well as the Caribbean (United Nations, 1981C:6).

Additional Protocol 1, for example, was negotiated among a Negotiating Committee of the Preparatory Commission of the Treaty and the powers referred to in the protocol (France, the Netherlands, the United Kingdom, and the United States). It provided for the extension of the nuclear-weapon-free status to certain territories lying in the zone of application of the treaty, which both *de jure* and *de facto* are under the jurisdiction of states outside the zone. The effect of Additional Protocol 1 is to delimit the confines of the system of control for those territories bound to the application of IAEA safeguards.

During the drafting of the treaty a clear commitment by the nuclear-weapon states to respect the nuclear-weapon-free status of the zone was considered an important precondition for rendering effective the terms of the treaty. The search for a formula to embody this commitment led to contacts between the preparatory commission of the treaty and the nuclear-weapon states and to the adoption of Additional Protocol 2. According to this protocol, nuclear-weapon states pledged to fully respect the "statute of denuclearization of Latin America for warlike purposes as defined, delimited and set forth in the Treaty" and "not to contribute in any way to the performance of acts involving a violation of the obligations of Article 1 of the Treaty in the territories to which the Treaty applies." Furthermore, and significantly, nuclear-weapon states undertook in accord with this protocol not to use or threaten to use nuclear weapons against the parties to the treaty.

A pause at this juncture is useful, to consider the basic reasons for Tlatelolco's achievements thus far. It is revealing that the Tlatelolco initiative was launched with the cooperation of all interested countries with common will. The initiative was perceived by all the countries of Latin America as being in their common interest and enhancing their security. This perception was critical in bringing the treaty to fruition, in part because it rationalized it and served as a catalyst for its inception. This perception assisted in the process of agreement, resulting in a multilateral, regional, concerted effort. Thus, the securing of consent among the parties concerned demonstrated to the five nuclear-weapon states the unwavering resolve of Latin American countries in implementing this regional denuclearization initiative. The demonstration of resolve helped, it may be contended, to involve the nuclear states in the process and to provoke them into making a meaningful contribution to the treaty's implementation.

For example, the United States declared its support for Tlatelolco mainly because the initiative originated in its geographical area and all states within the region participated (Arms Control and Disarmament Agency, 1982:59). This regional, unified commitment in itself became a facilitative factor in obtaining negative security assurances from nuclear-weapon states pledging not only their support for the zone but their commitments not to use or threaten to use nuclear weapons against the parties to the treaty.

Tlatelolco also demonstrated the paramount importance of ad hoc preparatory efforts such as those carried out by COPREDAL (Robles, 1979:21). Recall that the treaty was facilitated (perhaps inadvertently) by the fears and threats stemming from the Cuban missile crisis, which worked to mobilize support for the treaty movement. Hence, in the discussions on a Middle East NWFZ, an attempt should be made to explore the possibilities of conducting similar ad hoc preparatory work, either in the form of appointing a Special Representative of the Secretary General of the United Nations to tour the region and discuss the initiative with the countries concerned or by conducting a preparatory expert-group study. It may be that such preparatory work will require, in the Middle East as well as in Latin America, not only actors committed to a NWFZ but a sense of danger, perhaps provoked by a crisis, to mobilize efforts for such preparatory work.

In this way, Tlatelolco may be seen as having been created before the incorporation and broad-range deployment of nuclear weapons into the Latin American continent. It is noteworthy that Tlatelolco was not totally perceived by the regional states and the nuclear-weapon states as altering any existing security arrangement or tilting the nuclear and military balance in favor of any of the major participants. Indeed, since the initiative emanated and matured intraregionally and was subsequently endorsed by extraregional powers, it appeared not to be aimed at any particular country. This was not unimportant. Because no state felt that Tlatelolco would place it in a disadvantageous position or jeopardize its military situation or national interests, no state felt threatened by the treaty regime, and accordingly, no state had incentives to oppose the treaty. On the contrary, Tlatelolco was seen as based on and capable of serving collective regional interests in the wake of a tense and polarized world undergoing an unabated quantitative and qualitative nuclear arms race. This in fact prompted the Unites States to acknowledge that Tlatelolco marked the first time the United States had "entered into an obligation that restricted the scope and use of nuclear weapons permissible by international law in defense of a country's security interests" (Arms Control and Disarmament Agency, 1982:63).

Tlatelolco was not circumscribed by a limited time factor. Unlike the Antarctic Treaty, for example, which is, upon request, subject to review and possible reconsideration after thirty years (1991), Tlatelolco was designed to remain permanent in nature (Article 30). This added a factor of stability and continuity. It also reflected the profound commitment of its members to permanently uphold the principle of denuclearization irrespective of changes within the international system.

The treaty codified the principle of verification by acquiring the approval from sovereign states for on-site inspection measures by international means (set out in Articles 12, 13, and 14 linking the Tlatelolco regime to IAEA safeguards). This added muscle and meaning to the treaty by enhancing its ability to identify potential violations.

TLATELOLCO: A CRITICAL ASSESSMENT

The treaty left some issues unresolved, however, because of pressures exerted by several nuclear threshold countries (namely, Argentina and Brazil) in addition to the status of territories lying in the zone of application (which were under the jurisdiction of states outside the zone, namely, France, the Netherlands, the United Kingdom, and the United States). The Soviet Union, for example, leveled three main criticisms against some of Tlatelolco's shortcomings (A/C.1/PV.1889; CCD/PV.553; UN, 1976B:16). It nevertheless must be noted that despite Moscow's criticism the Soviet Union signed and notified Additional Protocol 2.

Still, the first criticism was directed against Article 18, which allowed for the possibility of conducting peaceful nuclear explosions (United Nations, 1976b:16). The issue here, then, was that Tlatelolco only regulated instead of prohibited altogether nuclear explosions in Latin America. This indicated that no strict measures against horizontal proliferation were in fact implemented by the treaty, according to this interpretation. According to the Soviet Union, Tlatelolco made no real difference in controlling the spread of nuclear weapons, since nuclear explosive devices for peaceful purposes (PNEs) were technically no different from military nuclear explosive devices; hence, the possibilities ultimately of manufacturing nuclear weapons through this alleged "peaceful" process remained high. It is interesting to note at this juncture that the United States delivered a similar opinion on this same issue upon its signature and ratification of Additional Protocol 2:

> The United States Government considers that the technology of making nuclear explosive devices for peaceful purposes is indistinguishable from the technology of making nuclear weapons and that nuclear weapons and nuclear explosive devices for peaceful purposes are both capable of releasing nuclear energy in an uncontrolled manner and have the common group of characteristics of large amounts of energy generated instantaneously from a compact source. (United Nations, 1983b:69–70)

This ambigious treatment of the issue concerning PNEs resulted in a conflicting interpretation by several signatory states (The Stanford Arms Control Group, 1976:294). Mexico, the architect of Tlatelolco, asserted in response that allowing for the possibility of carrying out and benefiting from PNEs was an inherent right, envisaged not only by Tlatelolco but also by Article 5 of the Nuclear Non-Proliferation Treaty. The issue of the prohibition of testing, use, production, and acquisition of nuclear weapons was, according to Mexico, clearly dealt with in Article 1 of Tlatelolco.

Second, the Soviets also referred to the fact that Tlatelolco contained no ban on the transit of nuclear weapons through the zone. To this particular point the Mexican government responded by stating that Tlatelolco did not imply that such transit was allowable (United Nations, 1976b:16). Additional Protocol 2 particularly Article 2, highlighted the responsibilities of the nuclear-weapon states to respect the statute of Tlatelolco. A symbiotic link also was established between this article and Article 1 concerning the prohibition of receipt, storage, installation, or deployment of nuclear weapons in the zone. Thus, according to Mexico, the undertakings of all nuclear-weapons states were clearly defined.

Finally, the Soviet Union addressed the fact that Tlatelolco permitted the possibility of extending the treaty to parts of the high seas, which was contrary to generally recognized norms of international law, including the principle of freedom of navigation on the high seas, stipulated by the 1958 Geneva Convention on the High Seas (United Nations, 1976b:16).

One crucial point remains to be clarified and it concerns the relationship between Tlatelolco and the Non-Proliferation Treaty (NPT). As is known, several Latin American countries—namely, the two nuclear threshold countries (Brazil and Argentina)—have held an adverse opinion on the NPT. This, however, did not inhibit the establishment of the zone. Accession to the NPT was not stipulated as a rigid prerequisite to its establishment. This point is important because it suggests the possible analogy that can be drawn between nuclear threshhold countries in Latin America and those in the Middle East, particularly Israel. It is recognized that Israel has as yet refused to accede to the treaty. Here the lesson of Tlatelolco is instructive. It indicates that linking the process of establishing a NWFZ in the Middle East to *a priori* accession by states in the Middle East to the NPT might not be necessary, if the historical analogy between the Middle East and Latin America is valid. A UN expert study group asserted:

> Other experts noted that, while adherence to the NPT is desirable, it cannot be considered a prerequisite for membership in a NWFZ and noted, as a precedent, that several states not yet parties to that treaty are, however, parties to the Treaty for the Prohibition of Nuclear Weapons in Latin America (Treaty of Tlatelolco). (United Nations, 1976b:50)

Tlatelolco remains at present the only treaty establishing a NWFZ in a densely populated region. Lessons should be drawn if we are to extrapolate from it and draw conclusions about the prospects for a NWFZ in the Middle East. Ambassador Alfonso Garcia Robles of Mexico, the original author of the treaty (and rightly called the father of Tlatelolco), and winner of the 1983 Nobel Peace Prize asserts:

> The Latin American NWFZ which is now nearing completion has become in several respects an example which, notwithstanding the different characteristics of each region, is rich in inspiration. It provides profitable lessons for all states wishing to contribute to the broadening of the areas of the world from which those terrible

instruments of mass destruction that are the nuclear weapons would be forever proscribed. (Robles, 1979:21)

CONCLUSION

Building on this thesis, the preceding discussion demonstrates the ingredient conducive to the achievement of the successful establishment of a NWFZ. If the experience of Tlatelolco speaks to the situation in the Middle East, then we may posit that a NWFZ in the Middle East may be rendered auspicious by the existence of a crisis that provokes action, by the concerted effort of those affected in the region to mobilize support for a solution, and by the cooperation and support of outside parties, including and especially the superpowers. However, and encouragingly, a NWFZ does not seem, on the basis of this experience, to require unanimity or prior support for the Non-Proliferation Treaty; whereas community consensus appears needed for a regime's establishment, not every state within the region must necessarily join the regime and be willing to abide by its terms without reservation. Again, if this pattern applies to the Middle East, then we can argue that the prospects are not unfavorable for the creation of a NWFZ there, despite the difficulties involved. A "window of opportunity" may exist there as well. Whether and how this opening will and can be penetrated remains to be seen. This thesis will be explored in the Middle East after the analysis is allowed to benefit further from the examination of the histories of other NWFZ proposals. It is to these cases that we now turn.

NOTES

1. At the final preparation stage of this study, the South Pacific Nuclear Free Zone Treaty had not yet entered into force. The draft treaty was signed on August 6, 1985, in Rarotonga, Cook Islands, by eight of the fourteen members of the South Pacific Forum— namely, Australia, Cook Islands, Fiji, Kiribati, New Zealand, Niue, Tuvalu, and Western Samoa. The South Pacific Nuclear Free Zone Treaty is dealt with in the next chapter.

2. Argentina, Australia, Belgium, Chile, France, Japan, New Zealand, Norway, the Union of South Africa, the Union of Soviet Republics, the United Kingdom, the United States (United Nations, 1983b:12).

3. A State Department publication presents the figure of eighty-nine signatory states, and 59 as depositing instruments of ratification. This variance is attributed to the fact the Belorussian SSR and Ukranian SSR incorporated by the United Nations as two independent states are considered by the United States as included under the signature and ratification of the Soviet Union (Arms Control and Disarmament Agency, 1982:56–58).

4. The Soviet Union presented its first draft on March 18, 1969, and the United States on May 22, 1969.

5. For further clarification see Roger Coate (1982) and the special issue of *International Organization* 36 (Spring, 1982).

6. The treaty is not in effect for Argentina, which has signed but not yet ratified; Brazil and Chile, which signed and ratified but have not waived the requirements for the entry into force laid down in Article 28, paragraph 1. The other twenty-two countries for which

the treaty is in force are the Bahamas, Barbados, Bolivia, Colombia, Costa Rica, the Dominican Republic, Ecuador, El Salvador, Grenada, Guatemala, Haiti, Honduras, Jamaica, Mexico, Nicaragua, Panama, Paraguay, Peru, Surinam, Trinidad and Tobago, Uruguay, and Venezuela.

3

NWFZs: PLANS AND PROPOSALS

INTRODUCTION

Unlike the previous chapter, in which a study of treaties establishing NWFZs in four different regions was presented, this chapter discusses those initiatives that have not culminated in treaties. The NWFZ proposals dealt with in this section remain in a deliberative form. They are still faced with a multitude of responses and various forms of oppositions. In some of the cases regional support for a NWFZ was not even possible to achieve. In others superpower refusal played an important role in defeating the purpose of a NWFZ, because of a linkage process whereby these proposals were tied to military posture and nuclear balance.

Owing to the diversity of regional differences, functional considerations, and military modes, some of these initiatives either have lost momentum or have been repetitively inscribed on the agenda of the UN General Assembly with no enforceable measures.

For conceptual purposes it is pertinent here to differentiate between these types of proposals. First are proposals to which the General Assembly devotes particular attention. These are alive and well. They are inscribed annually on the agenda of the General Assembly and are therefore under consideration by the international community. Examples of these concern the denuclearization of Africa, South Asia, implementation of Tlatelolco, and the Middle East. Second, we have proposals that are, as of today, absent from the agenda. Some of them seem to have been abandoned because of the exigencies and nuclear setting of the regions involved, such as central Europe. Others, such as the Nordic initiative and the Balkans, remain the object of discussion among states in the region (Delcoigne, 1982:50).

It would be inaccurate, however, to argue that whereas the previous chapter deals with cases of success, this chapter deals with failures. On the contrary, the present chapter offers a historical overview on the evolution of different NWFZ proposals. Collective efforts for regional disarmament measures should be encouraged instead of restrained. The fact that such efforts did not culminate in treaties does not preclude the possibilities of retrial and success.

Throughout this survey valuable lessons can be drawn to enrich our discussion of the establishment of a NWFZ in the Middle East. Later, chapter 6 will concentrate on precisely that. It is important to demonstrate that the Central European, Nordic, and Balkan proposals have so far been inhibited because of linkages to the central European nuclear theater balance: NATO versus Warsaw. If we acknowledge that fact and then compare it with the Middle Eastern setting for which a NWFZ is proposed, we can measure an important margin of success already working in favor of a NWFZ in the Middle East. The same could be said concerning the NWFZ proposal for South Asia, where, in contrast to the Middle East, the various countries are still split on the initiative. It is to this task we now turn.

CENTRAL EUROPE

The purpose of this section is to highlight the dangers augmented by the presence of large arsenals of nuclear weapons in Central Europe. This section will avoid indulging in a hypothetical debate or value judgment of various power configurations and balances in Europe. Two views, however, emerge. One is centered on the premise that power concentration including nuclear weapon buildup has inhibited war in Central Europe. Proponents of this view have relied heavily on deterrence theory, defined in terms of "reliance on the ownership of strategic weapons, to curtail other powers from attacking" (Kegley and Wittkopf, 1981:336). Thus, deterrence is the process of "persuasion of one's opponents that the costs and/or risks of a given course of action he might take, outweigh its benefits" (George and Smoke, 1974:11). U.S. Secretary of Defense Casper Weinberger observed that in order for deterrence to succeed, "We must convince any potential adversaries that the cost of aggression by them would be far higher than any possible benefit" (*U.S. News and World Report,* December 12, 1983).

The most conventional analysis of this topic proceeds from the assumption that both Western and Eastern camps, once fully cognizant of the potential risks entailed in the use of nuclear weapons, would seek the equilibrium afforded by a condition in mutual assured destruction (MAD), since both camps under those circumstances would be inhibited from using nuclear weapons. That is, that condition would produce "self-deterrence" on the part of each superpower. This is often proclaimed as a reason for deterrence having succeeded so far.[1]

An alternate group of analysts follows a different line of reasoning[2]—namely, that power concentration in central Europe will eventually enhance the likelihood of a nuclear exchange. This group believes that war could result from a technological failure, miscalculation, or by accident. They also feel that increasing the arms race brings both camps closer to the brink of a nuclear exchange.

The report of the Independent Commission on Disarmament and Security Issues lists three factors that may contribute to the breakdown of deterrence:

> First, the cumulative impact of thirty-seven years of accommodation to nuclear weapons may have made policymakers less sensitive to their dangers psychologically; second, technological developments falsely suggest that it may be possible to limit nuclear war; and third, there is a danger that nuclear war may begin inadvertently during a crisis. (United Nations, 1983a:41)

The most recent Non-Aligned Summit Conference, held in India (1983), offered a similar assertion in its final communiqué: "Nuclear deterrence is unlike deterrence in the prenuclear age. Where the entire civilian populations of the world are held hostage to the strategic interests of one or another nuclear weapon states, such policies represent nuclear terrorism rather than deterrence" (United Nations document A/38/495 of October 12, 1983:7). Against this backdrop of existing conditions and rival theories, we can look more closely at the setting within which contemporary proposals for NWFZs are under discussion and receiving attention.

THE SETTING

Three points, at this juncture, appear especially salient and relevant. First, from a historical perspective, Europe has witnessed the outbreak and costly conduct of two devastating world wars. It is reported that the First World War claimed the high human toll of 8.5 million soldiers, whereas an estimated 15 million soldiers and 65 million civilians died during the Second World War (Kegley and Wittkopf, 1981:360). The casualties included 20 million citizens of the Soviet Union, 6 million Poles, 4 million Germans, and 2 million Chinese (United Nations, 1983a:65). Although it is safe to say that some of these casualties occurred in regions outside the central European theater, it must also be noted that European intraregional disputes were a primary factor underlying the outbreak of both world wars.

Second, at present two opposed superpowers and their military alliances (NATO and the Warsaw Pact) remain in a state of tense military confrontation in Europe, targeting nuclear and conventional weapons at one another. With respect to the global stockpile of nuclear weapons, the figure of 50,000 warheads has been estimated and confirmed by different sources (Sivard, 1982:10; United Nations, 1983a:16). This is equivalent to 16 billion tons of TNT. In the Second World War the limited use of 3 million tons of TNT resulted in 40–50 million deaths (Sivard, 1982:5).

In short, the prospects for the outbreak of military conflict has intensified in Europe because of the exacerbation of the international climate, the increase in weapons numbers and destructive potential, and the suspension of arms-reduction talks between both superpowers. The summit conference between Reagan and Gorbachev in 1985 did little to defuse the situation.

Finally, while several unresolved international problems and conflicts involving both superpowers impact detrimentally on the security balance in central Europe, that region is not without its own endemic problems and volatile circumstances (such as, *inter alia,* the hypothetical possibilities of a military intervention in Poland either unilaterally by the USSR—a tactic used before in 1956 against Hungary and in 1968 against Czechoslovakia—or through a multilateral Warsaw Pact force). Another unresolved intraregional problem is Europe's search for ways and means to respond to calls for the unification of both Germanies, a contentious issue still separating Warsaw and NATO countries. The tense situation surrounding the city of Berlin constitutes yet another grave threat to world peace and security.

These complex political and power configuration problems are confounded by a variety of other issues. For instance, in Europe the military situation is particularly complex. The force levels are exceptionally high; military posture rests, more directly than anywhere else in the world, on an intricate combination of conventional forces, short-range and medium-range nuclear weapons as well as intercontinental strategic missiles, and finally on the direct involvement of four nuclear-weapon states whose security interests in the region are defined there as fundamental. Achieving total victory under these circumstances has become exceedingly difficult, if not impossible; consequently, nations have opted instead to seek strength and bargaining power through armament (Kissinger, 1962:11–12; Schelling, 1966:31; Halperin, 1967:10).

There has been speculation, on the one hand, about the potential circumscribed use of nuclear weapons in Europe. In fact, noted personalities have advanced a scenario of a limited nuclear war in Europe following the eruption of any of the above-mentioned problems (Kissinger, 1957:89; 1962:63–171). On the other hand, some studies have asserted that conducting a limited nuclear war could never be successfully confined to specific military targets, since civilian populations would eventually become victims of this process. Additionally, the use of nuclear weapons is acknowledged to automatically carry with it the risk of further escalation. A UN study (1983a:59–141) observed that

> the dynamics of the interaction between governments would lead inexorably to larger and more intense nuclear exchange. . . . [O]nce the nuclear threshold has been crossed the dynamics of escalation would inexorably propel events towards

catastrophe. Doctrines and strategies of limited nuclear war thus carry dangerous connotations. Their acceptance would diminish the fears and perceived risks of nuclear war and blur the distinction between nuclear and conventional armed conflict, thus lowering the nuclear threshold. (59,141)

Different studies have estimated possible casualties in the event of a nuclear war in Europe. Some of these are instructive, albeit alarming. For example, a military simulation code-named Sage Brush, held in Louisiana in 1955, studied the effect of use in Europe of 275 warheads ranging from two to forty kilotons. The study concluded that "the destruction was so great that no such thing as limited or purely tactical nuclear war was possible in such an area" (Blackett, 1962:63; Record, 1974).

Also, an exercise code-named Carte Blanche was undertaken in Western Europe itself in the same year in which the use of 335 nuclear weapons, 80 percent targeting German soil, was simulated. It was concluded that "in terms of immediate German casualties alone, and so excluding the victims of radiation disease and other secondary effects, it is estimated that between 1.5 and 1.7 million would die and 3.5 million would be wounded" (United Nations, 1983a:60). As a result of this exercise, Chancellor Helmut Schmidt asserted that the use of tactical nuclear weapons "will not defend Europe but destroy it" (Schmidt, 1962:101).

In the 1960s additional simulations were conducted. The hypothesis that even a limited nuclear war would inflict almost unlimited destruction was confirmed, as stated by Alain C. Enthoven and K. Wayne Smith, two defense specialists: "[E]ven under the most favorable assumptions it appeared that between two and 20 million Europeans would be killed, with widespread damage to the economy of the affected area and a high risk of 100 million dead if the war escalated to attacks on the cities" (Enthoven and Smith, 1971:128).

In a United Nations (1981d) study published in 1981 entitled *A Comprehensive Study on Nuclear Weapons,* the concept of possible use of modern nuclear-weapon technology was explored. The study advanced a scenario in which both opposed alliances would use a total of 1,700 nuclear weapons (ranging from one to five kilotons) against each other's ground forces and nuclear arsenals in Europe. It was assumed that no such warheads would be used against cities. The study concluded that a minimum of 5 to 6 million civilian casualties would result from the immediate effects of the explosion alone, with an additional 1.1 million civilians who would suffer from radiation disease. These fatalities would occur within a period of days (Document A/35/392).

The underlying assumption is that a nuclear-weapon confrontation in Europe cannot be contained or prevented from spilling over to a holistic nuclear exchange with apocalyptic proportions. A crisis of this scale could escalate swiftly to incorporate the whole world, and before long, man could be faced with genuine dangers of complete annihilation. The genius of Albert Einstein was apparent when he refused to speculate on the type of weapons of a third world war. "But

Table 3.1
The Current Strategic Nuclear Balance (Estimated Figures)

	United States	Soviet Union	China	United Kingdom	France
Intercontinental ballistic missiles (ICBMs)	1,052	1,398			
ICBM warheads	2,152	6,170			
Sea-launched ballistic missiles (SLBMs)	520	969			
SLBM warheads	4,768	1,809			
Strategic bombers	376	150			
Bomber warheads	2,348	300			
Total strategic missiles	1,572	2,367			
Total strategic warheads	10,000	7,400	4	192	80
Total tactical warheads	20,000	20,000	300	250	300

Source: International Institute for Strategic Studies (1982–83); U.S. Department of Defense; Sivard (1982).

in a fourth war,'' he remarked, ''they would be sticks and stones'' (Kegley and Wittkopf, 1981:322). This prophecy, then, dramatizes the threat that nuclear weapons pose while underscoring the need to prevent their use and contain their further proliferation. Tables 3.1 and 3.2 underscore this reality and the dangers inherent.

THE CENTRAL EUROPEAN NWFZ INITIATIVE

As early as 1957 Poland proposed to the UN General Assembly a plan named after its foreign minister, A. Rapaki, which was subsequently endorsed by other members of the Warsaw Pact. It aimed to place a prohibition on the production and stockpiling of nuclear weapons on Polish territory if ''West and East Germany would accept, simultaneously, the same restrictions on their own territory'' (United Nations, 1970:328; 1976b:20).

After both Czechoslovakia and East Germany endorsed the plan, the Polish government extended its proposal in 1958 by advocating the creation of a ''nuclear free zone covering Poland, Czechoslovakia, East Germany and West Germany.'' The proposal called for the prevention of stockpiling or secondary installations of nuclear weapons, and called for the prohibition of the use of nuclear weapons against this area. It also called for a ''broad system'' of ground and air control and the establishment of a policing apparatus consisting jointly of NATO, Warsaw, and nonaligned states capable of verifying the observance of these commitments (United Nations, 1970:328). In order to avoid the intricacies involving the request for the conclusion of a formal treaty comprising

Table 3.2
The Current Nuclear Balance in Europe

U.S.	
Missiles	0
F111 fighter bombers	164
F-4s	265
A-6s and -7s	68
FB-111s (in U.S. for use in Europe)	63
	560
British	
Polaris missiles	64
Vulcan bombers	56
	120
French	
Land-based missiles	18
Submarine missiles	80
Mirage-4 bombers	33
	251
Soviet	
SS-20s (100 targeted on Asia)	345
SS-4s and -5s	260
SS-12s and -22s	120
SS N-5s	30
TU-26 backfire bombers	100
TU-16s and -22s	435
SU-17s, -24s, and MIG-17 fighter bombers	1,788
	3,078

Source: International Institute for Strategic Studies (1982–83); U.S. Department of Defense; Sivard (1982).

both Germanies, it was deemed that a unilateral declaration by the countries concerned would be sufficient. However, this Polish proposal was unacceptable to main Western countries, since it "contained no limitation of conventional forces" (United Nations, 1970:329).

Since then, the Polish proposal has undergone several revisions and modifications. In 1958, for example, Poland suggested a two-stage implementation plan: a freeze on nuclear weapons in the designated zone coupled with a simultaneous reduction of conventional forces. This plan, however, requested that the reduction of conventional forces be carried out simultaneously with the "complete denuclearization of the zone" (United Nations, 1970:330), a caviat or precondition ultimately rejected by NATO.

In 1959 Ireland responded to the challenge by proposing an "area by area" approach to prevent the proliferation of nuclear weapons in Central Europe

(United Nations, 1976b:19). This implied that non–nuclear-weapon states in a given area would undertake the following: first, not to manufacture or acquire nuclear weapons and second, to agree to verification and inspection measures by the United Nations. The Irish proposal asserted that in return the nuclear-weapon states and all the other members would undertake to assist these members in case of an attack by means of a "standing United Nations force" (United Nations, 1976b:20).

Following that in 1964, Poland submitted yet another new plan proposing to "freeze at existing levels of nuclear and thermo nuclear charges irrespective of the means of their employment and delivery, accompanied by controls to be established in nuclear plants in the area and at points of access by road, rail, sea and air" (United Nations, 1970:32a). The control procedures envisaged were to be exercised on a "parity basis" by representatives from NATO and Warsaw (United Nations, 1976b:21). At the time, the United States and her Western allies considered the thrust of this initiative to be aimed exclusively at the reduction of Western European nuclear-weapon capabilities while ignoring Moscow's superiority in the conventional-weapon field. Western European nuclear-weapon states affirmed three preconditions for the success of such a NWFZ: (1) its formation with the consent of all parties, (2) nonalteration of the delicate balance of forces between NATO and the Warsaw Pact, and (3) the necessity of implementing and recognizing effective controls (United Nations, 1976b:20).

One of the most recent proposals concerning a NWFZ in Central Europe has been put forward by a group of noted worldwide experts who issued a study entitled *Common Security: A Blueprint for Survival* (United Nations, 1983a). In this study, previously referred to, the experts proposed the establishment of a battlefield–nuclear-weapon-free zone. The new addition to the concept of a NWFZ was the use of the term *battlefield;* large portions of NATO and the Warsaw Pact's nuclear munitions in Europe were and still are of this type. In this respect they stressed that the weapons were "designed and deployed to provide support to ground forces in direct contact with the forces of the opponent. Their delivery systems have ranges up to 150 kilometers, and are primarily short range rockets, mines and artillery" (United Nations, 1983a:147).

For this purpose these experts recommended the establishment of a battlefield NWFZ in Central Europe "extending ultimately from the northern to the southern flanks of the two alliances." According to this proposal, this denuclerized battlefield zone would ultimately become free of nuclear munitions, storage sites, maneuvers simulating nuclear operations, and any storage of atomic demolition munitions (United Nations, 1983a:149). As for the geographic definition of the zone, the study proposed 150 kilometers on both sides but left the final geographic status to be determined through negotiations. Following the issuance of this report, Tass—the Soviet news agency—reported that given the range and mobility of contemporary battlefield nuclear weapons, the proposed 150 kilometers would be inadequate. Tass urged a zone of between 250 and 300 kilometers, or 155 to 185 miles on each side of the line (*The New York Times*, January 28,

1983). Commenting on this dispatch, Western experts voiced their own misgivings, noting that tactical, nuclear surface-to-surface missiles have ranges of more than 400 miles and can be transported on mobile launcher vehicles.

The study in fact went one step further by recommending, for the first time ever, the establishment of a chemical-weapon-free zone in Europe. The report recommended "a declaration of the whereabouts of existing depots and stockpiles in Europe, adequate means to verify their construction and procedures for monitoring compliance" (United Nations, 1983a:151). It became evident that this zonal arms-limitation approach, starting with a NWFZ, had its own appeal and was beginning to spill over into other arms-control sectors, at least from a theoretical standpoint.

The official United States response on this issue came on January 29, 1983, just one day after Tass's announcement. The chief spokesman for the State Department, John Hughes, contended that such a proposed NWFZ in Central Europe would not be realistic and would not contribute to security and stability in Europe: "Indeed, we are concerned that such a proposal can only divert attention from the serious efforts we are making in Geneva and Vienna to achieve dramatic reductions in nuclear and conventional forces in Europe" (*The State*, January 29, 1983).

Hughes's statement reflected, without any doubt, the difficulties facing such a Central European NWFZ initiative. One obstacle was the United States and Western European conviction that such Soviet proposals were practically presented for propaganda purposes and were in essence void, since they were directed primarily at United States and Western European peace and nuclear-freeze movements in order to hamper NATO's deployment of medium-range nuclear weapons.

The entanglement of this NWFZ initiative in the complex web of both East-West tension and a nuclear- and conventional-arms race was another obstacle. This point deserves elaboration. It must be noted that parity in the nuclear-weapon field became further complicated by simultaneous accusations that each superpower's rival had gained superiority in the conventional weapons field. In fact it is noted that one pragmatic explanation for the Western European rejection of the 1957 Rapacki plan was NATO's decision to offset what it considered to be a Warsaw Pact superiority in conventional weapons by means of tactical nuclear weapons stationed in Western Europe. A United Nations study asserts:

> The formal decision to this effect was taken at the North Atlantic Council meeting on 19 December 1957. This decision by which the use of 'tactical' nuclear weapons in Europe became part of NATO defense planning, as well as the conviction that the proposed zones would give unilateral military advantage to the Warsaw Treaty, remained all along the decisive factor in the reticence of the NATO states towards the establishment of denuclearized zones in any part of Europe. (United Nations, 1981c:20)

Table 3.3
Conventional Military Balance in Europe

	NATO	Warsaw Pact
Manpower (in millions)	2.6	4.0
Divisions	84	173
Tanks	13,000	42,500
Anti-tank guided-weapon launchers	8,100	24,300
Armored personnel carriers and infantry fighting vehicles	10,750	31,500
Artillery/mortars	30,000	78,800
Combat aircraft	2,975	7,240
Fighter bombers	1,950	1,920
Interceptors	740	4,370
Reconnaissance	285	600
Bombers	—	350
Helicopters	1,800	1,000

Source: NATO (1982b); International Institute for Strategic Studies (1982–83); *U.S. News and World Report*, December 12, 1983; Larson and Bodie (1983).

Judging from the discussions held throughout the meetings of the Conference on Security and Cooperation in Europe, the Helsinki accords of August 1975, and the ongoing talks of the Mutual Reduction of Forces and Armament meetings on this subject and that of associated measures in Central Europe, two independent views emerged.

NATO countries asserted that there existed a considerable disparity of forces in terms of manpower and equipment, which, along with geographic factors, favored the Warsaw Pact. NATO accordingly requested that any agreement on reduction, and/or limitation, designed to achieve a more stable relationship should provide for the "elimination of the existing imbalance by adequate reductions which should not necessarily be the same for both sides" (United Nations, 1981c:12). This prompted the Soviets along with its Warsaw Pact allies to temporarily suspend the Vienna-held talks on troop reduction in Central Europe.[3] These talks, as is known, originally began in October 1973 to discuss the issue of conventional troops and equipment reduction in the region of Central Europe.

With respect to conventional-power distribution in Europe, the figures in table 3.3 are self-explanatory.[4] They reflect the superiority and growing number of Warsaw armies in the conventional field. This is an added factor complicating the prospects for establishing a NWFZ in Central Europe. These figures also reflect the fact that the nuclear-arms race in Central Europe is further confounded by its linkage to a growing and spiraling arms race in the conventional field.

The third difficulty associated with the establishment of such a NWFZ is the concept of verification. Needless to say, verifying compliance with arms-control agreements has always been an uncertain task. Compliance, therefore, can prove to be either a failure or success depending on the specific type or design of the weapon. A UN study observes: "Mobile systems, smaller systems that can be fitted with nuclear or conventional warheads, all can complicate the negotiations and verification of arms agreements" (United Nations, 1983a:135).

To ensure the success of arms-control agreements, therefore, verification measures must be coupled with confidence- and security-building measures along with a favorable political climate between contracting members. Thus, it is cardinal that all contractual parties receive assurances that all undertakings are carried out and that these agreements do not create a unilateral advantage for any state or group of states (United Nations, 1970:327). Confidentiality cloaking military establishments has also made verification measures, particularly on-site inspections, extremely difficult to achieve in Central Europe.

By way of conclusion, the dangers created by nuclear weapons would seem to constitute a strong incentive for their abolishment. And yet the history of such efforts to eliminate nuclear weapons from Central Europe is one of failure—a failure that illustrates the obstacles, political and technological, to the creation of such a NWFZ.

A NORDIC NWFZ: THE NORTHERN EUROPE INITIATIVE

The idea of a Nordic NWFZ was initially suggested by Soviet Premier Nikolay Bulganin to his Norwegian counterpart in January 1958, when the United States deployed plans for the stationing of Thor and Jupiter intermediate- and medium-range missiles in Europe (Milton Leitenberg, 1982:17–28). Later the concept of a Nordic NWFZ evolved as a response to a Swedish proposal submitted to the UN General Assembly in 1961 (United Nations, 1970:262). Sweden then called for an inquiry conducted by the Secretary General "as to the conditions under which countries not possessing nuclear weapons might be willing to enter into specific undertakings to refrain from manufacturing or otherwise acquiring such weapons and to refuse to receive in the future, nuclear weapons on their territories on behalf of any other country" (United Nations, 1976b:20). Sweden contended that if the results of this inquiry were favorable, a conference should be convened in order to work out some arrangements that could meet with the approval of all countries (Resolution 1664 [16] of December 4, 1961).

In May of 1963 the President of Finland voiced a call for the establishment of a NWFZ among the Nordic countries. President Urho Kekkonen stated that "despite differences in their security policy none of the Nordic countries had acquired nuclear weapons or accepted those belonging to another State on its territory." He added that in principle this meant that the zone will "only confirm, through mutual undertakings, the existing de facto situation of absence of nuclear weapons without impairing the security of the Nordic countries or affecting the balance of power in the world" (United Nations, 1976b:25).

Finland continued to push its initiative at the twenty-sixth, twenty-seventh, and twenty-eighth UN General Assemblies (1971–1973) and in the Conference on Security and Cooperation in Europe in 1975. Finland asserted that a NWFZ should be studied in connection with the negotiations on force reductions in Europe and the introduction of methods by which the nuclear-weapon states could provide guarantees to countries of this zone (United Nations, 1976b:25). In 1974 the USSR welcomed the Finnish proposal and declared readiness to serve as a "guarantor of the status" of such a NWFZ.

Explaining Soviet support for this proposal, Dr. Oleg Bykov, Deputy Director of the Institute of World Economy and International Relations (IMEMO) of the USSR Academy of Sciences in Moscow, listed three main preconditions for the establishment of such a zone. First was the maintenance of the existing parity of nuclear weapons between East and West in Europe. He observed that the nuclear equilibrium stabilized the military-political situation in the continent. Second was a continuation of the political climate generated by the Helsinki accords, which could be accomplished by safeguarding security and promoting cooperation in Europe. Third was the development of political will in Northern Europe. He cautioned, however, against the deployment of a new generation of American nuclear weapons in Western Europe that could "disrupt the existing balance of power and raise nuclear confrontation to a higher and more dangerous level" (Oleg Bykov, 1983:29). It is for these reasons Dr. Bykov described a NWFZ in Northern Europe as possessing "great importance for the stabilization of the situation [which] would contribute to the limitation and reduction of nuclear armaments in Europe, strengthen mutual confidence, further the process of improving security in Europe and enlarge cooperation" (Bykov, 1983:30–31).

A Swedish scholar, Milton Leitenberg (1982), presented a counterargument for the Soviet view. Leitenberg asserted that Moscow's support for this NWFZ should be taken with a grain of salt, since it entails involving the Soviets with further obligations for nuclear-arms reduction on Soviet territories bordering this proposed Nordic NWFZ. He observed that Moscow was not even prepared to approve this NWFZ and dismantle any nuclear weapons from the Kola Peninsula bordering Finland and Norway nor to have this peninsula included in a Nordic NWFZ in any respect. The Soviets, on the other hand, rejected this assertion and stated in response, "As far as Soviet territory is concerned the military potential on the Kola Peninsula is part of the global strategic balance between the United States and the USSR and is not aimed at the Nordic Countries" (*The New York Times,* July 24, 1981). This Soviet response, however, avoided responding to the main criticism embodied in Leitenberg's assertions.

If we were to examine the United States' response to the Central European NWFZ initiative, suffice it here to quote some of President Reagan's remarks given at a reception for Baltic Americans on June 13, 1983:

> It seems ironic that those responsible for the repression I have been describing are now proposing what they call an atom-free Baltic, a Nordic nuclear free zone, especially since unidentified submarines have repeatedly violated the territorial

waters of Norway and neutral Sweden. This kind of conduct doesn't lend itself to a spirit of trust. As a matter of fact, the curious thing is, if you really stop to think about it, their description of a nuclear free zone is that there won't be nuclear weapons in that zone. The kind of nuclear free zones we want in the world are zones where nuclear weapons will not be landing and exploding. I urge the Soviets to concentrate on the serious negotiations in Geneva instead of making meaningless gestures. (Mottola, 1983:87)

On July 2, 1983, U.S. Vice President George Bush declared in Helsinki that United States' difficulties with this proposed zone lie with the process of "verification and how Soviet nuclear weapons in the Nordic area and the Baltic area are accounted for." Mr. Bush added that unless many details were worked out, "the United States would oppose such a zone until there was satisfaction on many points" (Mottola, 1983:87). The messages embraced in these statements were directed towards the Nordic countries following the incident involving a Soviet diesel-powered "Whisky"-class submarine (Number 137), which ran aground in Gasofjarden outside a Swedish naval base. According to the Reagan administration, Soviet support for this NWFZ initiative was incompatible with Soviet behavior, as demonstrated by the detection of ten kilograms (twenty-two pounds) of U-238 in the submarine's torpedo section, which was sufficient to indicate the presence on board of nuclear weapons (Leitenberg, 1982:18). This incident, then, clarified how close and vulnerable the Nordic countries were to Soviet nuclear weapons.

This initiative, however, remains strong in the wake of intraregional European support (Sverre Lodgaard and Marek Thee, 1983). The President of Finland in May 1978, for example, suggested the elaboration of a Nordic arms-control arrangement, the main purpose of which was to isolate the Nordic countries from the effects of nuclear strategy in general and from that of new nuclear-weapons technology in particular. In this respect the Finnish President emphasized that

> the initiative for negotiations must come from the States in the region, and that they must themselves conduct the negotiations in good faith without coercion or pressure, that they alone were qualified to interpret their respective security needs, and that in Finland's view the necessary arrangements could be made within the framework of the existing security policy solutions. Because a security arrangement concerning the Nordic countries would in one way or another affect the security interests of the leading nuclear-weapon states, it would be most natural and necessary that they should participate in the negotiations at an early stage, and also the countries in the region would have to receive assurances against the use or threat of use against them of the weapons they could commit themselves not to acquire or station in their territories. (United Nations, 1981c:29)

A variation on this same proposal was put forward by a noted Swedish personality, Ambassador Alva Myrdal, winner of the 1983 Nobel Peace Prize, who suggested a reduced version of this NWFZ including only Sweden and Finland, since both were at present nuclear-weapon free and neutral. Ambassador Myrdal suggested the exclusion of NATO allies Norway and Denmark from the proposed zone, as well as the exclusion of issues involving Soviet territories, while proposing the inclusion of guarantees from the nuclear-weapon states to both Sweden and Finland (Leitenberg, 1982:20).

Although past experience would suggest that this reasoning is wise, it is not without its difficulties. Some of these difficulties can be enumerated. First, it should be noted that unlike the Middle East, the Nordic region is already integrated in the overall nuclear-weapon security balance between East and West. Even though Norway, Denmark, and Iceland have refused to place special munition sites for nuclear weapons on their territories, the geographic proximity of this group of Nordic states to NATO and Warsaw forces places them as potential targets. Johan Jørgen Holst of the Norwegian Institute of International Affairs confirms what has just been stated: The fallout from a nuclear war in Europe in general, and particularly one involving Soviet territory in the northwest, would certainly extend to Nordic Europe (1983:5). He, in fact, cautions that the Nordic area is located at the interface of three separate but partly overlapping balances, the theater balance in Central Europe, the global naval balance and the central balance of deterrence (Holst, 1983:7–11).

The Nordic region is therefore part and parcel of the military posture and competition between East and West, and as a result cannot be extricated from that process. That is why the difficult ties underlying the establishment of a NWFZ in the Nordic region must advance in tandem with the broader process of arms regulation and reduction in Europe. That broader process involves negotiations on several issues, such as the establishment of confidence-building measures and a restructuring and reduction of the deployment of battlefield nuclear weapons in "forward areas" (Holst, 1983:11).

This also illustrates the functional differences between a region such as Northern Europe and the Middle East or Latin America. Leitenberg (1982:17–28) describes this Nordic zone as "restricted" in the sense that this area is surrounded on all sides by nuclear weapons, which is quite different from a declared NWFZ on an entire continent such as Latin America. We should, however, apprehend those differences and contrast them with the Middle East. The net outcome will be encouraging. The direct political and military confrontational setting between NATO and Warsaw nuclear forces in Europe does not exist today in the Middle East. This sine qua non fact, in contrast, demonstrates how difficult it is to fully implement such a NWFZ proposal in the Nordic region.

Another difficulty peculiar to this Nordic NWFZ initiative is the fact that three Nordic countries are members of NATO, two of which, Norway and Denmark, have qualified their position on the subject of nonstationing of nuclear weapons. A Finnish professor, Osmo Apunen (1983:25) states: "The meaning of this self-imposed limitation depends on what is meant by the concept of a nuclear weapon. This implies that the question of nuclear defense is left open with respect to crisis situations and warfare." Since the nuclear defense plans of NATO cover

Norway and Denmark, Apunen (1983:26) adds: "the Norwegian and Danish qualifications do not actually exclude all the different means of nuclear delivery from their territory in peacetime." In essence Norway and Denmark cannot, therefore, consider a Nordic NWFZ without the approval of their NATO allies (Leitenberg, 1982:26). The essential distinction that should be kept in mind centers on the "qualified" positions taken by Norway and Denmark. Notwithstanding their respective positions against the placement of nuclear weapons on their territories during peace times, both countries have reserved their right to invite foreign forces (NATO) to use their territories for placing and/or launching nuclear weapons in times of war.

Additionally, since three of the Nordic states are members of NATO, they draw on the nuclear umbrella provided by the United States. In this connection Holst states:

> Complete nuclear abstinence is incompatible with alignment with nuclear-weapon states. Airfields may be used by nuclear capable aircraft, naval ships with nuclear weapons may call on ports, navigation aids may be used by nuclear weapon carriers, etc. Hence Norway's policy on nuclear weapons, like that of not permitting the basing of foreign troops during peacetime, has never been defined in inclusive terms, but rather in terms of explicit exclusions. (Holst, 1983:5)

What this means is that the explication of the Nordic region as totally free of nuclear weapons is not altogether descriptive. A better delineation would be to describe it as seminuclear (Apunen, 1983:27). This constitutes a major obstacle facing the establishment of such a zone. In the Middle East, on the other hand, the delineation of seminuclear does not even apply. It seems, however, that the closer the initiative is to the delicate balance of terror between NATO and Warsaw, the less are the chances of its immediate success. Geographic proximity to the European nuclear theater seems to confound the initiative.

THE BALKANS AND THE MEDITERRANEAN

Proposals for a NWFZ in these regions have been advanced repeatedly for the past three decades. They remain, however, in an embryonic stage intermittently brought back to center stage and emphasized by various governmental declarations. None of these proposals at present has been elaborated into a comprehensive plan. In addition, no concrete steps have been taken towards their implementation. These proposals, as such, should not be mistaken for a worked-out, formal plan. Even their phrasing remains in the most general abstract terms.

The Balkan initiative was launched on September 10, 1957, after Romania suggested the establishment of an area of peace in the Balkans free of foreign military bases. To that effect, Romania suggested the convening of a Balkan conference to be attended by the prime ministers of all the concerned countries.

In May 1959 the Soviet Union supported the initiative, announcing that its reason for support was to facilitate the conversion of the Balkan peninsula into a zone of peace free of nuclear weapons. Towards that end, Romania proposed that agreement be reached on a Balkan treaty of security providing for the establishment of a NWFZ in that region, guaranteed by and agreed to by all the major powers (United Nations, 1976b:22).

Later, in June 1959, the Soviet Union again embraced the Romanian initiative. Subsequently, Moscow dispatched messages to the governments of the Balkan states and others (namely, France, the United States, and the United Kingdom) formally proposing the establishment of a NWFZ in the Balkans and the Adriatic, and declaring its readiness to assume the role of a guarantor of the zone. This formal Soviet proposal, however, was never presented in a treaty or a declaration format. A UN study asserts: "The Soviet proposal was worded in general terms. Questions regarding the control system or guarantee mechanism were left to be solved through negotiations" (United Nations, 1981c:27). The rationale behind this kind of presentation might have been to secure at the outset the approval of the United States and its NATO allies on the general thrust of this initiative, leaving the details to later stages of negotiations.

The United States, however, viewed this initiative from its own standpoint, depicting it as altering the existing military balance at the expense of NATO forces. George Delcoigne (1982:51) Director of the International Atomic Energy Agency's Division of Public Information asserted that the United States at the time believed ample guarantees of nonagression already existed in the United Nations Charter, that the Soviet proposal neglected to deal with the issue of production and stockpiling of nuclear weapons; Delcoigne went on to state that, at the time, the U.S. believed that the Soviet proposal made insufficient references to verification measures.

The crux of this argument centered on the notion that such an initiative was not addressed for disarmament purposes but was intended only as a quid pro quo procedure against the deployment of new missile systems in Western Europe. Examples to that effect were frequently cited. On May 13, 1959, for example, in a message to the government of Greece, the Soviet Union expressed the hope that "Greece would not allow the establishment of NATO nuclear bases on its territory and the conviction that the Balkan peninsula can and must become a zone of peace and friendly cooperation among the Balkan states" (United Nations, 1981c:27).

Furthermore, in 1963, following news of the replacement of U.S. missile bases in Italy and Turkey with missile-carrying submarines in the Mediterranean, the Soviet Union revived the concept by including the Mediterranean as a zone free of nuclear weapons. The Soviet Union declared that it was "ready not to deploy nuclear weapons in the designated waters provided the similar obligations were assumed by the other powers" (United Nations, 1976b:23).

Whatever our net assessment is concerning the evaluation of this initiative, it must be noted that without Soviet and American concurrence no fruitful outcome could be expected. At least, that pattern has not yet been broken in any previous endeavor.

In subsequent years the Balkan initiative was advanced at different forums. For example, at the conference of the Non-Nuclear Weapon States in 1968, Yugoslavia, Romania, and Bulgaria stressed the necessity for a NWFZ in both the Balkans and the Mediterranean. In 1972 Romania proposed the convening of a conference of the Balkan states. Romania envisioned several crucial factors to guarantee the success of this initiative—namely, that the initiative should provide for mutual obligations on the part of all parties, that it should offer security guarantees from all nuclear-weapon states, and that it should not limit the peaceful use of nuclear energy and the establishment of a system of equitable control (United Nations, 1976b:23). In 1978 and during the First United Nations Special Session devoted to disarmament, Romania made references to its previous proposals and reiterated its desire to establish such a NWFZ.

Early in 1984 representatives from four Balkan countries met in Greece to discuss the possibilities of converting the Balkans into a NWFZ. The conference, convened by the Greek Premier Andreas Papandreou, was attended by Bulgaria, Yugoslavia, Romania and Greece. Albania and Turkey did not attend (*The Christian Science Monitor*, January 16, 1984; *The Wall Street Journal*, January 17, 1984). Albania's refusal stemmed from her "disbelief" in the practicality of the initiative as long as some Balkan countries belonged to either NATO or the Warsaw Pact. It was reported that President Reagan in response to a joint letter from the Greek Prime Minister and President Nicolae Ceausescu of Romania, asserted that "the United States favored a general agreement for Europe and not denuclearized zones for specific areas" (*The New York Times*, January 17, 1984:A3). It is pertinent to recall here that such United States objections do not exist per se against the concept of establishing a NWFZ in the region of the Middle East. But this underscores once again that the posture either superpower assumes towards any NWFZ initiative will play a critical role in determining the subsequent course of development for that initiative.

DENUCLEARIZATION OF AFRICA

The genesis of the proposal to establish a NWFZ in Africa occurred in 1960, following a French nuclear test in the African Sahara. One year later a resolution calling on all states to refrain from conducting any nuclear tests in Africa, from using the continent to test, store, or transport nuclear weapons, and to respect the status of Africa as a NWFZ was adopted by the General Assembly (Resolution 1652, November 24, 1961).

In Cairo in 1964 the heads of state and governments of the Organization of African Unity (OAU) adopted the Declaration on the Denuclearization of Africa. The declaration stipulated two basic obligations: concluding an agreement under UN auspices not to manufacture nuclear weapons, and calling on all major nuclear powers to respect the principles and provisions of the declaration (United Nations,

1976b:24). In 1965 the General Assembly endorsed the declaration and called upon all states to desist from testing, manufacturing, or deploying nuclear weapons in Africa (Resolution 2033, December 3, 1965).

The resolution continued to be tabled annually on the agenda of the General Assembly. The resolution, however, underwent several changes. None of these changes were drastic to the extent of departing from the genesis of the 1964 Cairo Declaration. The two basic principles (namely, that of calling on all states to respect the African NWFZ and that of the Declaration on the Denuclearization of Africa) were upheld and have been repeatedly voiced from 1965 until today. On the other hand, several additions have been incorporated as a reaction to regional anxieties surrounding South Africa's capabilities in the nuclear field. Concomitantly, the political setting became increasingly heightened and polarized as a result of South Africa's policy and potential capabilities. Some of these developments are summarized below.

First, South Africa's refusal to conclude an adequate safeguard agreement with the International Atomic Energy Agency (IAEA) to safeguard against the diversion of nuclear material from peaceful to military purposes is noteworthy. South Africa's ample supply of uranium coupled with several reports concerning the development of facilities for uranium enrichment invited the assertion that South Africa may be a short distance from producing a nuclear device (Spence, 1974:210). Second, South Africa's continued military incursions into territories of the front-line states, particularly Angola, exhibits further reason for concern about South Africa's external aspirations. Third, South Africa's continued policy of apartheid, which generates extensive hostilities, spurred South Africa to maximize security by spending heavily on defense (Spence, 1974:210). Fourth, international concerns over South Africa's growing military and nuclear capabilities have played a role. This in fact prompted the UN General Assembly to adopt resolution 34/76B of December 11, 1979, by which a group of six experts from Sweden, the Soviet Union, Venezuela, Nigeria, France, and the Philippines were requested to present a study entitled "South Africa's Plan and Capability in the Nuclear Field" (United Nations, 1981b).

Two indicators of an imminent South African nuclear explosion aroused international concerns over South African nuclear intentions. The first was disclosed by the Soviet Union when the discovery of a nuclear-weapon underground test site in the Kalahari Desert in 1977 was made public. It is interesting to note at this juncture the immediate reaction of the Western countries. France threatened to condemn the test if the test was verified and promised to take retaliatory measures. The United States referred to the "serious implications" of the possible test and labeled the situation of "gravest concern." While Western countries sought assurances from South Africa, it was reported that privately they threatened to sever diplomatic relations if South Africa detonated a nuclear weapon (*The New York Times*, August 21, 22, and 31, 1977; United Nations, 1981b:30). J. E. Spence (1974:229) author of several books and articles on South Africa, shows why: "a decision to take up the nuclear option might have adverse diplomatic effects on South Africa's relations with the Western Powers. . . . On the other hand, both Britain and the United States would come under severe pressure from the more militant of the African states should South Africa develop nuclear weapons." Although it is difficult to attribute South Africa's retrogression to the intervention by major Western powers, it must be registered that such collective and unified effort ultimately brought positive results, inhibiting further pursuits by South Africa. Hence, it would appear that necessary channels should be constructed in order to bring similar collective efforts to bear on the prevention of nuclear weapon proliferation in the Middle East. Perhaps a declaration by the five permanent members of the Security Council to that effect would be the most fungible parallel mechanism for this purpose.

The second indicator involved an explosion detected by an American VELA satellite placed in orbit to monitor compliance with the partial Nuclear Test Ban Treaty of 1963. The explosion of 1979 was thought to be a South African nuclear detonation. Later several investigations proved inconclusive. One point of interest here which could relate to the Middle East is the presence of the VELA satellite. Without any doubt its presence has proved successful in monitoring the provision of the Partial Test Ban Treaty since 1963. The concept of utilizing similar appropriate satellites, with the consent of all parties concerned and preferably under UN auspices, could be studied and possibly extended as a verification mechanism to secure the implementation of a Middle East NWFZ. The information retrieved could be dispatched to a joint scientific committee comprising countries that are parties to this NWFZ. Imminent violations could therefore be detected, and escalation could be prevented through this "technological" approach to the verification problem.

Astonishingly, while these basic provisions governed the position of African states in their annual resolutions presented to the General Assembly, the African states neglected to incorporate a paragraph (preambular or operative) calling on South Africa to accede to the Non-Proliferation Treaty of 1968. Perhaps the reason for this oversight stems from intra-African disagreement and division over the treaty itself. It must be noted that fifteen states, in addition to South Africa, are not parties to the NPT (Epstein, 1977a:19; United Nations, 1983b:170–76).

Apart from the declaration little has been achieved in the physical process of denuclearizing Africa. This in fact prompted the outgoing Secretary General of the Organization of African Unity, Adam Kodjo, to call on African states to acquire nuclear weapons in order to balance South Africa's nuclear capabilities. Kodjo stated before OAU's 1983 summit conference, "Let us not be told about denuclearizing Africa . . . [T]he duty of African states . . . is to resolutely embark on the nuclear path" (Puchala, 1983:64).

One additional flaw with this NWFZ initiative has been the manner in which it was managed. At present, Africans have yet to determine the necessary and appropriate procedures to define and implement such a NWFZ in the continent. However, instead of capitalizing on the concrete and successful step of possessing the Declaration on the Denuclearization of Africa approved by the General

Assembly, African states instead substituted mere rhetorical condemnation of "certain" states for their collaboration with South Africa in the nuclear field. This shift in focus, while justifiable, came at the expense of the concept of establishing a NWFZ in Africa. As a result, no preparatory steps or consultations among the states of the region for drawing a draft treaty for the denuclearization of the continent were ever carried out (Delcoigne, 1982:52).

This issue of South Africa's collaboration with some Western countries (including France, the Netherlands, Federal Republic of Germany, United Kingdom, and the United States) has been downplayed by South Africa's surge for independence and self-sufficiency. In other words, it could be argued that this collaboration was not responsible for South Africa's development of a nuclear program. Spence (1974) and Edouard Bustin (1975) have both indicated that South Africa's ostracism and sense of isolation inspired by the United Nations' 1963 imposition of an arms embargo have led South Africa towards self-reliance and self-sufficiency in order to achieve enhanced bargaining power in relation to the West.

Hence, what should be highlighted is the prescription that the issue of condemning Western collaboration with South Africa should not take precedence over or be carried out at the expense of enforcing the initiative to denuclearize the continent. African diplomacy should therefore be geared towards utilizing and working through—not excluding—Western countries in order to bring pressure to bear on South Africa to implement the 1964 declaration as a practical and concrete step towards the establishment of a NWFZ. Ostensibly, the interplay of alternate approaches to containing the nuclear aspirations of a nuclear-ambitious country should be taken into account, as this history suggests. For one mode of deterring a nuclear aspirant may either reinforce or interfere with the effectiveness of another.

THE PACIFIC

China in the late 1950s and early 1960s proposed the establishment of a NWFZ in the Pacific. Since China was absent then from the body of the United Nations, little was done to develop this initiative (United Nations, 1976b:20; *Peking Review,* August 2, 1963, and December 13, 1974). This initiative in the early 1960s is reported to have been actively considered by the Labor party in Australia. The impetus for the establishment of such a zone emerged out of the opposition engendered by French nuclear-weapon tests in the Pacific. Governments of Australia, New Zealand, and the Association of South-East Asian Nations (ASEAN) launched several protests to the French government in order to stop these atmospheric tests. Furthermore, New Zealand in 1975 sought the support of its regional neighbors in the South Pacific Forum, where representatives from Nauru, Fiji, New Zealand, Tonga, the Cook Islands, Niue, Papua New Guinea, Australia, and Western Samoa supported the establishment of a NWFZ in the South Pacific.

It was not until late 1975 that Fiji and New Zealand introduced a draft resolution

(A/10192 of August 15, 1975) to the General Assembly to this effect. Four out of five nuclear-weapon states abstained on the resolution, which dramatically weakened this initiative. China, the fifth nuclear-weapon state, voted in favor, expressing only reservations concerning the possible extension of such a zone to include areas of the high seas or international straits. At this stage the physical outline of what might constitute such a NWFZ was never spelled out by the parties concerned. Crucial issues such as the geographic scope of the region were also not clearly defined. The fact that four out of five nuclear-weapon states were not in favor of the proposal hurt its credibility. This meant that before any consultation these four powers refused to offer any obligation towards any such future treaty. The Soviet Union, for instance, voiced reservations on the issue of transit of nuclear weapons in the zone (Delcoigne, 1982:51). The United States, on the other hand, saw the zone as hampering its nuclear combat vessels from entry into local ports (Alley, 1977:48). France had territorial interests to protect (New Caledonia and French Polynesia). Evidently, the Soviet Union and the United States were also worried about such a zone's possible repercussions on their military and naval bases in the Pacific and the possible hindrance of their own fleet movement in this designated region.

Since the adoption of resolution 3477 on December 11, 1975, the initiative was dropped from the agenda of the General Assembly. However, during a meeting of the South Pacific Forum held in Australia on August 19–30, 1983, the participants revived the issue of French nuclear testing in French Polynesia and the issue of dumping nuclear waste in the Pacific. It was decided to restore the initiative once more, by tabling a resolution on the issue on the agenda of the thirty-ninth (1984) UN General Assembly.

In Canberra in 1983 the South Pacific Forum approved an Australian request that consideration be given to the drafting of a treaty on a nuclear-free zone in the South Pacific. In 1984, at its meeting in Tuvalu, the forum endorsed a set of principles for such a treaty and directed a working group of officials from forum members to undertake an examination of the issues and to prepare a draft treaty for consideration at its next meeting. The working group held five meetings.

Following extensive consultations and negotiations, on August 6, 1985, the heads of governments of member states of the South Pacific Forum (comprising Australia, Cook Islands, Federated States of Micronesia [as an observer], Fiji, Kiribati, Nauru, New Zealand, Niue, Papau New Guinea, Tonga, Tuvalu, Vanuatu, and Western Samoa), meeting in Rarotonga, Cook Islands, endorsed the South Pacific Nuclear Free Zone Treaty. Eight countries signed the treaty in Rarotonga, namely Australia, Cook Islands, Fiji, Kiribati, New Zealand, Niue, Tuvalu, and Western Samoa. This treaty became the second, following Tlatelolco, to establish a NWFZ in a permanently inhabited region. It also established a NWFZ bordering two other similar zones: those of Tlatelolco and the Antarctic. Basil Bolt, leader of the New Zealand delegation to the Third Review Conference of the Parties to the Treaty on the Non-Proliferation of Nuclear Weapons described the treaty in Geneva on August 29, 1985, by stating that it "meant that a large area of the Southern Hemisphere was committed to the goal of being free of nuclear weapons'' (Bolt, 1985:10).

In brief, the treaty provides for a nuclear-free zone in an area bounded by the Indian Ocean coast of the Australian continent in the West, the boundary of the Treaty of Tlatelolco in the east, the equator in the north, and the boundary of the Antarctic Treaty in the south. The treaty also stipulates that no South Pacific country that becomes a party to the treaty will develop, manufacture, acquire or receive from others any nuclear explosive device.

Second, there will be no testing of nuclear devices in the territories of participating states, nor will these states assist any other state to to test such devices.

Third, there will be no stationing of nuclear explosive devices in the territories of participating states.

Fourth, all peaceful nuclear activities in territory of the parties to the treaty will be subject to full-scope safeguards, and the export of nuclear material will be in accordance with strict nonproliferation measures. Parties also commit themselves to supporting the continued effectiveness of the international non-proliferation regime based on the NPT and IAEA safeguards.

Fifth, international law with regard to freedom of the seas will be fully respected.

And finally, performance of obligations by parties will be verified by IAEA safeguards under agreements with the agency and through a system of consultations, including provision for on-site inspections subject to the directions of a consultative committee provided for in the treaty.

The treaty also reflects the forum's strong opposition to the dumping at sea in the region of nuclear waste.

There are three protocols to the treaty. The first of these invites France, the United States, and the United Kingdom to apply key provisions of the treaty to their South Pacific territories. The other two protocols respectively invite the five nuclear-weapon states not to use or threaten to use nuclear explosive devices against parties to the treaty and not to test nuclear explosive devices within the zone.

Until the time this study was being concluded, the treaty had not yet entered into force, since eight instruments of ratification were not yet deposited as stipulated in Article 15 of the treaty.

Despite the significance of this treaty insofar as it establishes a NWFZ after Tlatelolco, it continues to face severe criticisms and challenges. Vanuatu, one member of the South Pacific Forum, said that it would not sign the treaty because it was too weak, partial, and noncomprehensive. Australian newspapers such as the *Sydney Morning Herald* said that the treaty had done nothing to make the possibility of nuclear war more remote. The *Melbourne Age* added that nuclear armed ships would continue to cruise the Pacific.

The challenge facing the South Pacific Nuclear Free Zone Treaty could be summed up in the following: First is the continuation by France of its nuclear testing program at Mururoa Atoll. An incident involving France and New Zealand in which the Greenpeace ship *Rainbow Warrior* was sunk in Auckland Harbour demonstrated the gravity of France's views concerning protests directed against the continuation of its nuclear explosions in French Polynesia and at Mururoa Atoll.

Second is the matter of the continuation of the dumping of radioactive wastes and material in the zone.

A third consideration is the refusal of two nuclear-weapon states—namely, the United States and France—to accept the provisions of the treaty and the attached protocols prohibiting nuclear explosive devices and nuclear testing. The Soviet Union is on record welcoming the treaty and declared its readiness to diminish its naval presence in this nuclear-free zone. Some analysts believe, however, that this Soviet position is for propaganda purposes given Soviet refusal of the concept since its inception and Soviet military interests in the region. Others feel that Moscow can capitalize on, if not exploit, antinuclear sentiments in the Pacific by endorsing the establishment of such a nuclear-free zone that would impact on U.S. ships and aircraft rather than on those of the Soviets.

Fourth is the difficulty posed by the position of New Zealand's Labor party not to allow port visits by U.S. nuclear-powered or nuclear-armed warships, a matter viewed by Washington as disturbing existing security arrangements. AN-ZUS, which has united Australia, New Zealand, and the United States since 1951, has been subject to strains because of the difference in views between two of its members. New Zealand believes that ANZUS does not oblige New Zealand to accept nuclear-armed ships, since it was not a nuclear alliance. Washington refused this assertion. As a result, New Zealand withdrew from ANZUS in 1986.

In conclusion, the South Pacific Nuclear Free Zone Treaty is an important contribution to the cause of establishing a NWFZ around the globe. It remains to be seen whether the treaty will enter into force and how its members will tolerate the challenges described above.

THE ESTABLISHMENT OF A NWFZ IN SOUTH ASIA

As with the African initiative to establish an African NWFZ, which followed the French nuclear test in the Sahara in 1960, Pakistan, following the Indian nuclear explosion of May 1974, inscribed a new item on the agenda of the twenty-ninth General Assembly. The item was entitled "The Establishment of a NWFZ in South Asia." This quid pro quo process was immediately met with dissent by India (the major nuclear power in the region). India's resistance levied a toll on the success of this initiative, as will be shown.

A brief examination of the positions of both countries concerned can help explain the dichotomy. With respect to Pakistan, the initiator of the proposal, several factors can be highlighted. Pakistan believed that there were no differences between a peaceful nuclear explosion—such as the one carried out and termed a PNE by India—and an explosion that was conducted to develop a nuclear weapon. Pakistan believed, therefore, that the May 1974 Indian explosion might have "removed the restraint on regional nuclear proliferation and hence it became necessary to establish a regime of security for South Asia to ensure against the proliferation of such nuclear weapons" (United Nations, 1976a:104).

Pakistan also believed that all generally recognized conditions for the establishment of a NWFZ in South Asia existed. They were, *inter alia,* the declaration by all states in the region, including India, of opposition to the ownership and introduction of nuclear weapons in the region, the qualified support given by the five major nuclear-weapon states to the NWFZ initiative, and the declaration made by South Asian states not to acquire nuclear weapons. Pakistan also stated that the presence of military alliances or friendship treaties with nuclear-weapon powers and the proximity of nuclear-weapon powers should not become an inhibiting factor against the establishment of such a zone.

India, on the other hand, expressed that it had no intention of developing a nuclear weapon. India differentiated between nuclear weapons and the use of nuclear energy and technology, including underground tests exclusively carried out for peaceful purposes.

According to India, South Asia would not be treated in isolation as a distinct zone. South Asia was depicted as only a subregion constituting an integral part of the Pacific and Asia, which was surrounded by nuclear-weapon states or countries belonging to alliances; and hence, it was imperative to take into account the security balance of the entire region. Perhaps one of the most complicating problems facing the establishment of this NWFZ was tied to the definition of its geographic scope. Ashok Kapur, Indian nuclear proliferation specialist, (1979:184) shows the conceptual implications of defining such a geographical boundary. He asserts that if we were to define South Asia as India and Pakistan alone, India would reject that definition on the grounds that such a limited two-party view fails to incorporate the potential nuclear threat posed by China to India. The presence, therefore, of nuclear weapons and foreign military bases in the region was alleged to confound the security environment of the region and make the entire situation inappropriate for the establishment of a NWFZ in South Asia. Additionally, India maintained that unlike Africa and Latin America, where there was an agreement by countries of the region to join a common effort, South Asia lacked that homogeneously unified accord. India stressed that as far as the South Asian NWFZ initiative was concerned, no prior consultations had taken place, and no agreement regarding the implications, feasibility, and acceptability of the initiative had been reached in a matter bearing on the vital national interests of all countries in the region (United Nations, 1976a:105; 1976b:28).

As a result of these differences in positions between Pakistan and India vis-à-vis this NWFZ initiative, each country presented a separate draft resolution to the twenty-ninth General Assembly in 1974. Both resolutions reflected, in essence, the national positions of India and Pakistan as previously described. The Indian draft, on the one hand, expressed the view that such a NWFZ initiative should emanate from states of the region after taking into consideration its special features and geographic extent (Resolution 3265A [29th]). The Pakistani draft, on the other hand, called for consultations between and among states of the South Asian region and other neighboring non–nuclear-weapon states, requested the Secretary General to convene a meeting for this purpose, and called on the General Assembly to endorse in principle the concept of establishing a NWFZ in South Asia (Resolution 3265B [29th]).

The fact that two opposed and competing draft resolutions on the same issue were presented to the General Assembly resulted in the loss of consensus and agreement among countries of the region. This led the Secretary General of the United Nations not to convene, in 1975, the meeting envisaged by the Pakistani resolution (United Nations, 1977a:75). This also eroded the support from key countries such as Sweden, France, Hungary, the Soviet Union, United Kingdom, United States, and Yugoslavia, who abstained on the Pakistani draft. By 1975 an almost exact repeat of the entire scenario took place, this time with the General Assembly adopting both resolutions without a vote. By 1976 India desisted from presenting a draft resolution, while Pakistan kept the item alive by doing so. However, India consistently voted against the Pakistani initiative—except in 1977, when it abstained—with an annual explanation for its vote not much different from its original position stated in 1974. The Pakistanis, however, watered down their call on the Secretary General to hold consultation and instead requested him to render assistance ''as may be required'' (Resolution 31/71). Throughout the years little has been achieved, as positions have remained rigid, unchanged, and divergent. From 1974 until 1983 the General Assembly adopted a total of twelve resolutions on the subject, all without consequence.

NUCLEAR PROLIFERATION IN SOUTH ASIA: PROSPECTS FOR ESTABLISHING A NWFZ

In order to reach an understanding of the prospects for establishing a NWFZ in South Asia, a brief summary of the factors contributing to the crisis governing Indo-Pakistani relations must be presented.

Since the 1965 and 1971 Indo-Pakistani wars, both countries have remained locked in a bitter rivalry. This adversarial stance has both communal and religious roots. The dispute over Jammu and Kashmir remains unresolved. Additionally, despite India's overwhelming Hindu majority, India has at least 80 million Moslems who feel religiously affiliated with Pakistan's 93 million Moslems. India's continued quest for regional predominance is also in constant clash with Pakistan's search for security, parity, and equality despite differences in size and population. India's successful detonation of a nuclear device in 1974 and its successful space programs (placing three satellites in orbit, *United Press International*, April 1, 1984) increased her chances of developing an intermediate-range ballistic missile. On the other hand, Pakistan has refused the concept of an Indian nuclear monopoly and has thus embarked on an ambitious program of her own. This prompted the Congressional Research Service for the Subcommittee on Arms Control, Oceans, International Operations and Environment of the U.S. Senate Foreign Relations Committee to report that Pakistan "might be able to produce as much as 50 kilograms of plutonium a year" (Cronin, 1983:611).

Pakistan's position has been partly motivated by fear that should India deploy a full-fledged nuclear deterrence force, that force could be utilized to coerce Pakistan into yielding to India's dictated demands. Additionally, Pakistan's smaller army (compared to India) could have forced Pakistan—driven by classic deterrence objectives to counter India's numerical superiority—to seek an equitable relationship (Dunn, 1982:45).

Having considered this complex political setting governing the relationship between India and Pakistan, it could be argued that the prospects for implementing a General Assembly resolution on the establishment of a NWFZ in South Asia are dim. Additionally, one may also postulate that the Pakistani initiative is only an interim initiative designed to embarrass India in international diplomatic circles until Pakistan reaches parity through developing her own nuclear status.

While we should not totally embrace these interpretations, they help shed light on some of the limitations confronting this NWFZ initiative. Hence, it would be safe to state that the prospects for the success of a NWFZ in this area depends on two factors. The first consists of regional nonproliferation incentives, which are primarily dependent on the actions of both countries, and second is the development of more cordial Indian-Pakistani relationships, to a degree that would at the least pave the way for conducting regional consultations or convening an international conference to discuss suitable ways and means to implement the NWFZ proposal in South Asia.

Within a regional context this implies that both parties are likely to become more susceptible to pressures exerted on them by other participants. China, for one, is destined to play that role and hence will likely be perceived by India as its primary strategic threat. Until today China has not surrendered its national claims to territory held by India, including the Arunachal Pradesh state. India, as a result, views China's nuclear advantage as a liability exerting pressure on India for a possible "capitulation" (Cronin, 1983:610). Moreover, India does not view favorably China's support, from 1974 until now, of the Pakistani draft in the General Assembly. This particular point is exacerbated by reports of Chinese-Pakistani ties in the nuclear field. Observers point to Prime Minister's Bhutto's visit to China in May 1976, which concluded with his statement that:

> In light of recent developments which have taken place, my single most important achievment which I believe will dominate the portrait of my public life is an agreement which I arrived at after an assiduous and tenacious endeavor spanning over eleven years of negotiations. In the present context the agreement of mine, concluded in June 1976, will perhaps be my greatest achievement and contribution to the survival of our people and nation. (Cronin, 1983:603)

These reports prompted the Reagan administration in 1981 to temporarily suspend discussions on nuclear cooperation with China, based on concern about possible Chinese assistance to Pakistan's nuclear enrichment program (*The New York Times*, September 19, 1982; Namboodiri, 1981:145–46).

Although it is correct to assert that international pressures for inspection of some of the Indian and Pakistani installations and that efforts at preventing further proliferation of nuclear weapons exerted by the United States 1978 Nonproliferation Act, have to a degree restrained both India and Pakistan, it remains true that incentives for—not against—nuclear proliferation remain strong in the region. Hypothetically, Pakistan might envision a single detonation as sufficient to establish a deterrent relationship with India, rally domestic opinion, and strengthen Pakistan's role in the Islamic world. India, on the other hand, seems to be under pressure to resume its nuclear-weapons program. Its fear of being placed at a political and military disadvantage in a crisis with Pakistan could further spur nuclear desires that distract attention from domestic difficulties and the China syndrome and that serve as a gesture of dissatisfaction with the United States for its military assistance to Pakistan, which could further spur Pakistan's nuclear desires for an additional, if not larger in magnitude, detonation.

Conversely, it could be argued that both parties may remain eager not to compromise their close links with the supplier countries who are keen not to encourage proliferation and who because of their *ad infinitum* position, may exert economic influence over both India and Pakistan. This influence can take the shape of withholding nuclear material, cutting bilateral economic aid, or obstructing multilateral aid coming from international agencies such as the International Bank for Reconstruction and Development (IBRD).

Perhaps the most rational speculation could be cited from Richard Cronin's work *Prospects for Nuclear Proliferation in South Asia*. He asserts:

> The best hope of deterring proliferation in both countries probably lies with India and Pakistan themselves. At the present time both seem to have a temporary interest in not moving beyond a certain point with a nuclear explosion[;] for instance, Pakistan stands to lose much that it has gained. Similarly, a premature Indian response to Pakistan's nuclear activities would destroy important relationships and risks losing more than it gains. It is very unlikely that either India or Pakistan can be forced to abandon this nuclear option. The overall security of the region, however, including the cause of nonproliferation, could be well served by a *modus vivendi*. This could encompass either an overt or tacit agreement on the limits of their respective nuclear activities. (1983:612)

The earnest hope, thus, would be to translate such a *modus vivendi* closer to the letter and spirit of establishing a NWFZ in South Asia.

Before concluding it is pertinent to recall here some of the unilateral initiatives to establish a NWFZ embracing only one state, which involves the original initiator of this initiative. Three examples in this context may be cited.

First, on May 24, 1986, Iceland's Parliament approved a resolution declaring Iceland a NATO member, nuclear free. On May 30, 1986, the Prime Minister of Iceland qualified this approval by stating that it merely meant that the government had to seek parliamentary approval before deploying nuclear weapons.

Second, a call was forwarded by North Korea to convene an international conference in 1986 for the establishment of a NWFZ in Korea.

Third, the small island of Belau (Palau) in the Pacific adopted, several years ago, a constitution declaring Belau to be a nuclear-free state. This constitution prohibits all nuclear activities, including the transport of nuclear weapons in the zone of Belau.

While little could be expected from those three initiatives, it remains clear that the concept of NWFZ was gaining worldwide recognition and momentum.

CONCLUSION

The purpose of the last two chapters has been to present a general overview and comparative descriptive survey of all NWFZ initiatives undertaken since the advent of the nuclear age. This survey is necessary in order to draw lessons and identify patterns applicable to and facilitating the establishment of a NWFZ in the Middle East. Each and every example studied provides valuable insights. In chapter 6 the task will be to filter those proposals and extract from them useful alternatives that could facilitate the establishment of a NWFZ in the Middle East. However, instead of expounding on some of those issues and lessons now, it is more useful to move directly to a discussion of the Middle Eastern NWFZ initiative as it has historically unfolded since its inception in 1974. Then, after that background has been supplied, a new basis will exist from which to reexamine NWFZ initiatives discussed in chapters 2 and 3. The purpose here is to identify lessons learned and to apply them to the Middle East NWFZ situation. Hence, extraregional ideas can be related to the modalities of establishing a NWFZ in the Middle East.

Before that, an overview of the danger of nuclear-weapon proliferation in the Middle East will be presented. The emphasis on Israel in such a discussion is intended to remind the parties that such dangers are real and close. Such a survey should provide a better understanding of the subject. "The only solution"—to quote an eminent Israeli scholar (Simha Flapan, 1982:6–11)—should be to rally collective efforts in order to establish a NWFZ in the Middle East, without delay.

We will turn to that goal now and then proceed, in chapter 6, to offer conclusions and evaluations based on the historical experience of previous NWFZ initiatives.

For summary purpose table 3.4 presents an overview of the standing of all NWFZ proposals discussed in chapters 2 and 3. This table summarizes the positions of both superpowers. Their concurrence was vital for the establishment of the NWFZs in Antartica, outer space, the seabed, and Tlatelolco. The table also demonstrates that their disagreement adds difficulties for the establishment of NWFZs in Central and Northern Europe, the Balkans, the South Pacific, and South Asia. The table identifies the presence of nuclear weapons and devices in

Table 3.4
Status of NWFZ Initiatives

Regions	Denuclear-ized by Treaty	Year of Entry into Force	Number of Signatories	Number of States Ratified	Scope (Sq. Mi.)	Population Density in Millions	Presence of Nuclear Weapons	Superpower Concurrence	UN Resolution
Antarctica	Yes	6/23/61	12	25	5,100,000		No	Yes	Yes
Outer space	Yes	10/10/67	90	83			No	Yes	Yes
Seabed	Yes	5/18/72	88	70			No	Yes	Yes
Latin America	Yes	4/25/69	31	30	7,500,000	259,000,000	No	Yes	Yes
Africa	No	—	—	—	11,688,000	513,000,000	No	USSR in favor U.S. abstains	Yes
South Asia	No	—	—	—	1,731,775	930,555,000	India's nuclear explosion	USSR abstains U.S. in favor	Yes
Central Europe	No	—	—	—	631,479	233,543,000	Yes	No	No
Nordic	No	—	—	—	491,474	22,542,000	Nuclear umbrella NATO & Warsaw Pact	No	No
Balkans	No	—	—	—	596,257	114,220,000	Yes	No	No
Mediterranean	No	—	—	—	969,100	318,808,000	Yes	No	Yes
South Pacific	Yes	—	9	3	3,276	22,958,421	Yes	No	Yes

the regions that remain undenuclearized. It also presents in figures the geographic scope and the population density of the regions under consideration. Following that, chapter 4 will study the dangers of nuclear-weapon proliferation in the Middle East.

NOTES

1. For instance, Soviet peace activist Andrei Sakharov, long known for his advocacy of disarmament goals, declared that parity between the United States and the Soviet Union should be maintained. He also described President Reagan's plan to deploy a new generation of MX missiles as suitable to counter Soviet military buildup (*Time*, June 4, 1983). Numerous scholars and policymakers alike have advanced premises such as peace through strength (Kissinger, 1957, 1961), preserving peace by preparing for war; and they offer that the history of arms control suggests that such international endeavors rarely reduce weapon levels, since, in actuality, they freeze existing levels while funds are diverted towards the development of new and technologically superior weapon systems. Thus, for these scholars the proliferation of nuclear weapons is stabilizing, and therefore, transplanting deterrence to other volatile regions of the world will eventually preserve peace (Steven Rosen [1977] has urged the establishment of a "stable system of mutual nuclear deterrence in the Arab-Israeli conflict"). Hedley Bull, in *Rethinking Non Proliferation* (1975) and *The Control of the Arms Race* (1961), has urged the maintenance of deterrence and the application of "selective proliferation" to certain regions. Leslie Gelb (1979) has demonstrated that following arms-control agreements a spiraling arms race usually occurred in areas not covered by those agreements. Eugene Rabinowich (1960) has stressed findings that war breaks out more easily between "disarmed" members than between members "governed by deterrence." David Zeigler (1977), Herbert Scoville (1977), S. Rosen (1973), and Glen Snyder (1969) have all asserted that arms-reduction talks supply a "false" security, since arms-control negotiations have become the best excuse for escalating military expenditures. In this regard Charles Kegley and Eugene Wittkopf (1981) have shown that following SALT I the combined military expenditures of both superpowers accelerated to an unprecedented $1 trillion, a facilitative factor towards economic recovery (Rosen, 1973; Bruce Russett, 1982).

2. Examples of this school of thought could be found in the multilateral approach to general and complete disarmament envisaged by numerous UN resolutions and studies. Scholars such as Karl Deutsch (1964) have shown that the core concept of deterrence theory, namely, rationality, assumes the impossible. Deutsch ponders how such parties expect to frighten their opponents and then rely on their "cool headedness" and rationality to react. Robert Jervis (1979) has shown that deterrence theory will not lead to stability, since it relies on punishments rather than incentives, overestimates rationality, and underestimates the crisis; and he has indicated that deterrence could not be carried transculturally. Charles E. Osgood (1963) noted that as fear and emotional stress increased, nonrational mechanisms prevailed over human thinking. Ole Holsti (1972) confirmed the same hypothesis in a study relating the factors of crisis, the effect of escalation, and the outbreak of war. Michael Wallace (1979) has shown quantitatively that in twenty-three out of twenty-eight wars coded, an arms race preceded the outbreak of hostilities. James A. Stegenga (1983), citing fifteen different reasons for the immorality of nuclear deterrence, demonstrated how deterrence transformed the United States into a "garrison state."

Even one of the major proponents of power and the realist school, George Kennan (1982) described deterrence as a "nuclear delusion." Jonathan Schell (1982; 1984) urged the world to get "rid of the bomb" and nuclear deterrence before it "gets rid of us."

3. The initials MBFR have been widely used, particularly by the Western press. The letter *B*, in fact, stands for the term *balanced*, a concept totally rejected by the Soviet Union and Warsaw Pact members. According to Moscow, before negotiating a balanced conventional-arms reduction, NATO must initiate reduction in the Western nuclear arsenal.

4. It must be noted that Warsaw Pact countries discredit most figures published by NATO countries. They have denied any disparities cited by NATO and have asserted that both sides were in approximate overall parity. As a result, a discrepancy between official data submitted by the Warsaw Pact countries on their own military manpower in the region and Western figures for the same seems destined to emerge.

4

THE DANGERS OF NUCLEAR-WEAPON PROLIFERATION IN THE MIDDLE EAST: THE ISRAELI CASE

The purpose of this chapter is to identify the dangers of nuclear-weapon proliferation in the Middle East and to explore the complications that arise in that region as a result of its unique characteristics. Emphasis will necessarily be placed on Israel because of its advanced status as not only a nuclear aspirant but a nuclear power in this domain. A review of the vast literature in the field demonstrates a high degree of consensus among scholars and policymakers alike that Israel has achieved dominance in the nuclear field in the Middle East. Israel has been described as only a "turn of a screwdriver" away from a nuclear weapon, and as "the most dominant military and nuclear state in the Middle East (Power, 1983a:5). To use the same words offered by Zbigniew Brzezinski in a private interview with the author in November 1983, Israel "undoubtedly possesses the scientific knowledge to assemble a nuclear device in a relatively short time."

In so doing, the ultimate goal should be approached from a clear, objective perspective, since no talk of denuclearization or the establishment of a NWFZ in the Middle East is possible without an accurate survey of the present status in the region. In other words, if we can describe validly the nuclear proliferation process in the Middle East, we can thus better estimate and anticipate its effects on an expectant regional nuclear-arms race, as well as on superpower involvement in such a race, and therefore on any international NWFZ regime that might be established. A word of caution is in order, however. The survey presented here is not intended to be exhaustive nor holistic. It simply is provided to present the reader with knowledge of the possibilities of nuclear-weapon proliferation in the Middle East, which is basic to an understanding of the current policy predicaments and prospects for a NWFZ. The intention of the author is not to sacrifice objectivity but lay out the facts as they are. The firm belief is that the possibility of establishing a NWFZ in the Middle East without the participation of Israel is nil. Since Israel is a primary actor, it is imperative to advance with accommodation in order to establish a verifiable and successful nuclear-weapon-free regime in the Middle East. However accommodating, Israel should not deter us from presenting arguments on all sides of the issue. It should be always remembered that opposition against a nuclear Israel, as much as support for a NWFZ in the Middle East, originates first from within Israel rather than from without, as the sources quoted throughout this survey indicate.

Hence, this survey does not lend itself to victimizing Israel. It seeks only to highlight a reality we intended either to ignore or neglect. An Israel avowedly armed with nuclear weapons would provoke drastic repercussions. There is no guarantee in a situation such as that that other major nuclear powers will remain idle. Before long the Middle East could become a replica of central Europe, its destiny not only based on a fragile nuclear posture but controlled by extraregional nuclear-weapon powers. The combination of such a setting with the complexities of the Arab-Israeli conflict could lead to drastic dangers. Even an unavowed Israeli nuclear posture is not without its dangers. Simha Flapan observed:

> The proponents of this strategy were wrong in their prognostications. The nuclear ingredient added a psychological dimension of deep distrust to the conflict, as well as fears and distorted images that reduced the prospects of reconciliation to a minimum and made peace efforts extremely difficult. It exacerbated relations to a degree whereby all attempts to find a way out of this impasse were doomed to failure. The nuclear 'deterrent' did not deter but instead stimulated and intensified the conventional arms race. "Israel's policy," added the Israeli scholar, increased "Arab fears and suspicions and the urge to accelerate the development of their nuclear program to catch up with Israel." (Flapan, 1982:7, 8)

Another Israeli scholar, Shlomo Aronson of the Hebrew University in Tel Aviv, demonstrated that despite Israel's nuclear threat, the Arabs launched an attack in 1973. He (1977:12) observed, "Accordingly, in this view, it was not Israel's nuclear threat that influenced Arab planning and operations but rather Israel's conventional power." The hope then is not only for a NWFZ proposal in the Middle East but also for a rallying of collective efforts towards its implementation before a balance of terror degenerates this region of turbulence, passionate conflict, and deep suspicion into a state of mutual destruction.

The relatively lengthy emphasis placed on Israel is not difficult to justify; in fact, no less than ten reasons may be advanced. Suffice it here to state that Israel alone in the region is in an advanced stage of nuclear development. And as mentioned earlier there are several reasons that make Israel a case sui generis. A demonstration of these factors will explain how it is invalid to equate Israel's nuclear stance and posture with any other state in the Middle East. These reasons may be summarized by the following features surrounding the Israeli program:

(1) Israel's active engagement in various aspects of nuclear research since 1949

(2) Israel's early cooperation agreements in the nuclear field with France in 1953 and with the United States in 1955, both resulting in Israel's early acquisition of nuclear facilities

(3) Israel's nonsignatory status with respect to the Non-Proliferation Treaty

(4) Israel's rejection of proposals to place the larger segment of its nuclear facilities under international IAEA safeguards

(5) The ambiguity surrounding Israel's intentions and incentives for developing a nuclear-weapon program

(6) Reports of Israel's acquisition of uranium by clandestine means

(7) The ambiguity surrounding Israel's effort in the field of uranium enrichment

(8) Israel's possession of the necessary skilled scientific infrastructure

(9) Israel's large investment in a costly and varied delivery system

(10) Israel's policy of establishing a regional "unilateral veto" on the possession of any nuclear capability by any state in the region

Thus, we will proceed by seeking to describe the Israeli factor in the nuclear-ization of the Middle East by concentrating on actions and achieved developments in the Israeli nuclear program, and we will leave aside questions concerning how and why these circumstances have arisen.

ISRAEL'S EARLY ENGAGEMENT IN NUCLEAR RESEARCH

Israel's nuclear research program is important and instructive for two reasons. First, it denotes Israel's early interest in a nuclear option. This is understandable, and some Israelis see it as justifiable given that Israel is surrounded by an Arab majority. Second, inasmuch as time is a critical element in building and developing nuclear technology and training personnel, what scientists label "time factor maturity" is already evident in the Israeli case. The purpose of this line of pursuit, however, is to present an indication of Israel's early established capabilities in the nuclear field.

This survey then attempts to demonstrate that Israel's nuclear research program is already a well-established fact and has clearly achieved an advanced stage relative to its neighbors in the Middle East. The fact that Israel has achieved what it has in the nuclear field is a critical component that should be considered in any negotiations aiming at establishing a NWFZ in the Middle East. By highlighting the dangers of nuclear proliferation in the Middle East, it can be demonstrated that such an Israeli policy could be detrimental to even Israel's national interests. Why? Basically, once an avowed Israeli nuclear-weapons policy takes place, a spurious nuclear-arms race in the region may then be ignited—a development that is in the interests of no nation, including Israel.

Nuclear weapons in the Middle East can be linked ultimately to the complexities of the unresolved Arab-Israeli conflict. Professor Fuad Jabber (1971:9) an expert on Israeli nuclear capabilities has suggested that "the open ended crisis that has characterized Arab-Israeli relations ever since the Jewish state was established in Palestine . . . invests a nuclear Middle East with ominous possibilities, the gravity of which is compounded by the greater likelihood of their realization."

Jabber (1971) also provides a fully detailed description of how Israel's early interests in the nuclear field evolved. It was estimated that as early as 1949, a group of scientists associated with the Ministry of Defense was dispatched to the Netherlands, Switzerland, United Kingdom, and the United States for training in nuclear physics. Later, in 1949, the Weizman Institute in Rehovoth established four laboratories for experimentations in the field of applied physics, spectroscopy, electronics, and nuclear magnetic resonance in the Department for Isotope Research. Because of uranium concentration in the Negev desert, experiments were conducted on the most economical means of extracting uranium from phosphate ores in the Negev (Jabber, 1971:17; United Nations, 1982b:8). The Weizman Institute—through the research work of Dr. Israel Dostrovsky—developed a chemical process for the production of heavy water (enrichment by fractional distillation), instead of producing it by means of electric power (a technique originally devised by a group of scientists at London University). This new technique, devised by Israel later, became a competitive alternative to the Norwegian system of producing heavy water through hydroelectric power.

In 1952 the government of David Ben-Gurion established a central authority to coordinate national-level research in atomic energy. Also that year, the Israel Atomic Energy Commission (IAEC) was established under the aegis of the Defense Ministry. Jabber (1971:17–18) has shown how the commission's functions were kept "fluid," had no decision-making powers, and lacked a definition of its *modus operandi*. This, according to Jabber made it

> possible to assign to it new tasks and prerogatives without having to go through the legislative machinery, with the avoidance of unwanted publicity and public debate. This would save the tight secrecy which has consistently surrounded Israel's atomic establishment ever since its inception from impairment through legislative intervention. (Jabber, 1971:18)

This policy was carried to the fullest, to the extent "that the existence itself of the IAEC was unknown to the Israeli public" (Jabber, 1971:19).

The linkage between Israel's nuclear activities and the Israeli Defense Ministry should not be overlooked. The justifications of these links at the start were made on the grounds that the army possessed the prerequisite technical, organizational, and administrative capabilities. To these Jabber (1971:19) adds three other factors: the army's influence at a time when Ben-Gurion was both Prime Minister and Minister of Defense (1948–1953 and 1955–1963), the open-ended state of war Israel was facing with its Arab neighbors, and the capabilities of the army to maintain confidentiality.

In sum, the two principal achievements of IAEC were, first, discovery of the means of achieving radioactive minerals for the industrial production of uranium and, second, the implementation of a process for the production of heavy water. This, according to Jabber (1971:19), opened a "new path to the obtainment of two of the most basic and scarce raw materials in the field of nuclear power, namely, uranium and heavy water."

ISRAEL'S EARLY COOPERATION AGREEMENTS WITH FRANCE AND THE UNITED STATES

Israel's early cooperation agreement with France was signed in 1953 but was kept secret until it was disclosed in 1954 by Abba Eban, Israel's representative to the United Nations. It was he who first confirmed the operation of a pilot plant for the production of heavy water in Israel and acknowledged that the procedure had been transplanted successfully in France. This agreement for cooperation in atomic research provided for the extensive exchange of nuclear scientists and information between the two countries.

From the Israeli point of view this agreement enabled its own scientists to obtain a "wealth of technical data" and an opportunity for training and research through the courtesy of a technologically advanced country, France (Jabber, 1971:23). For the French the agreement provided two essential elements that it needed: knowledge concerning heavy water production and the technical means to process low-grade uranium ores. Hence, there was a community of interests that was nurtured by several other world events. Roger Pajak, arms control and Middle East specialist (1982) has demonstrated how the Egyptian president Gamal Abdel Nasser was considered a facilitative factor towards the solidification of that communion. Nasser at that stage was equally regarded by both Israel and France as a staunch enemy. France remained bitter over his involvement in the Algerian situation, for Nasser had exported the principles of the Egyptian revolution in supporting the Algerian Liberation Movement. Israel, on the other hand, feared an Egyptian military action (Pajak, 1982:31; see also Jabber 1971:27).

In the absence of disclosures about the details of that joint agreement, the rest of the world was left to speculate. What is certain, however, was the fact that this French-Israeli agreement to supply the Dimona reactor, near Beersheba in Southern Israel, aroused criticism and anger not only in the Arab world but also domestically in Israel, resulting in the resignation of all the members of Israel's

IAEC in 1957. Israel's two reactors are Nahal Soreq and Dimona. Each reactor will be described briefly below.

NAHAL SOREQ

As a result of U.S. President Eisenhower's 1953 Atoms for Peace Plan, Israel acquired, for the first time in 1955, a small one-megawatt (Mw), pool-type light-water reactor. The United States contributed $350,000 toward the original cost of this project. The reactor was built at Nahal Soreq, south of Tel Aviv, close to the Weizmann Nuclear Research Centre in Rehovoth. It became operative in June 1960. The reactor burns highly enriched uranium (90 percent). It was also reported that the amount of U-235 provided yearly for the installation reached ten kilograms. The reactor consists of "six Kilograms of fuel . . . ensconced at the bottom of a 25 feet-deep pool filled with filtered natural water and surrounded by a concrete wall 8–feet thick at the base. The pile is controlled by a series of rods coated with cadmium and baron which regulates the flow of neutrons" (Jabber 1971:30). By 1969 the reactor's capacity was increased to five (Mws).

Until 1965 the United States stipulated a system of inspection in accordance with its Atomic Energy Act of 1954. The purpose of this act was to ensure that no nuclear material offered by the United States could be diverted for military use. By April 1965 the United States, in an effort to strengthen the safeguards system of the IAEA signed a trilateral agreement with Israel and the IAEA. This agreement was renewed in 1975 and was extended by a 1977 protocol, still in effect.

DIMONA

One of the critical factors affecting any measurable scientific estimate of the effects and importance of the Dimona plant has been rendered obsolete by the tight measures of security enforced by Israel on this particular nuclear installa-tion.[1] The origin of Israel's policy of psychological deterrence or calculated ambiguity can be traced to this installation. Not until December 1960 did the world learn of Dimona, notwithstanding the fact that construction began in 1957, after France agreed to supply Israel with the reactor and its fuel supplies. After originally claiming the installation was simply a "textile plant," both Israel and France confirmed the construction of a natural uranium fueled reactor (Pajak, 1982:32). It should be noted that such a disclosure came in relation to strong international pressures and questioning. Some of this pressure in fact came from the United States itself following a closed meeting of the joint Congressional Committee on Atomic Energy on December 9, 1960. That meeting, also attended by State Department and Intelligence officials, resulted in a formal request for clarification on whether Israel was on the verge of producing nuclear weapons (Jabber, 1971:34; Pajak, 1982:32).

Dimona has been placed strictly out of bounds for inquiry for almost every observer, including members of the Israeli Knesset (Jabber, 1971:33). Several independent reports demonstrate how Israel has reacted to those seeking access to Dimona. The first of these reports was published by *Time* (April 12, 1976:39). That report illustrated how Israel came close to downing a U.S. surveillance plane (SR-71, known as the *American Blackbird*). According to this report the plane, which was on a surveillance mission in 1973 over the Middle East, came close to "discovering what Israel sought to keep covered" (39). A high-ranking Israeli Air Force commander instructed his pilots to "down it." The plane, however, flying at an altitude of 85,000 feet, escaped unharmed. (This report was also confirmed by the *Middle East Journal* (June 1976:27; see also Pajak, 1982:37).

Dimona is reportedly protected not only by the combined forces of the Israeli army, air force, and intelligence, but also by a sophisticated electronic and radar system. No flying is allowed over Dimona, even by Israeli military aircraft. It is reported that during the Six-Day War in 1967, an Israeli Mirage III—either out of control or with its communications gear inoperative—inadvertently flew over Dimona. Israeli defenders shot it down with a ground-to-air missile (*Time*, April 12, 1976:40). Also, in 1973 a Libyan civilian airliner carrying 113 passengers strayed off course due to a navigational error and flew close to Dimona. The plane was shot down by several Israeli interceptors, causing 108 casualties (Pajak, 1982:37; *Time*, April 12, 1976:40). The Israelis, however, deny this allegation and argue that they had feared a terrorist had commandeered the plane and had planned to crash into an Israeli city.

As far as inspection measures are concerned, it is known that Dimona was unofficially visited by a small number of United States scientists from 1961 until 1969. In fact, it is reported that these visits were transient (scheduled only once a year) and were limited by the Israeli government. *The New York Times* (July 18, 1970) reported that a United States team, irritated by the Israeli-imposed limitation, concluded that as a result they "could not guarantee that there was no weapons related work at Dimona." It is important to note that such limited inspection measures allowed to the United States were presented only as a compromise measure in order to ensure the flow of United States assistance in the nuclear field (Jabber, 1971:37).

Since 1969 no further visits were allowed. Repeated requests from the United States to visit the facility were denied. In 1976, for example, a U.S. Senate delegation studying the issue of nuclear proliferation was barred from visiting Dimona. The Israeli government charged that Dimona was a national security facility, and that Dimona "had neither been built [n]or assisted by the United States" (Shaker, 1980:837)

It must be recalled that in protest over the close association of Dimona with the Ministry of Defense, several statements were issued by leading members of the Mapai party, describing Dimona as a "political, economic and military catastrophe." In 1980 *The Economist* (see also Quester, 1983:548) reported that there were indications to support the assertion that Dimona's capacity may have been almost tripled to seventy megawatts. A United Nations (1982b:11) study asserts, "If this is correct, annual plutonium production could have increased to about 25 kilograms, which would be enough to produce 3 bombs.

It must be noted, however, that plutonium, before it can be used in nuclear weapons, must go through a chemical separation process to separate it from other fuel elements. Two international bodies have reported that a pilot plant for the reprocessing of spent fuel exists in Israel (Stockholm International Peace Research Institute [SIPRI] 1979 and *IAEA Bulletin*, 1979). SIPRI, in particular, reported that the elementary equipment necessary for such a facility was purchased from a French company. Such a facility would be capable of handling up to 3,400 kilograms of irradiated fuel a year, from which it could extract from 4.5 kilograms of plutonium (United Nations, 1982b:12).

Another means for plutonium separation is through radiochemistry laboratories, widely known as "hot cells." Such facilities are known to exist in Israel. These laboratories reportedly have been built near Nahal Soreq. Mohamed Shaker, Egypt's Ambassador in the Vienna headquarters of the IAEA (1980:839) asserts: "These laboratories are equipped—through American aid—with special remote control and automatic instruments necessary to handle highly toxic material. Similar facilities have been constructed as part of the Dimona complex to deal with the irradiated elements produced by the reactor there" (see also United Nations, 1982b:12 for confirming evidence).

As far as testing such nuclear devices, the literature surveyed allows for three interpretations. First, Shaker posits that testing is no longer an absolute necessity before deployment. After all, "The Hiroshima bomb was not pre-tested" (1980:839). Second, George Quester of the University of Maryland (1973:101), studying the possibilities of conducting laboratory tests or computer simulations of such an explosive device, referred to unconfirmed reports of Israel's success with such experimentation. Third, there are those who believe that the explosion detected by a U.S. VELA satellite on September 22, 1979, in Southern Africa was a joint Israeli–South African nuclear venture (Shaker, 1980:840). Even though later studies conducted by the science advisor to U.S. President Carter (United Nations, 1981b:31) reported that the VELA recording could have been caused by "signals of unknown origins," it is noteworthy that on October 25, 1979, the U.S. State Department issued a somewhat conflicting statement:

> The United States Government has an indication suggesting the possibility that a low yield nuclear explosion occurred on September 22 in the area of the Indian Ocean and South Atlantic including portions of the Antarctic continent and the Southern part of Africa. No corroborating evidence has been received to date. We are continuing to assess whether such an event took place. (*The Department of State Bulletin*, October 25, 1979)

Notwithstanding the results of the inconclusive investigation conducted by Frank Press, special science advisor to President Carter, a discrepancy and an unexplained time lag still remains between the findings reported by Dr. Press and the statement issued by the State Department. Such considerations have given impetus to a great deal of speculation.

On the issue of Israel–South African collaboration, there exists a wealth of literature. Suffice it to quote in this context Robert Harkavy (1977b:78), who served with the United States Atomic Energy Commission:

> In 1976, there were adumbrations of a growing Israeli–South African military nexus. Some commentators pointed out the obvious points of convergence between Israel and South African security requirements and the possibilities for exchange and mutual assistance. Israel presumably has nuclear weapons design expertise and a highly developed arms industry capable of producing Jericho missiles, among other things; South Africa, of course, has one of the world's largest uranium reserves and capital assets which could be used to expand Israel's war industries. There were rumors of Kfir fighter sales to South Africa—to follow the reshef missile patrol boats already purchased—and the imports of South Africa's successful development of the nozzle process for producing U-235 is obvious. In short, the potential of a nuclear nexus of Israel and South Africa needs little elaboration. (Harkavy, 1977b:78; also see *The New York Times,* August 18, 1976:9; Bustin, 1975:205–27; *The Washington Post,* July 8, 1975:A14)

A UN study on South Africa's plan and capability in the nuclear field asserted furthermore:

> Particularly in recent years, there has been growing concern about possible nuclear cooperation between South Africa and Israel. Such speculations grew particularly persistent after Prime Minister John Vorster visited Israel in 1976 and signed various agreements of cooperation. (United Nations, 1981b:17)

A variety of other scholars and news reports support these findings. Lewis Dunn, specialist on nuclear proliferation problems (1982:38) confirmed the possibility of an Israeli–South African connection entailing an exchange of nuclear-weapon design information from Israel in exchange for uranium or enrichment technology from South Africa. Furthermore, *The Washington Post* (December 8, 1980) has reported that an Israeli–South African–Taiwanese consortium that produced a version of a cruise missile with a 150–mile range exists.

ISRAEL'S NONSIGNATORY STATUS OF THE NON-PROLIFERATION TREATY

The position of Israel vis-à-vis the NPT has, until now, remained unchanged. Israel has persistently refused to become a party, either as a signatory state or a ratifying member of the treaty. It should be underscored that a NWFZ initiative is a complementary measure to the NPT. Article 7 of the treaty states, ''Nothing in this Treaty affects the right of any group of States to conclude regional treaties in order to assure the total absence of nuclear weapons in their respective territories."

At present Israel remains unwilling to sign the NPT, claiming that it "does not provide it with adequate security guarantees" (Lefever, 1979:68). International pressures on Israel to join the treaty have also failed. Israeli scholar Shlomo Aronson (1977:4) states that these pressures came as early as 1968, the year the NPT was signed. During that time Israel requested F-4 planes from the United States. However, U.S. President Lyndon Johnson reportedly attempted to link the supplies to an Israeli approval of the treaty. These endeavors, according to Aronson, failed; nevertheless, the F-4 shipment was approved.

The arguments most commonly used in support of such a policy is that cutting any type of assistance to countries whose security is in the United States' national interest will have detrimental effects on U.S. strategic objectives. A second argument centers on the necessity of maintaining such assistance in order to achieve a leverage (Schelling, 1966) over the Israelis. Third, it is argued that any type of excessive pressure on Israel, such as preventing conventional-arms shipments, might accelerate Israel's search for a latent nuclear threat (Feldmen, 1982a:211). Israel has, however, signed (1963) and ratified (1964) the 1963 Treaty Banning Nuclear Weapon Tests in the Atmosphere, in Outer Space and Under Water (Partial Test Ban Treaty) as well as the Treaty on Principles Governing the Activities of States in the Exploration and Use of Outer Space including the Moon and Other Celestial Bodies (signed 1967, ratified 1977).

There are other possible interpretations of Israeli objections to the NPT. These stem from Israel's declining faith in international institutions. For example, the imposition of safeguards eventually might curtail Israel's free hand in her nuclear research program. Also there appears to exist a "special aversion" by Israel to the IAEA, which, because of its "sympathies to the Arab World," could generate charges of military diversions or request shutdowns of certain facilities for verification purposes. In such a process "controlled by IAEA," leaks could occur, and Israel's nuclear secrets could be compromised and used to orchestrate an "Arab conventional reprisal attack" (Quester, 1973:85).

Quester (1973) provides one explanation of Israel's refusal to sign the NPT. He asserts that such a refusal is based on several factors: Israel's acquisition of additional boundaries after the 1967 war; the tendency in the Arab world not to recognize Israel; and Soviet moral and material support for the Arabs, coupled with a French embargo in 1967 that forced Israel to turn to the United States for arms supply. This atmosphere, asserts Quester (1973:82), has "precluded many of the supposed advantages of the NPT," to the degree that "Israel might thus find enough advantages in witholding signature to outweigh any marginal loss."

In retrospect, two of Quester's arguments have broken down. First, the tendency in the Arab world not to recognize Israel has changed, especially in view of the Egyptian-Israeli Peace Treaty of 1979. This development, however, did not encourage Israel to shift its position on the NPT. In fact, reports from

Washington indicate that the Israeli delegation to Camp David in 1978 refused even to discuss an Egyptian proposal on this issue (Shaker, 1980:843). Second, an Arab reprisal attack never occurred; Israel, however, launched a reprisal attack against a nuclear reactor in Iraq in June 1981, despite the fact that Iraq was a full-fledged NPT member and had placed all its nuclear facilities under IAEA safeguard and international control system.

Concomitantly, Israel's nonsignatory status of the NPT should be viewed in conjunction with the ambiguity surrounding the intentions of the Israeli nuclear program. This situation is destined to hold Arabs hostage to an Israeli nuclear blackmail policy. Scholars, on the other hand, describe that policy as one of psychological nuclear deterrence. Quester (1973:84) explains: "By refusing to sign the NPT . . . Israelis do not guide the Arabs, but rather cow them with a vaguer sense of power which can be furthered by periodic rumors of bomb projects." This assertion is further confirmed: "Israel's main preoccupation seems to be that the psychological deterrence value of the country's potential nuclear capacity would be compromised if it were to adhere to the NPT" (Jabber, 1972:18).

What is interesting to note at this juncture is that Israel seems to enjoy a most-preferred status with the United States when it comes to matters related to arms shipment, irrespective of Israel's nuclear policy. A U.S. Senate delegation visiting the Middle East in 1977, studying possible repercussions of President Richard Nixon's proposal to sell nuclear power reactors to Egypt and Israel reported that

> Notwithstanding the adequacy of assurances against diversion in the proposed agreements for Egypt and Israel, the delegation believes that the ratification of the NPT by Israel and Egypt and the placement by Israel of its Dimona facility under IAEA safeguards, would provide added reassurances. Nonetheless, the delegation believes it would be counterproductive to require such measures as a pre-condition to the pending sales. (U.S. Senate, *Senate Delegation Report on Foreign Policy and Non-Proliferation Interests in the Middle East*, 1977:51)

This recommendation, according to an Israeli scholar, amounted "to an exemption of Israel from the spirit of existing antiproliferation legislation as well as from the precise provisions of an antiproliferation bill already introduced by President Carter" (Feldman, 1982a:222). The fact remains, however, that Egypt alone in 1981 ratified the NPT a priori to delivery of any components for a nuclear power reactor.

Despite Israel's attack on the Iraqi nuclear reactor on June 7, 1981—which will be discussed later—and Israel's refusal to join the NPT and place its nuclear activities under IAEA inspections, the U.S. policy in this field underwent little changes. The United States, however, cut off shipment of F-16 planes to Israel following the attack. Paul F. Power of the University of Cincinnati (1983b:627), asserts that a State Department official "advised two Congressmen sponsoring an amendment to a foreign aid authorization bill that would cut off United States aid to any State manufacturing a nuclear bomb that Israel might fall into the vulnerable category, thereby causing the anti-proliferation Representatives to withdraw their proposals" (also see *The New York Times,* December 9, 1981).

It is pertinent to recall here that some Arab States have neither signed nor ratified the NPT. Hence, if the Arab states want Israel to fully accede to the NPT regime, it is imperative that they set the example by joining the NPT. Their argument that they shall join once Israel does so does not serve the cause of nuclear weapon nonproliferation in the Middle East.

ISRAEL AND THE INTERNATIONAL ATOMIC ENERGY AGENCY

Currently the Nahal Soreq reactor remains the only Israeli reactor under IAEA safeguards. It might be pertinent to recall that this reactor supplied by the United States under the Atoms for Peace Program went into operation in June 1960. Until 1965 this reactor remained under United States inspection, visited twice a year by United States inspectors, and was later, in the same year, placed under IAEA safeguards in accordance with the trilateral agreement concluded by the United States, Israel, and the IAEA. A decade later this agreement was updated and extended by a 1977 protocol (United Nations, 1982b:14)

The United States as a result has established a relative but temporary degree of control over Nahal Soreq. The fact that the spent fuel is sent back to the United States for reprocessing, coupled by the "near absence of plutonium," precludes Nahal Soreq's becoming an immediate international concern (Shaker, 1980:837).

It is the Dimona reactor that is creating a great deal of speculation and fear, since it is not covered by international safeguards. A group of UN experts asserted:

> Since Israel is not a party to any agreement by which it would undertake to notify the IAEA of such further nuclear facilities, there is no official information about the larger part of Israel's present nuclear program. In this situation it is impossible to ascertain authoritatively to what extent, if any, Israel's unsafeguarded nuclear facilities, including in particular the Dimona reactor and its associated installations, are used for the purpose of producing weapon grade material. (United Nations, 1982b:14)

Israel's relationship with the IAEA has been further undermined by the former's destructive air raid and bombardment of a safeguarded nuclear facility in Iraq in June 1981. The representative of Iraq stated before the UN Security Council that Israel's military aggression was also an attack on the IAEA, the international safeguard system, the NPT, and the internationally established principles concerning the peaceful uses of nuclear energy (United Nations,

1981a:174). This assertion was further stressed by the same group of experts mentioned earlier who were reporting to the UN Secretary General on the issue of Israeli nuclear armament.

> In the opinion of the group of experts, Israel has not only fallen short of subjecting all its own nuclear facilities to international inspection but has also acted to undermine the credibility of IAEA safeguards elsewhere in the region. The most dramatic Israeli attack on the credibility of IAEA safeguards was the bombing of the Iraqi nuclear facility in June 1981, despite IAEA assurances that it inspected the Iraqi reactors and had not found evidence of any activity which was not in conformity with NPT. (United Nations, 1982b:14)

As the IAEA Director General put it, "from a point of principle, one can only conclude that it is the Agency's safeguarded regime which has also been attacked" (United Nations, 1982b:14).

The Israeli raid prompted the IAEA Board of Governors to adopt a resolution (S/14532) on June 12, 1981. This resolution "condemned Israel and recommended to the IAEA General Conference that Israel's privileges and rights of membership be suspended." Furthermore, it urged agency members to provide emergency assistance to Iraq and reaffirmed the board's confidence in the effectiveness of the agency's safeguard system as a reliable means of verifying the peaceful use of a nuclear facility.

It must be mentioned that Israel justified her attack on the Iraqi nuclear reactor in a lengthy UN document entitled "The Iraqi Nuclear Threat—Why Israel Had to Act." In this document Israel made clear that Iraq was destined to produce nuclear weapons, that its nuclear facility was capable of producing plutonium, and that the existing safeguards on Osirak were insufficient and ineffective.

AMBIGUITY SURROUNDING ISRAEL'S INTENTIONS AND INCENTIVES FOR DEVELOPING A NUCLEAR WEAPON

In order to anticipate the probable future, it is important to identify some of the hypothetical nuclear-policy options available to Israel. For example, Israel could altogether eschew nuclear weapons. It could also openly cross the threshold by exploding a device. Or it could announce that it already possess such a device. Alternatively, it could acquire a weapon but deny that acquisition. Or Israel might acquire the know-how just short of the actual possession and maintain a posture of ambiguity.

With respect to Israel's declared posture, Israel has repeatedly gone on record stating that it would not be the first to introduce nuclear weapons in the Middle East. On the other hand, until now Israel has not categorically renounced nuclear weapons, even though it has joined the consensus on UN General Assembly Resolution 35/147 of 1980 (see appendix A) concerning the establishment of a NWFZ in the Middle East. This resolution says in its second operative paragraph that states should, "pending the establishment of such a zone in the Middle East and during the process of its establishment, declare solemnly that they will refrain, on a reciprocal basis, from producing, acquiring or in any other way possessing nuclear weapons and nuclear explosive devices."

Shai Feldman of Tel Aviv University explains three policies of nuclear posture associated with Israel:

> The first is the "nuclear option" posture. The second is a "bomb in the basement" posture. The third is "disclosed" or "overt" deterrence. A nuclear option posture implies that operational nuclear weapons have not yet been assembled but that the capability exists to do so within a relatively short time. A bomb in the basement posture implies that nuclear weapons have been assembled but not disclosed. Finally, overt deterrence implies that the acquisition of nuclear weapons is disclosed and becomes part of the public domain. (Feldman, 1982a:8–53)

It would appear, therefore, that Israel has chosen to maintain a posture of calculated ambiguity. Through refusing to deny or confirm reports concerning nuclear activities, and by refusing to join the Non-Proliferation Treaty and allow for IAEA safeguards, Israel has created what has been termed a process or posture of psychological deterrence. The world at large has been left to speculate whether Israel's policy is that of a "nuclear option" or "a bomb in the basement." This has been termed as "deterrence through uncertainty" (Harkavy, 1977b:70).

The incentives to Israel for promoting and maintaining such a posture could be summed up in the following: Israel feels the need to prevent the Arabs from crossing the threshold into Israel's land proper. Israel's policy of ambiguity could be explained as more cost effective. Rather than a declared nuclear policy that could either invite "the Soviets or Chinese to furnish some Arab regimes with a counterforce" or invite external pressures possibly from the United States to bear on Israel, the policy of an unavowed nuclear posture prevents such repercussion (Pajak, 1982:35; Harkavy, 1977b:70). Israel might also regard a decision to cross the nuclear-weapon "threshold as irreversible, [and its standing] back from the acquisition of nuclear weapons allows it to keep its options open" (United Nations, 1982b:19). Additionally, a policy of nuclear ambiguity offers Israel a valuable "bargaining chip" usable on many fronts, especially on the Arab front, in order to promote "Arab anxiety and caution in a climate of uncertainty" (Harkavy, 1977b:71). This "bargaining chip" could be used also in the case of an all-out peaceful settlement.

REPORTS OF ISRAELI ACQUISITION OF URANIUM AND THE AMBIGUITY SURROUNDING ISRAELI EFFORTS IN THE FIELD OF URANIUM ENRICHMENT

Two distinct reports should be highlighted about Israel's search for uranium. The first deals with an incident in 1968 concerning a shipment of 400,000 pounds of uranium that never reached its originally planned destination. The second involves the disappearance of about 200 pounds of highly enriched uranium from a processing plant in Apollo, Pennsylvania. It is important to consider these reports, since they were made public by Western sources. These reports have added to the fear and ambiguity surrounding Israel's goals for its nuclear program.

As far as the first incident is concerned, *The New York Times* (April 29, 1977) reported that a Central Intelligence Agency (CIA) official declared that the incident had its beginning November 16–December 2, 1968, when a German flag freighter with a cargo of 400,000 pounds (200 tons) of uranium ore extracted from Belgian-owned mines in Zaire departed from Antwerp, Belgium, headed for Genoa, Italy, after a stop in Rotterdam, Holland. The ship was loaded with about 200 tons of uranium sold in 1968 by a Belgian company based in Zaire— *Union Minière du Haut Katanga*—to an Italian firm (United Nations, 1982b:13). Instead of delivering the payload to Genoa, Italy, it has been confirmed that neither the ship nor its cargo reached its scheduled destination. Instead, the ship (the *Scheersberg A*) was next seen at the Turkish port of Iskenderun, flying the flag of a different country, bearing a new name, and manned by a different crew. Italy along with other members of the European Atomic Energy Commission (EURATOM) and the United States conducted an investigation. The findings, however, were inconclusive. Some analysts theorized that the cargo might have been transferred at sea sometime between November 16 and December 2, 1968, to an Israeli ship or that the *Sheersberg A* might have made an unscheduled visit to the Israeli port city of Haifa, where the cargo could have been unloaded (The *Los Angeles Times*, April 29, 1979).

In 1968 the ownership of the *Sheersberg A* was linked, according to the records of Lloyd's Register of Shipping in London, to Biscayne Traders Shipping Corporation—a company owned by Dan Aerbel, an admitted agent of the Israeli Secret Service: MOSSAD. Aerbel, who was held in a Norwegian jail on charges of murdering a Moroccan worker in Lillehammer, informed the Norwegian Attorney General about that ship throughout the course of his interrogation. Later Haakon Wiker, the same Norwegian Attorney General, described Aerbel: "In my mind, there was no doubt that he was a Mossad officer. . . . The Israeli government has, in fact, established that he worked for them" (The *Los Angeles Times*, April 29, 1979).

Paul Leventhal (1977), a former staff member for the U.S. Senate's Government Operations Committee, has offered an interpretation of such data (quoted in *The New York Times*, January 27, 1978). The assessment was that the 200 tons were unenriched natural uranium, not readily usable for weapon purposes but that it could have been fed into the unsafeguarded heavy-water reactor (Dimona). The resulting spent fuel could have been used as a source for producing weapon-grade plutonium. Dimona is known to use the same kind of uranium that disappeared (*The New York Times*, April 29, 1977). The link between uranium and unsafeguarded nuclear facilities is described by Fuad Jabber (1971:87): "Were a country to embark on a weapons programme, one of its first and most urgent tasks would be to ensure a suitable and continuing supply of control-free uranium for its reactor in the face of the many obstacles that have been created by the international community in general'' (see United Nations, 1982b:11 for a detailed study on Israeli plants for uranium extraction and production).

The second incident involved the disappearance of almost 200 pounds of enriched uranium from the plant of the Nuclear Materials and Equipment Company (NUMEC) at Apollo, Pennsylvania, which was fabricating fuel for U.S. submarines. David Burnham, a reporter for the *New York Times*, and John Fialka, a reporter for the *Washington Star* (1979) have detailed how "the nation's most vital safeguard system had been penetrated by one of our closest allies'' (Fialka, 1979:50).

NUMEC was originally formed by Dr. Zalman Shapiro, a chemist, veteran of the Manhattan project, and a "Zionist'' (Burnham, 1979:82). The ties between NUMEC and Israel were described as strong. One of these ties was an arrangement for NUMEC to serve as a "technical consultant, training and procurement agency'' for Israel in the United States. This mother company later gave birth to ISORAD, a "NUMEC subsidiary half owned by the Israeli government.'' NUMEC's annual financial report described its ties with Israel as involving the development of machinery to preserve strawberries and citrus fruits by irradiation (Fialka, 1979:53). Also, it was reported that NUMEC hired Baruch Cinai, an Israeli metallurgist. In addition, the company frequently hosted Ephraim Lahav, a scientific attaché to the Israeli Embassy in Washington. It should be noted that at this time NUMEC housed more than 2,400 classified documents, possessing detailed descriptions of confidential U.S. military research in the nuclear-weapons field.

In 1968 Fialka reported that the CIA attempted to investigate these frequent losses of uranium from NUMEC after achieving scientific evidence that Israel was using highly enriched uranium near Dimona (Fialka, 1979). The directors of both the CIA and the FBI, Richard Helms and J. Edgar Hoover, decided to place Shapiro under FBI surveillance. Shapiro was described as traveling "throughout the United States recruiting scientists, all of whom were Jews, for work on various technical problems confronting Israel'' (Fialka, 1979:56). According to an FBI report to the U.S. Congress, this investigation was hindered by "Shapiro's use of an encoded phone[,] a device in an Israeli Embassy office in New York. Several attempts to crack the code reportedly failed'' (Fialka, 1979:57; also see Stephen Green, 1984:148–180).

As a result NUMEC became the focus of repeated investigations. The United States Energy Research and Development Administration (AEC) estimated that about 206 pounds of highly enriched uranium had disappeared from the plant between 1957 and 1965. Fialka (1979) offers several theories pertaining to this analysis. The first centers on President Johnson, who reportedly read a CIA national intelligence estimate on Israel's entry into the nuclear club. Johnson reportedly instructed CIA director Helms "not to tell anyone else, not even Dean

Rusk (then Secretary of State) or Robert McNamara (then Secretary of Defense)'' (Fialka, 1979:51). Fialka theorizes that Johnson, possibly aided by the CIA, acquiesced to the diversion to aid Israel in preparing for what culminated in the 1967 Six-Day War.

The second theory portrays MUMEC as a "free lance" operation conducted by the "CIA's powerful pro-Israeli lobby" (Fialka, 1979:51). Harkavy (1977b:14) also confirmed these early relationships between the CIA and Israel. Quoting two prominent columnists, Tad Szulc and ex–Defense Department official William Beecher, it was argued that elements within the CIA acting independently had presented Israel's nuclear program with overt help in the wake of the 1956 Suez war. Harkavy (1977b:14) stated that both men have implied "that United States aid had been given (in the wake of the government's strong opposition to the Anglo-French-Israeli operation, which coincided with and indirectly facilitated the Soviet invasion of Hungary) as a quid-pro-quo for Israel's territorial withdrawals after the 1956 victory and its future cooperation." The third theory offered depicts the diversion as an operation exclusively carried out by Israel with help from Shapiro.

What must be underlined, as a result, is the common denominator shared by those three theories. All three focus on Israel's alleged links and possible role in such an operation. In an insightful study published by the Brookings Institution, Lefever (1979:65) asserted that we should consider these reports with a great deal of concern, since they "appear to be substantially correct, indicate that Israel, not India, became the sixth nuclear weapon state."

To be used in an explosive device, uranium must be "enriched." This means that the easily fissionable form of this heavy metal, uranium 235, must be concentrated from its natural level of 0.7 percent U-235 to almost 90 percent. While once it took a multimillion-dollar gaseous diffusion plant to enrich uranium, today there are cheaper, more compact, and less conspicuous centrifuge techniques. Israel is reported to have considered the use of laser beams for isotope separation (Gillette, 1974). A United Nations study (1982b:12) asserted that developing such a method could have high economic advantages "including their potential efficiency and the savings of electricity in relation to other uranium enrichment techniques." There is no indication, however, that this research has been completed. In fact the reports indicate that it is still at a laboratory stage (also see *Los Angeles Times,* April 29, 1979).

Israel is also reported to have devised its own technique for extracting uranium from the phosphate deposits in the Negev desert (Jabber, 1971:89). A survey of the Negev deposits places the phosphate deposits at "220 million tons with an average uranium concentration of 100–170 parts per million. The uranium availability is thus computed at 25,000 tons" (Chari, 1977:346). A noted Israeli scientist and former director of the Nahal Soreq Research Center declared in 1975 that Israel owned up to 60,000 tons of uranium and could extract 60 tons per year at the Arad Chemical works for use in nuclear reactors (Jabber, 1977:77).

Recent reports of the smuggling of 800 Krytrons, devices that could be used as triggers in nuclear weapons, to Israel by a California businessman increased the anxieties in the region over Israel's clandestine means and dangerous intentions.

ISRAEL'S SCIENTIFIC INFRASTRUCTURE

It is important to consider Israel's scientific infrastructure and to explore the extent to which such know-how has played a salient role in allowing Israel to expand in the field of nuclear research. Roger Pajak (1982) has shown how Israeli scientists in the early 1950s managed to "perfect a technique for producing heavy water." Pajak (1982:30–31) adds, "In exchange for information on this process, France in 1953 permitted the Israelis to study its own nuclear research program. The French subsequently invited Israeli scientists to participate as observers in their nuclear weapons testing in the Sahara Desert" (see also *The Middle East*, June 1976:2). Lefever (1979) asserted that this process of cooperation between Israel and France was beneficial to both countries. Israel presented France with its knowledge on "how to produce heavy water and to extract uranium from low-grade ores both reportedly of considerable help to the French in decreasing their reliance on American technology" (Lefever, 1979:68). Lefever postulates that it is even possible that the French nuclear test in the Sahara desert in the late 1960s was carried out using "a bomb of a French-Israeli design" (see Harkavy, 1977b:5).

A United Nations (1982b:6) study lists three requirements for the manufacture of nuclear weapons. They are these: (1) the availability of enough amounts of nuclear material of weapon-grade quality, (2) the possession of skilled personnel, and (3) the presence of the necessary technology and equipment. These technical requirements are all reported to be within Israel's possession.

In a comparative study conducted by Theodor Winkler (1981) and published by the London-based International Institute of Strategic Studies, Winkler compared the scientific capabilities of eight nuclear-threshold countries (Pakistan, India, Israel, South Africa, Libya, Iraq, South Korea, and Taiwan). The study listed Israel as the only country with "excellent" scientific and technological knowledge. India (a country that has already exploded what it termed a peaceful nuclear device) in addition to Pakistan and South Africa were all rated lower than Israel on this category.

Jabber (1971) discusses a symbiotic parallel between science and technology, and research and development, on the one hand, and the founders of the State of Israel and the primary objectives of that state, on the other. Jabber refers to the role played by Chaim Weizmann, Israel's first president and a noted scientist in the field of organic chemistry, and by science itself in the attainment of Zionist and later Israeli objectives.

The Israeli government's early interest in nuclear power was not an isolated development or an example of remarkable perspicacity and long-range vision, but only one expression of the primordial role science and technology have been assigned in facing the development and security problems of the country. This important factor should be constantly kept in mind in any study. (Jabber, 1971:16)

Weizmann believed that science was Israel's "mighty weapon," her "vessel of strength . . . and source of defence" (cited in Jabber, 1971:16). His assertion helps to clarify the fundamental role played by and assigned to science in the thinking of Israeli leaders.

In this assessment Israel's active engagement in different aspects of nuclear research, including the development of its own source of uranium and the acquisition of the necessary expertise for the different processes that make up the nuclear fuel cycle, has placed Israel as a donor or exporter of its own scientific knowledge in this field. This is an important consideration for assessing Israel's nuclear capabilities. Whether Israel is only a "screwdriver's turn" away from producing nuclear weapons, or whether it already has produced them may reside in this attribute. A United Nations (1982b:21) study observes that Israel "has the technological skills and expertise as well as the technical infrastructure required to manufacture nuclear weapons."

It is important in this respect to differentiate between Israel's decision to follow a policy of calculated ambiguity and its policy of scientific development. It is safe to state that while Israel did not allow the former to restrain the latter, scientific development proceeded unaffected by policy options. Quester (1973:87) elaborates: "It would be one thing for a country like Israel to postpone any explicit decision to manufacture and demonstrate its possession of nuclear weapons; it would be another to halt the scientific progress which inevitably draws the nation closer to weapons production."

DELIVERY SYSTEMS

As far as delivery systems are concerned, Israel possesses a sophisticated combination of missiles and advanced aircrafts that could carry and deliver nuclear warheads (see figure 4.1). In fact, *Time Magazine* (April 12, 1976:39) reported that during the 1973 Middle East war, Israel possessed "a nuclear arsenal of 13 atomic bombs, assembled, stored and ready to be dropped on enemy forces from specially equipped Kfir and Phantom fighters or Jericho missiles."

The British publication *All the World's Aircraft* (Jane's, 1984) reports that the Israeli Air Force possesses A-4 Skyhawk attack bombers (maximum range, 2,055 miles; maximum weapon load, 10,000 pounds); F-4 E Phantom fighter-bombers (maximum range, 2,300 miles; maximum weapon load, 16,000 pounds); and Mirage III B fighter-bombers (maximum combat radius, 745 miles; maximum weapon load, 8,000 pounds). All these figures make these aircrafts suitable and potential delivery vehicles (Chari, 1977:349). The United States has also armed Israel with the latest and most sophisticated F-16 AS fighter striker and F-15 A

Figure 4.1

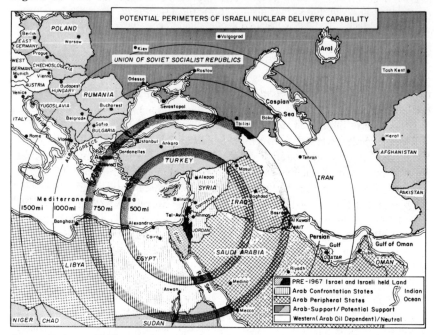

Source: Harkavy (1977:41). Reproduced with the permission of the University of Denver.

Eagle fighter/interceptor aircraft. These types of planes, using advanced avionic technology, were used in destroying the Iraqi nuclear reactor in 1981. Their high technology capabilities enabled them to fly towards their target in Iraq some 600 miles away unnoticed, even by 4 American Air Borne Warning and Control System (AWACS) surveillance planes that had been delivered to Saudi Arabia after the outbreak of hostilities between Iraq and Iran. (*US News and World Report,* June 22, 1981:18–21). SIPRI reports that 40 F-15 Eagles ordered in 1978 were delivered to Israel by 1982. That same year Israel requested 11 more to compensate for the sale of extra equipment to Saudi Arabia. In addition to 75 F-16 A aircraft already delivered, Israel placed an additional order of 75 more in 1982 (SIPRI 1983:319).

Israel's indigenous knowledge in avionics has also placed it as one of the most advanced countries in the Middle East in aircraft industries. According to reports from Washington following Prime Minister Yitzhak Shamir's visit to the United States in 1983, a new United States–Israeli partnership or strategic co-operation agreement allotted additional U.S. military aid to Israel in the form of grants rather than loans. Israel is said to have requested a large sum of this package for the development of its own LAVI fighter (*US News and World*

Report, December 12, 1983:34). Recent reports have indicated that the LAVI project is facing difficulties because of high financial costs.

A parallel project with the LAVI is the production of the Kfir (Lion Cub) fighter. Powered by a General Electric J79 afterburning turbojet, the Kfir has appeared in many versions (Kfir-C2; two-seater Kfir-TC2; the Kfir-C7, an improved version of the C2 with an increased payload/range capability; and the two-seater Kfir-TC7). It is reported that approximately 200 Kfirs of all versions had been produced by 1983 with production continuing (Jane's, 1984:125).

Israel's early interest in missiles could be traced back to 1963, according to an Israeli scholar, when the government of Levi Eshkol worked with the French Dessault Company on a mutual project to develop a short- to medium-range ballistic missile with nuclear-weapon-carrying capability (Aronson, 1977:2).

Two noted Indian scholars (Chari, 1977; Subrahmanyam, 1975) have also confirmed that Israel was engaged in confidential negotiations with the government of France in order to develop a surface-to-surface missile. Originally designated MD-660, this missile uses a solid fuel, has a range of 240 nautical miles, can be fired from a mobile camp, and is capable of carrying a 1,200–pound warhead. Firing trials were carried out off Toulon in the spring of 1968 (Harkavy, 1977b:33).

After the 1967 French arms embargo, Israel indigenously developed the two-stage Jericho missile, which is reported to have a range of 280 nautical miles (see figure 4.2). Chari (1977) asserts that Israel has been manufacturing three to six Jericho missiles a month. Jericho is believed to be capable of carrying a 1,000–pound to 1,500–pound warhead (*Stockholm International Peace Research Institute Yearbook,* 1973:371). Some military analysts have contended that the Jericho's production could be explained only in connection with a nuclear-weapon program, since in terms of payload and costs it represents an uneconomical investment if used with conventional warheads (Dowty, 1978:82). *The New York Times,* quoting "well placed American and Western intelligence reports," wrote that this production "would not make much sense to manufacture a costly weapon like the Jericho merely to carry the equivalent of two or three 500–pound bombs. The decision to go into production strongly suggests that Israel has, or believes it could soon have, nuclear warheads for the system. . . . Israel may have a number of nuclear weapon components that could be assembled quickly in crisis for use on the Jericho'' (Haselkorn, 1974:159).

Speculations have also emerged concerning Israel's development of a "cross breed" rocket engine that could use liquid or solid fuel. The project is reported to be "destined chiefly for guided missiles" (Friedman, 1974:33).

Israel has also received Lance surface-to-surface missiles from the United States. These missiles have a versatile range of 70 miles and are capable of carrying nuclear warheads (*The Christian Science Monitor,* December 3, 1981:16). The order for these U.S.-made missiles came amid reports of Israel's problems with its own Jericho guidance system (Dowty, 1978:82). The Lance

Figure 4.2

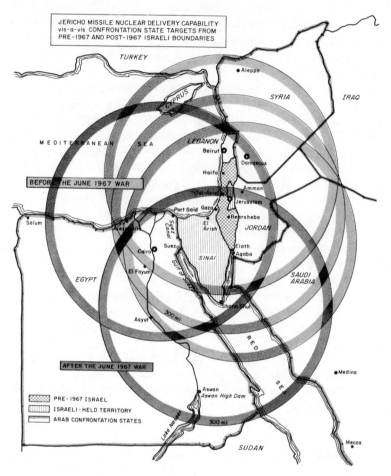

Source: Harkavy (1977:35). Reproduced with the permission of the University of Denver.

missile, however, is specifically used with nuclear warheads. In fact the U.S. Congress for cost-effective purposes, prohibited the Pentagon from producing a conventional warhead for the Lance missile until it could prove cost effective, a proof never presented, at least in public (Pranger and Tahtinen, 1975:31).

Even though the concept of an Israeli nuclear naval force has not received much attention, strategy and military analysts such as Harkavy (1977b:37) assert that a nuclear-tipped missile could be mounted on some of Israel's Saar or Reshef patrol boats presently armed with Gabriel ship-to-ship missiles. It is also reported that experiments have been carried out for the production of Gabriel III A/S, an air-to-surface weapon equipped with a fully active radar-seeker incorporating features. This version has a range of 25 miles, whereas the extended version

Gabriel III A/S ER has a longer range of 37 miles. Both versions are "smart," since they can be launched either in "fire and forget" or "fire and update" mode. The "fire and forget" descends to a low cruising altitude and follows an inertial course originally programmed for homing. The "fire and update" mode permits the launcher to deliver en route correction from the launch site, thus increasing accuracy (Jane's, 1984:740).

In 1975, as an "incentive" for Israel's approval of the Sinai interim accord, Israel officially demanded that the United States sell Pershing missiles. This order, which was met with a heated debate and was later withdrawn, raised speculations on the strategic purpose and use of this complex missile system (Lefever, 1979:71). It is known that the Pershing has a range of 100 to 540 miles and costs $1.8 million apiece. Furthermore, it has been deployed only as a strategic weapon in NATO.

Robert Harkavy (1977b), analyzing Israel's potential nuclear delivery systems, adds two components. First is the possibility of prepositioning nuclear weapons through a covert intelligence operation known as the bomb-in-the-suitcase theory. To support his argument, Harkavy cites previous daring Israeli operations such as Entebbe and the Beirut airport raid. He asserts that such an "esoteric means of delivery cannot discount Israeli willingness and capacity to make the attempt" (Harkavy, 1977b:38). Second, Israel's advanced production of remotely piloted vehicles (RPVs), which had proved successful in 1983 against Syrian SAM sites in the Bekaa Valley, would allow Israel to deploy a much more dispersed and mobile nuclear force.

It is important to highlight this mix between tactical aircraft and missile-delivery systems already possessed by Israel. Such a force has several advantages. First, it could allow for better penetration into hostile territories. Second, it could not become a victim of sophisticated, Soviet-made, anti-aircraft SAM interdiction, which proved effective in the 1973 war and during the war in Lebanon. Harkavy (1977b:34) supports this assertion: "As in the case of the superpower's 'triad' systems such a mixed delivery force would be effective in several complementary dimensions, which complicates defenses designed to cope with each form of threat." Third, in the event of an Israeli air force immobilization by a preemptive attack, its missiles could be ready to launch a counterattack (Chari, 1977:349). Fourth, particularly in a situation in which preemptive attacks are feared, a nuclear configured air force allows for an airborne alert. Further, a fighter aircraft provides for a "greater punch" than missiles (Harkavy, 1977b:36).

ISRAEL'S REGIONAL POLICY OF ESTABLISHING A UNILATERAL VETO ON THE POSSESSION OF NUCLEAR CAPABILITIES IN THE MIDDLE EAST

The Israeli raid on June 7, 1981, that culminated in the total destruction of the Iraqi nuclear installation has demonstrated that Israel can go to far limits in order to uphold its policy of establishing a unilateral veto on the possession of nuclear capabilities by any country in the Middle East. The IAEA Director General helped clarify the issue on June 9, 1981:

> Iraq has been a party to the Non-Proliferation Treaty since it came into force in 1970. In accordance with that Treaty, Iraq accepts agency safeguards on all its nuclear activities. These safeguards have been satisfactorily applied to date. The last safeguard inspection at the Iraqi nuclear center took place January of this year, and all material there was satisfactorily accounted for. This material included the fuel so far delivered for the Tamuz reactors. (IAEA press release/988:2)

The Egyptian scholar E. Galal (1982:75) argues that such an act has demonstrated Israel's determination to "supersede the international non proliferation system by attempting to impose a regional military nuclear monopoly by military means."

Understandably, there are international concerns over the issue of horizontal proliferation. However, questioning the efficacy of the IAEA safeguard system or the value of the NPT is no license for such attacks. Again, we would be avoiding the main issue—namely, the presence of Dimona as the only unsafeguarded nuclear installation in the Middle East.

An Israeli colonel (ret.) Meir Pa'il (1982:61) argues, "Since Israel would not be able to play for long the role of the nuclear policeman who destroys Arab nuclear reactors undisturbed, Israel must initiate a nuclear demilitarization of the Middle East and offer to open its nuclear option to efficient international inspection."

CONCLUSION

In sum, Israel's nuclear policy could be described as one of deterrence, yet unavowed, nondeclarative, unilateral, ambigious, and relying on psychological threats. The study offered here is important, since it demonstrates the relationship between Israel's nuclear option and Israel's foreign policy-making. E. Galal, writing for an Israeli publication, explains:

> Israel's nuclear strategy has clear, well established characteristics:
>
> a) The acquisition of full nuclear capabilities to cover the whole region with both strategic and tactical capabilities.
>
> b) Safeguarding full autonomy and independence for this nuclear capability.
>
> c) Assuring a perpetual monopoly in the region.
>
> d) Avoiding open declaration or overt demonstration of this capability as long as military dominance is assured by conventional weapon superiority while clandestinely using all non-conventional methods to develop this capability. (Galal, 1982:77)

Some question the viability of establishing a NWFZ in the Middle East and in fact argue against Israel's relinquishing its nuclear posture. They contend that a treaty establishing a NWFZ in the Middle East would be in the Arab world's favor and would force Israel into relinquishing an important bargaining chip. In response to these critics this study wishes to postulate the following. First, this study understands Israel's security preoccupation and does not wish to render Israel in a disadvantageous position. This study asserts, however, that security for Israel does not lie in a fragile system of undeclared nuclear deterrence, but rather that security should rest on a legally binding instrument to free the Middle East from nuclear menace. History has proved that peace with Egypt remains strong, alive, and well. Egypt considers its peace with Israel as one vital cornerstone of its foreign policy. Peace should be allowed to broaden in order to encompass other parties and to spill over into other fields. Israel's acceptance of—coupled with forthcoming moves from other Arab countries—and aligning with the NPT regime could help achieve a cardinal step towards realizing a just, lasting, and comprehensive peace in the regime. Second, Israel's policy of implementing a unilateral veto on countries in the region aspiring for the nuclear option is not without flaws, for soon Israel may be faced with a situation whereby an Arab country could possess nuclear capabilities. Lessons from history could be drawn to avert the repetition of Israel's successful attack on the Iraqi nuclear installation. In this case the NWFZ approach can serve best Israel's intentions and prevent such a situation from occurring. The rationale for denuclearizing the Middle East as a result gains topicality and urgency.

It is to this task we now turn. In chapter 5 a survey of the Middle East NWFZ initiative from 1974 to the present will be presented. Positions will be analyzed and events scrutinized. Since the thrust of this study focuses on the NWFZ approach as the "only solution," it is time to examine that solution analytically and thoroughly.

Table 4.1 demonstrates the position taken by the majority of states in the Middle East on effective international control and safeguard measures to prevent the proliferation of nuclear weapons to the region. As shown, major states (some bordering Israel) such as Egypt, Iraq, Iran, Syria, Jordan, Lebanon, and Libya have all signed and ratified the NPT and have concluded safeguard agreements with the IAEA.

The following chapter outlines the requirements for prevention of nuclear-weapon proliferation in the Middle East, which center around the establishment of a NWFZ. Since the genesis of this proposal has been encompassed since 1974 by the United Nations, this chapter will trace historically the evolution of a specific issue—the establishment of a NWFZ—in the Middle East. The positions of states in the region will be surveyed and contrasted to important political events that governed the area. A summary of the positions taken by both superpowers will also be advanced.

Table 4.1
Status of Non-Proliferation Treaties and Disarmament Agreements:
The Middle East Case

Countries	Partial Test Ban		NPT		Safeguards Agreement with International Atomic Energy Agency in Connection with NPT
	S	R	S	R	
Algeria	X				
Bahrain					
Djibouti					
Egypt	X	X	X	X	In force: June 30, 1982
Iran	X	X	X	X	In force: May 15, 1974
Iraq	X	X	X	X	In force: February 29, 1972
Israel	X	X			
Jordan	X	X	X	X	In force: February 21, 1978
Kuwait	X	X	X		
Lebanon	X	X	X	X	In force: March 5, 1973
Libya	X	X	X	X	In force: July 8, 1980
Mauritania	X	X			
Morocco	X	X	X	X	In force: February 18, 1975
Oman					
Qatar					
Saudi Arabia					
Somalia	X	X	X	X	
Sudan	X	X	X	X	In force: January 7, 1977
Syria	X	X	X	X	
Tunisia	X	X	X	X	
United Arab Emirates					
Yemen	X		X	X	
Democratic Yemen		X	X	X	

Source: United Nations (1983b); International Atomic Energy Agency (1982).

NOTE

1. The Dimona reactor or (IRR-2) is a natural uranium research reactor, heavy-water moderated, with a 25–megawatt thermal capacity. It became operative in December 1963, with the help of French scientists. Dimona has an annual plutonium production rate of some 8–10 kilograms, which is within the vicinity of what is considered to be required for the production of one plutonium weapon. In 1981 a Swiss expert on nuclear physics, Theodor Winkler, using the same data and figures, estimated that Israel could have produced as many as twenty nuclear-weapon cores (*Christian Science Monitor*, December 3, 1981).

5

THE UNITED NATIONS AND THE ESTABLISHMENT OF A NWFZ IN THE MIDDLE EAST: PATTERNS OF INVOLVEMENT, 1974–1985

INTRODUCTION

The problems and prospects for the establishment of a NWFZ can be best considered and evaluated against the background of the evolutionary history of developments in the Middle East, especially recently. And for this purpose that history is no better revealed than in the twists and turns of efforts and initiatives as they have unfolded in the United Nations since 1974. Accordingly, the purpose of this chapter is to chronologically trace the stages and phases that have governed the process within the United Nations with regard to this item on the agenda of the UN General Assembly between 1974 and 1985. We will now turn to survey that history sequentially.

The item bearing the title "Establishment of a Nuclear Free Zone in the Region of the Middle East" was included on the General Assembly's agenda in the twenty-ninth session. In response, on July 15, 1974, Iran dispatched an Explanatory Memorandum (A/9693) in which it stated three main points. First, the point was made that developments in the region imparted a sense of urgency to this proposal because "greater access by states to nuclear technology has rendered the danger of nuclear weapon proliferation and a concomitant collapse of the non-proliferation structure, a more acute problem.'' Second was the point that the General Assembly was the most suitable organ in which a proposal of this nature could be discussed. Third was the statement that as a result of the ambiguity surrounding the geographic designation of the region and its security interests, the decision on the precise delimitation of such a zone should be left to the General Assembly. Iran, however, asserted that the preference was for the zone to include "as wide an area as possible.''

Eight days later and following extensive consultations between Egypt and Iran, Egypt decided to cosponsor the Iranian request (A/9693/Add.1 of July 23, 1974). These consultations resulted in a bilateral understanding between both countries to change the title of the item from "Establishment of a Nuclear Free Zone'' to "Establishment of a Nuclear Weapon Free Zone'' (A/9693/Add.2 of August 22, 1974). Both countries had agreed that the thrust of the initiative should be directed against the dangers of nuclear weapons and should not hamper their mutual quest for the use of nuclear energy for peaceful purposes, which resulted in adding the word *Weapon* to the title of the item. A message sent by the shah of Iran, Mohamed-Reza Pahlavi, to the UN Secretary General clarified that position:

> Atomic science represents man's best hopes for survival and his worst fears of doom. If coming generations are to enjoy the blessing of that technology and be free of its burdens, if we want to open new doorways to peace, we must be as bold and as imaginative in curbing the spread of nuclear arms as we have been in creating them. (A/9693/Add.3 of September 17, 1974).

This same letter went on to discuss the conditions governing the proliferation of nuclear technology and to caution against processing fissile material and the wider dissemination of scientific knowledge that could make acquisition of nuclear weapons a "less burdensome undertaking.'' The letter stated that "within the political setting of our region this might mean more than a mere involvement of adversaries in a senseless and wasteful nuclear arms race.''

Several conditions governed the position of both countries and served as an incentive for the introduction of this item. First, the emergence of a conducive climate of understanding between Egypt and Iran followed the 1973 Arab-Israeli war. The late President Anwar el-Sadat described this new relationship in his book *In Search of Identity*. He described how the relationship evolved from one of animosity between both countries under Gamal Abdel Nasser to that of mutual understanding under his own presidency.

> Today I am proud to state that Egypt's relations with Iran and with the whole world are based on mutual respect and trust. I shall never forget the day when the Egyptian Petroleum reserves fell to a dangerously low level, after the October 1973 War due to the closure of our oilfields. I sent word to the Shah of Iran and he immediately supplied us with more than 500,000 tons. He actually ordered Iranian oil tankers that were at sea to change course and go directly to Egypt to offer help.

He said: 'El-Sadat is a brother to me, I shall respond to his request on the spot. (Sadat, 1978:212–13)

Second, it became evident during and following the 1973 Arab-Israeli war that the region came close to the brink of a nuclear exchange. This was underscored by the fact that regionally Israel did not dismiss altogether the nuclear alternative as a last resort, in the event of a defeat with conventional weapons or in a situation whereby Israel's heartland became endangered. Reports to this effect were cited by *Time* magazine (April 12, 1976:39), in which it was reported that thirteen Israeli nuclear warheads were "hastily assembled at a secret underground tunnel during a 78–hour period at the start of the 1973 October War and were sent to desert arsenals where they remain today, still ready for use" (39). The crossing of the Suez Canal by the Egyptian army was considered an unparalled victory by worldwide military experts (including many Israelis such as Professor Shlomo Aronson [1977:11] of the Hebrew University in Jerusalem, who described this operation as a "tremendous success"). During that phase of the war, Israel faced an unprecedented defeat on the Egyptian and Syrian fronts, compelling Israeli Prime Minister Golda Meir to cable Washington on the fourth day of the war to "Save Israel" (Sadat, 1978:268).

Third, this same war also demonstrated the dangers of drawing both the Soviet Union and the United States to the edge of a nuclear holocaust. Both superpowers airlifted supplies and supplied military hardware and technology to the opposing sides, and were thus involved in the war. The global perspective of that war was in essence one of East-West confrontation through third parties or "pawns" (Russett, 1971). This prompted Henry Kissinger to assert to President Sadat in November 1973 that the United States would never tolerate a Soviet weapons victory over American equipment (Sadat, 1978:264).

Perhaps the most dangerous moments of that war came when the United States went on a worldwide general mobilization of its forces. As U.S. President Richard Nixon 1980:93 described the situation, "Our airlift to Israel and the alert of our forces which I ordered in 1973 with the knowledge that these actions might lead to an Arab oil embargo were a demonstration of how far the United States will go to keep our commitment to Israel's survival." Henry Kissinger observed that the American worldwide alert prompted the Soviets to place elements of the East German army on alert. This in turn forced the United States, according to Kissinger, to alert the Eighty-second Airborne Division and to dispatch two aircraft carriers, the *F.D. Roosevelt* and the *J.F. Kennedy,* to join the carrier *Independence* east of the Mediterranean. The U.S. forces were ordered to a state of alert, known as DefConIII, which "increases readiness without the determination that war is likely." Nixon cabled Sadat, requesting him "to consider the consequences for your country if the two great nuclear countries were thus to confront each other on your soil" (Kissinger, 1982:588). A lesson to be deduced from such actions is that both superpowers seemed willing to go to dangerous limits in order to honor their commitments and secure their interests in the region (Russett, 1971).

Finally, the period of the early 1970s coincided with the launching of ambitious programs by Egypt and Iran for the peaceful uses of nuclear energy. Both countries had requested nuclear-power reactors from the United States and thus were in need of demonstrating the seriousness of their intentions to the American legislative branch. The pro-Israeli lobby in the U.S. Congress argued against the approval of the sale of reactors to Egypt. John F. Roehm, Professor of Military Science (cited in Spanier and Nogee, 1981:31) demonstrated how the Egyptian request for a nuclear reactor ''raised a storm of controversy in Congress,'' which resulted in a provision in the 1974 Foreign Military Sales Act (the Nelson-Bingham bill), authorizing Congress to ''veto U.S. arms sales to foreign governments of $25 million or more'' (*Congressional Quarterly Almanac*, 93rd Cong., 2nd sess., 1974:30, 1975:542, 546). The introduction, therefore, of the NWFZ initiative by both Egypt and Iran could be viewed as a means of demonstrating the good will of both parties, thus, softening opposition to their demands for peaceful nuclear reactors. (Egypt at that time, it may be recalled, had not yet ratified the Non-Proliferation Treaty.)

In 1974 a draft resolution was presented to the First Committee of the UN General Assembly by Egypt and Iran. The issue subsequently was opened for a debate. Egypt argued three fundamental principles pertinent to the discussion about a Middle East NWFZ: (1) the states of the region should refrain from producing, acquiring, or processing nuclear weapons; (2) the nuclear-weapon states should refrain from introducing nuclear weapons into the area or using nuclear weapons against any state of the region; and (3) an effective international safeguard system affecting both the nuclear-weapon states and the states of the region should be established. Egypt also emphasized that the establishment of NWFZ should not hamper states from enjoying the benefits of the peaceful uses of nuclear energy, especially given the economic needs of the developing countries (United Nations, 1976a:108). With respect to the general debate that ensued, several observations can be made.

First, most states in the region supported the initiative, which in turn became a strong factor in demonstrating intraregional agreement, a factor missing from the South Asian NWFZ initiative, for example.

Second, all five nuclear states supported and voted in favor of the resolution (see appendix A for text).[1] The United States, for example, supported the resolution, stating that the zone ''could make a considerable contribution to stability and non proliferation'' (United Nations, 1976a:108). The United States cautioned, however, that requesting regional states to undertake commitments with regard to the establishment of such a zone a priori of actual negotiations and an agreement was a dubious procedure (United Nations, 1976a:108).

Third, most of the reservations presented were in connection with paragraphs 13 and 14 of the preamble and operative paragraph 3, all dealing with the NPT.

The resolution called on concerned parties in the area to accede to the Non-Proliferation Treaty, and towards such an end, recalled resolution 2373 of June 12, 1968, which requested the widest possible adherence to the NPT. As a matter of fact this resolution was not accepted by numerous non-NPT members. Concomitantly, countries such as India, Argentina, China, and France all expressed reservations about the paragraphs referring to the NPT (United Nations, 1976a:108). However, following consultations conducted by the Egyptian and Iranian representatives with the aforementioned countries, an agreement was reached to secure the widest possible support for the initiative by allowing these delegations to register their reservations in an explanation of their votes, but to vote in favor of the resolution as a whole.

Fourth, although Israel did not vote in favor, it did not vote against the resolution. Israel's abstention, on the other hand, may be explained in the light of two factors. The first factor is domestic. Internal opposition to Israel's nuclear option and support for a NWFZ in the Middle East dates back to the early 1960s, when the Committee for the Denuclearization of the Israeli-Arab Conflict was formed. The committee argued that the "adoption of a nuclear option was a fundamental mistake." Additionally, the Mapam party started a debate in the Knesset and is on record calling for a NWFZ in the Middle East. Pajak (1982:33) has described how this initiative was widely endorsed by the public by noting, "These objectives met with considerable sympathy from among the public and some leading members of the major political parties."

The second factor is political and is tied to an apparent policy of nuclear ambiguity or psychological deterrence. An Israeli vote against the resolution might have directed world attention to its unsafeguarded nuclear facilities. On the other hand, a vote in favor would have dissipated Arab fears, thus affecting the psychological deterrent. Hence, the abstention provided a convenient way to reiterate the original Israeli position that the countries concerned in the Middle East must conduct direct preparatory negotiations. Such a proviso has been considered by many to be unfeasible as long as Israel occupies territories of three Arab states, including the holy religious city of Jerusalem.

The Israeli abstention in the United Nations was explained in terms of the necessity of holding direct consultations between states in the Middle East and ultimately convening a regional conference. At this stage the Arabs stated they could not accept that stipulation, since direct consultations implied recognition of Israel, an issue closely related to the complexities of the Arab-Israeli conflict. As a way out of the emergent dilemma, Egypt introduced an amendment calling for a "preliminary process of consultations between the Secretary General and the states of the region" (United Nations, 1976a:108). Israel, however, considered such a step an "impractical" starter (United Nations, 1976a:108). It is interesting to note here the similarity between the positions of Israel and the United States on this issue. That convergence resulted in the removal of the Egyptian amendment from the body of the resolution in order to avoid an American negative vote on the issue. Operative paragraph 5 requested only that the Secretary General ascertain views with respect to the implementation of this resolution.

On December 9, 1974, the General Assembly adopted the draft as amended (Resolution 3263) by 128 votes to none, with only 2 abstentions (Israel and Burma). The resolution "commended the idea of establishing a NWFZ in the Middle East, considered that it was indispensable that all parties concerned in the area to proclaim solemnly and immediately their intention to refrain, on a reciprocal basis, from producing, testing, obtaining, acquiring or in any other way possessing nuclear weapons" (see appendix A for full text). Additionally, the General Assembly called upon the parties concerned in the area to "accede to the Treaty on the Non-Proliferation of Nuclear Weapons [and] requested the Secretary General to ascertain the views of the parties concerned with respect to the implementation of the resolution, and to inform the Security Council at an early date and the General Assembly at its thirtieth session (Resolution 3263). This phraseology envisaged a link between the Secretary General and the Security Council concerning the implementation of the resolution.

Implementing operative paragraph 5 of Resolution 3263, the UN Secretary General in 1975 invited several countries in the Middle East[2] to convey to him their views on the implementation of the resolution, particularly in reference to operative paragraphs 2 and 3. These paragraphs related to two basic ideas: a proclamation by the countries concerned to refrain, on a reciprocal basis, from producing, testing, obtaining, and acquiring nuclear weapons; and a call to all parties in the region to accede to the NPT.

Seven governments[3] responded to the Secretary General. Their replies were reproduced in Document S/11778 of July 28, 1975, entitled "Report of the Secretary-General." In all seven replies there was a clear-cut endorsement of the idea of a NWFZ in the Middle East. All countries stated their readiness to proclaim their intentions to refrain from producing, testing, and acquiring nuclear weapons, provided that Israel undertook a similar commitment. Syria elaborated on this by requesting "all parties concerned in the region to proclaim officially their undertaking [and] that adequate international control measures should be established to ensure the constant respect by these parties concerned for their commitments" (S/11778 of July 28, 1975).

With respect to accession to the NPT, some governments stressed that they had already joined, while others indicated that they had signed and would ratify once Israel had joined the NPT. The Egyptian reply, contained in the document S/11778 of July 18, 1975, however, referred to the necessity of accession to the NPT as an indispensable measure towards the establishment of such a NWFZ in the Middle East. The Egyptian reply went on to highlight the importance of securing the cooperation of all states, particularly the nuclear-weapon states, in agreeing to a solemn obligation neither to use nuclear weapons against countries in the Middle East nor to introduce or place nuclear weapons in the Middle East.

According to this proposal, Egypt called for the establishment of an effective international control system for the supervision of these commitments.

Consequently, Israel sent her reply to the Secretary General on September 22, 1975, several days following the opening of the General Assembly. The Israeli reply (UN document A/10221/Add.1 of October 8, 1975) contained the following elements:

(1) The establishment of a NWFZ in the Middle East was termed a "desirable further step towards a just and durable peace in the region, *in the light of the new climate created by the recent agreement between Israel and Egypt*" (A/10221/Add.1 of October 8, 1975:2–3).

(2) A parallel was drawn between Tlatelolco and the Middle East NWFZ. The success of the latter was seen to rely on direct negotiations, a facilitative factor proposed towards the success of the former.

(3) Israel proclaimed her readiness to participate in a conference of all states in the region, linking the proclamation called for in paragraph 2 of the resolution with the successful outcome of the negotiations for the establishment of such a NWFZ.

(4) No promises were made concerning the Non-Proliferation Treaty.

This reply revealed Israel's effort to link Egypt's proposal for the establishment of a NWFZ with recent disengagement agreements that had been worked out between Egypt and Israel.[4] Thus, the mention of such a "new climate created by the recent agreement between Israel and Egypt" appeared as an attempt to ostracize Egypt intraregionally, thereby diminishing crucial Arab support for this NWFZ proposal.

The Israeli reply also logically carried the insinuation that since "direct negotiations" had succeeded in bringing into being the Tlatelolco Treaty, two disengagement agreements with Egypt and one with Syria, then the success of a NWFZ would be facilitated best through direct negotiations. The absence, however, in Latin America of a historic conflict similar to the Arab-Israel conflict in the Middle East provided an environment conducive to direct negotiations between Latin American countries. Also, the Israeli reply made the disengagement agreements between the military forces of Egypt and Syria on one side and Israel on the other look like a disarmament agreement, when in reality they were not. Hence, calling for direct negotiations on the basis of these two points was invalid.

The Israeli response to the concept of a proclamation declaring a willingness to "refrain from producing, testing, obtaining or acquiring nuclear weapons" was a classic example of diplomatic ambiguity. Israel's support for such a proclamation was made conditional on "the successful outcome of negotiations for the establishment of a NWFZ in the region" (A/10221/Add.1, 1975:3). Hence, Israel insisted not only on conducting "direct negotiations" but also on a priori assurances of "successful outcomes" even before such negotiations started.

In addition, the efforts to persuade Israel to join the NPT were swiftly brushed aside. The Israeli response contained in the same document stated that "at present" Israel was "studying its legal and other implications." Even within this context the reference to studying the legal implications of the NPT was ambiguous. No support for the treaty was ever mentioned in the Israeli reply.

This reply prompted Ismael Fahmy, Egypt's Deputy Prime Minister and Minister for Foreign Affairs, to dispatch an additional memorandum to the UN Secretary General stating two basic points. The first was in conjunction with Israel's reference to its vote in favor of General Assembly Resolution 2373 adopting the text of the Non-Proliferation Treaty:

> This position . . . is meaningless unless followed by Israel's accession to the Treaty through signature, ratification and observance of all the provisions thereof. Israel also rejects any international inspection with regard to its nuclear reactor at Dimona, and is determined to acquire sophisticated weapons with nuclear potential. Moreover, Israel's indication that it is at present studying the legal and other implications of the Non-Proliferation Treaty does not make the well known Israeli position any more serious. More than seven years have elapsed since the establishment of the Treaty, thus Israel has had ample time to examine and re-examine the implications of the Treaty instead of evading accession to it, and of doing nothing except indicating that it is studying the Treaty and its legal and other implications. . . . As regards Israel's demand that negotiations between the States of the region should be the only means by which a nuclear-weapon-free zone could be established, Israel thereby lays down conditions which it realizes are rejected *a priori,* with a view to evading accession to the Treaty on the Non-Proliferation of Nuclear Weapons. There is a host of methods which can be followed if the intentions are truly good, such as the accession of all the States of the region to the Treaty on the Non-Proliferation of Nuclear Weapons. This method alone would ensure that the region will be free from nuclear weapons; that may be followed, for example, by a binding declaration to refrain from introducing or using nuclear weapons, to be issued by all the States of the region which are Members of the United Nations or members of the International Atomic Energy Agency, Vienna. (A/10221/Add.2 of October 15, 1975)

During the thirtieth session of the General Assembly in 1975, the same item was reinscribed on the agenda on the basis of the last operative paragraphs of Resolution 3263 of 1974. Bahrain, Jordan, Kuwait, and Tunisia cosponsored the Egyptian-Iranian resolution. This increase in the number of cosponsors was viewed as an indication that the initiative was being received favorably by other states in the Middle East.

In substance the 1975 draft was not much different from its predecessor. In fact, this draft reiterated all of the basic provisions of Resolution 3263. The only substantive change came in a paragraph recommending that the member states with which the Secretary General consulted "should exert efforts towards the

realization of a nuclear-weapon-free zone in the region of the Middle East''
(United Nations, 1977:71).

Throughout the debate on the resolution the same basic positions were repeated. Israel again requested preparatory negotiations. The United States ques-
tioned the method whereby governments were requested to pledge a priori
commitments before the initiation of the actual process of negotiations for the
establishment of the zone. In the end, however, the draft was adopted as Resolution 3474 by an overwhelming majority (125 votes in favor to none against
it, with 2 abstentions—Israel and Cameroon).

During the thirty-first General Assembly in 1976, Egypt, Iran, and Kuwait
submitted a draft resolution, cosponsored later by Bahrain, Jordan, Mauritania,
Sudan, and the United Arab Emirates. The inclusion of Mauritania was an
indication of the enlargement of the geographic scope and support for such a
NWFZ, even though the process for defining the zone per se was not referred
to in the body of the text itself.

Although the same basic governmental positions were reiterated, the draft
reflected the encouragement of the cosponsors resulting from the wide support
given to the 1974 and 1975 resolutions. Several basic ammendments were incorporated. First, the reference to Tlatelolco as a "notable achievement" incorporated in both the 1974 and 1975 texts was deleted following consultations
between the Egyptian and Soviet delegations.[5] Egypt and Iran, attempting to
minimize opposition to the text, decided to withdraw altogether any reference
to Tlatelolco in order to avoid Soviet reservations.

Second, the resolution, for the first time, focused its attention on *ad interim*
arrangements, pending the final stage of establishing the zone. These measures,
basically taken from previous years, stipulated the need to refrain, on a reciprocal
basis, from the production, acquisition, or possession of any nuclear weapons.
A new phrase was added here and referred to "nuclear explosive devices." This
language was inspired by India's "peaceful nuclear explosion." Hence, the
cosponsors, attempting to rid the Middle East of any such dangers, incorporated
in the 1976 text explicit reference to the prohibition of "nuclear explosive
devices" as well as nuclear weapons. The resolution also called on all parties
to adhere to the NPT, to place their nuclear activities under IAEA safeguards,
and to reaffirm the responsibilities of the nuclear-weapon states towards the zone.

The treatment of these fundamental provisions as *ad interim* measures reflected
the realization of the problematic difficulties facing the initiative. The cosponsors
and their respective capitals felt, however, that support for the initiative was
large enough to enable the eventual establishment of the zone and to convince
Israel to join the NPT and accept IAEA safeguards. The resolution was adopted
in 1976 as Resolution 31/71 by a vote of 130 to none, with one abstention—
Israel.

A separate vote, however, was requested by India on paragraphs 2 and 3,
referring to the NPT, but the paragraphs were adopted by 117 votes to none,
with 13 abstentions, mainly from non-NPT states.[6]

In 1977 (thirty-second session) the General Assembly had before it the same item, with Egypt, Iran, Bahrain, Kuwait, Qatar, and Yemen presenting a draft resolution on the issue to the First Committee. The resolution, in substance, was not different from the one adopted in 1976. The changes incorporated were cosmetic in nature and did not affect the thrust of the initiative. In the debate Egypt stressed that the conditions in the Middle East made the issue worthy of concern. Toward this end, principles had been devised to ensure the safety of the region from the dangers of nuclear proliferation. These included requesting regional states to pledge, *inter alia,* their support for this NWFZ, not to acquire nuclear weapons, to adhere to the NPT, and to place all activities under IAEA safeguards. Egypt stated that a nuclear threat was hovering over the region, and if "Israel obtained nuclear weapons, Egypt could not be expected to stand idly by in the face of that development" (United Nations, 1978b:175).

Israel expressed throughout the debate its support for such a NWFZ. However, the Israeli representative reiterated the necessity of establishing such a zone through negotiations. Towards this end Israel called on the Arab states to join in such "direct negotiations with a view to establishing such a zone by the conclusion of a formal, contractual, and multilateral convention between all states in the region" (United Nations, 1978b:176). The position of all other parties including the Unites States remained unchanged.

It seemed, however, that the momentum generated in previous years was difficult to maintain, especially in regard to actual steps to be taken towards the implementation of this UN resolution. Regional parties seemed deadlocked in unchanged and unyielding positions, while the five nuclear-weapon states, particularly the two superpowers, presented face-saving support without exerting any pressure on the parties.

Numerically, the 1977 text (Resolution 32/82) was still adopted by an overwhelming majority (131 to none, with Israel the only state abstaining). A seperate vote was again requested on the paragraphs dealing with accession to the NPT[7] and references to the necessity of placing nuclear activities under IAEA safeguards[8] (operative paragraphs 1 and 2).

One important historic development occurred on November 19, 1977. That was the date of President Sadat's historic journey to Jerusalem. For the first time the President of Egypt, the strongest and oldest country in the region, crossed the psychological barrier into a *de jure* recognition of Israel. While this trip had an unprecedented impact on the General Assembly, such an impact was not totally manifested in the language of the resolution. Since the trip coincided with the later meetings of the thirty-second General Assembly, it did not affect the language of the resolution itself.

A different form and shape of Egyptian-Israeli relations, however, started to emerge. With such changes came a variety of expectations, among them that Israel would finally feel obliged to reciprocate and work collaboratively towards the long-sought-for just and durable peace in the Middle East.

On the Israeli side there was euphoria, whereas guarded optimism marked the position of the Egyptian delegation to the United Nations. The trip to Jerusalem was seen as just a beginning, for several paramount issues remained unresolved.[9]

This new environment created a situation calling for the Egyptian UN delegation to strike a magic formula among several interrelated concerns. These factors included the following:

(1) Egypt's quest to keep the Middle East NWFZ initiative alive and well by scoring progress towards its implementation

(2) Adjusting to the new reality created by President Sadat's initiative, especially in connection with the Egyptian-Israeli relationship in the United Nations

(3) Maintaining regional support for the initiative by preventing its entanglement in intra-Arab discord and conflicting interpretations of the Jerusalem trip

(4) Preventing Israel from practicing a divide-and-rule policy by playing Egypt against its Arab colleagues and vice versa

(5) Utilizing the momentum generated by the United States' constructive involvement in bringing about peace in the Middle East in order to achieve progress in denuclearizing the Middle East.

In 1978 the United Nations convened its First Special Session on Disarmament. From May 23 to July 1 the General Assembly, following arduous negotiations, approved the Final Document (A/S-10/4) by consensus. In part 3 of that document, entitled "Program of Action," paragraphs 60–64 dealt with NWFZs. Paragraph 63 (d), in particular, observed the following on a NWFZ in the Middle East:

> The serious consideration of the practical and urgent steps, as described in paragraphs above, required for the implementation of the proposal to establish a nuclear-weapon-free zone in the Middle East, in accordance with the relevant General Assembly resolutions, where all parties directly concerned have expressed their support for the concept and where the danger of nuclear-weapon proliferation exists. The establishment of a nuclear-weapon-free zone in the Middle East would greatly enhance international peace and security. Pending the establishment of such a zone in the region, States of the region should solemnly declare that they will refrain on a reciprocal basis from producing, acquiring or in any other way possessing nuclear weapons and nuclear explosive devices and from permitting the stationing of nuclear weapons on their territory by any third party, and agree to place all their nuclear activities under International Atomic Energy Agency safeguards. Consideration should be given to a Security Council role in advancing the establishment of a nuclear-weapon-free zone in the Middle East. (A/S-10/4, 1978:12–13)

The developments specific to this phraseology are twofold. First, reference to the Non-Proliferation Treaty was deleted altogether, since it became evident that getting the General Assembly to approve the document by consensus entailed accommodating non-NPT states. Second, attempting to invigorate the initiative, Egypt proposed a wider role for the Security Council in promoting this NWFZ in the Middle East. This proposal was met with consternation, as it became evident that both superpowers were apprehensive of any such linkage. The paragraph adopted accordingly represented a compromise that left open the question of an enhanced Security Council role in advancing the initiative. However, this issue became the cornerstone of numerous deliberations in the years that followed.

In 1978 another resolution was tabled for consideration. Again the debate in the First Committee reflected substantial support for the initiative, both in the context of maintaining the Middle East free of nuclear weapons and strengthening the security of non–nuclear-weapon states (United Nations, 1979:290).

The issue of devising a stronger role for the Security Council was raised agian by Egypt. Egypt observed that such a role was crucial for the establishment of such a NWFZ and in dealing with any violations of such a zone. Reference was made to Security Council Resolution 255 of 1968, in which the nuclear-weapon states recognized that any nuclear aggression or threat of such aggression against a non–nuclear-weapon state would force them to react "in accordance with their obligations under the United Nations Charter." Iran supported the Egyptian proposal and explained that the resolution under debate contained a notable substantive change, involving paragraph 63 (d) of the Final Document of the First Special Session on Disarmament. This change centered on inviting the parties concerned to declare their support for the establishment of a NWFZ in the Middle East and to deposit those declarations with the Security Council. The representative of Iran explained:

> The process of depositing those declarations with the Security Council would put the whole undertaking on a more solid foundation. The Security Council role [is] perceived in a flexible manner as applying both to the methods by which the purpose of the paragraph would be implemented and to the time frame and necessary stages towards the establishment of a nuclear-weapon-free zone. (United Nations, 1979:291)

The efforts, however, either to establish a more active role for the Security Council or to extract specific assurances from the nuclear-weapon states for this NWFZ failed. The role of the Security Council remained reactive. But it appeared that insisting on such an issue would jeopardize the support given by the nuclear-weapon states to this initiative since 1974.

In terms of substance the resolution contained the same basic principles carried from previous texts. Again, changes were cosmetic in nature, except for the reference to depositing declarations with the Security Council. The cosponsors also decided again to dilute reference to adherence to the Non-Proliferation Treaty, substituting the verb *invites* for *urges* (the language of the previous resolutions). The reason for this was that strong reference to the NPT resulted in undue opposition and reservations from extraregional states not party to the treaty.

This development subsequently gave Egypt enough diplomatic leverage to avoid a separate vote on paragraphs referring to the NPT, enabling it to convince other non-NPT states that the language of such paragraphs were not directed against them. However, in 1978 these changes could not be accommodated, and India again requested a separate vote on two paragraphs dealing with accession to the NPT and the placement of nuclear activities under IAEA safeguards. These paragraphs were adopted (103 to none, with fifteen states abstaining).[10] The General Assembly adopted the draft on December 14, 1978, as Resolution 33/64, by 138 to none, with but one abstention—Israel (United Nations, 1979:292).

In 1979 two important developments occurred. The first was the signature of a peace treaty between Egypt and Israel on March 26. The second was the downfall of the shah of Iran. The Iranian revolt created a situation of disarray at the Iranian Mission to the United Nations. Experienced diplomats were displaced by figures who had little knowledge of the fabric, functioning, and mechanics of the United Nations. It soon became evident that Iran was neither capable of nor inclined to present the annual resolution or even to cosponsor it with Egypt.

Egypt consequently was faced with a difficult decision. The delegation could either present the initiative alone and stand the risk of criticism and revocation from a hostile "rejectionist"[11] Arab front—then comprising Syria, Libya, the PLO, and Yemen—or could withdraw (since Iran, the original cosponsor of the resolution, was not in a position to cosponsor the resolution with Egypt at that time).

The decision, taken at the highest level, was that Egypt should present the resolution independently. Consequently, Egypt presented a draft resolution to the First Committee of the General Assembly. To avoid any surprises, the decision was reached to keep the resolution in line with those adopted in previous years. An intensive cycle of informal consultations was conducted with the African group; the nonaligned, individual Arab representatives; and groups in other geographic regions, including Latin America, Asia, Eastern and Western Europe. Egypt referred to the growing international support for a NWFZ initiative in the Middle East and pointed to the dangers of nuclear-weapon proliferation in the region (United Nations, 1980:179).

Despite the inflammatory rhetoric referring to Egypt's peace with Israel that was emanating from certain rejectionist delegations, the resolution was approved by an unprecedented 136 votes to none, with one abstention—Israel (Resolution 34/77 of December 11, 1979). For the first time, as a result of extensive lobbying and consultations, no separate vote was requested on either paragraph dealing with the Non-Proliferation Treaty or with placing nuclear activities under IAEA safeguards. Instead, several explanations of votes were requested. The debate demonstrated that Egypt's peace with Israel had not circumscribed Egypt's quest for a just and lasting peace in the region and in fact may have been part and parcel of that quest. Thus, while Egypt welcomed its new peace with Israel, this did not inhibit Egypt from negotiating the unresolved differences in a firm but orderly manner at the negotiating table.

By 1980 additional developments had taken place. Egypt's successful efforts to bolster its NWFZ initiative and to separate the overwhelming international numerical support for its 1979 resolution from the intricacies of the Arab-Israeli dispute were facing challenges. The representatives of Egypt to the First Committee of the General Assembly explained to Arab colleagues that bringing intra-Arab disputes into a committee that dealt exclusively with matters of disarmament would weaken an initiative designed to protect the non–nuclear-weapon states of the Middle East from the dangers of nuclear-weapon threat and proliferation. Thus, Egypt maintained a policy of keeping the momentum in high gear. In this regard an effort was made to avoid tabling any other controversial resolution under the same item of establishing a NWFZ in the region of the Middle East.

On December 11, 1979, the General Assembly, upon an Iraqi proposal, adopted Resolution 34/89, entitled "Israeli Nuclear Armament." In this proposal the conviction was expressed that the development of nuclear capabilities by Israel would aggravate the dangerous situation in the Middle East, as well as international security in general. The proposal requested the Secretary General, with the assistance of qualified experts, to prepare a study on Israeli nuclear armament.

The genesis of this proposal was a series of mysterious mishaps related to the Iraqi nuclear program. Such difficulties were preceded by statements of concern from Washington and Tel Aviv concerning Iraq's nuclear agreements with some governments, including France. In response to such concerns the French Foreign Ministry reassured the United States regarding a reactor agreement signed with Iraq. The French government asserted that France's intention was to maintain control over "its nuclear export policy" and that the agreement with Iraq conformed to the Nuclear Suppliers Group Guidelines (*Nucleaonics Week,* January 19, 1978:10). France also contended that there was no basis for concern, since Iraq's purchase of a 70–MW reactor was governed by bilateral safeguard assurances. Under this agreement France was allowed to place 100 technicians at the site to monitor the reactor. In addition, it was recalled that Iraq was a member of the NPT and had agreed to place its nuclear facilities under IAEA international inspection (*Washington Post,* February 27, 1978).

In April 1979 a team of skilled but unknown saboteurs, "widely believed to be Israelis or Israeli sympathizers" (Pajak, 1982:47), entered the French plant at Seyne-sur-Mer and destroyed the reactor core that was ready to be shipped to Baghdad. This action caused an estimated two-year serious setback to the Iraqi nuclear program. Additional accidents of mysterious origin followed, including the assassination in Paris of the Egyptian-born and -educated physicist Yehia el-Mashad (Weissman and Krosney, 1981:239–43). Also, in September 1980 a raid was carried out by three U.S.-built F-4 Phantoms, bearing Iranian markings, on the Iraqi Tuwaitha nuclear complex, inflicting slight damage.

Suggestions were presented that this was an Israeli experimental raid (*U.S. News and World Report,* June 22, 1981:21).

Israel's official position on the UN decision to conduct a study entitled *Israeli Nuclear Armament* is best illustrated by Ambassador Arieh Eilan, Israel's representative to the First Committee, who stated on two separate occasions his government's position:

> To prepare a study on the Israel nuclear armament, in essence makes impartial research impossible by prejudicing the issue on the assumption that such nuclear armament in fact exists. The rest—if one may say so—of the scenario is clearly discernable. If draft resolutions A/C. 1/34/L. 12 Rev. 1 is adopted, the Arab propaganda machine, fed by petrodollars, will see to it that suitable articles appear in various publications all over the world, giving new "facts" about "Israel's nuclear armament." These articles will have to be collected, analyzed and quoted by the Secretariat of the United Nations and reported to the thirty-sixth session of the General Assembly. This report will then be quoted as so-called authoritative proof of Arab allegations against Israel. The pattern is both transparent and familiar. (United Nations document A/C.1/34/PV.37 of November 19, 1979)

Commenting on the mandate of the group of experts preparing the study, Ambassador Eilan observed:

> The group was not asked to investigate whether or not Israel possesses nuclear arms but was instructed to study "Israeli nuclear armament." Small wonder that under those terms reputable nuclear scientists, when approached, refused to participate in the work of the Group of Experts.
>
> It is certainly interesting to note that the report, which dwells upon technological and scientific aspects of nuclear capability, was written by five experts, four of whom are political scientists, while the only nuclear physicist happens to be an Arab. (United Nations document A/C.1/36/PV.24 of November 3, 1981)

Yet a confrontational stance between Israel and Iraq set the stage for a bitter feud. It seemed evident, however, that Israel's repeated threats to Iraq were bound to levy a toll on the Middle East NWFZ initiative. Thus, the job of Egypt became more difficult.

By July 29, 1980, Iraq's Acting Minister for Foreign Affairs dispatched a letter to the UN Secretary General (S/14073), referring to threats directed against Iraq by Israel and warning of a threat of military aggression against Iraq. The letter charged that Israel had "American manufactured aircraft whose range is capable of extending to Iraqi territory and which may be kept in readiness for an air strike against Iraq's nuclear reactors in order to halt scientific and technical progress in Iraq and prevent the Arabs from keeping up with advances in this field" (S/14073). Responding to Iraq's letter, Israel dispatched its own on October 15, 1980 (A/35/537). In that letter Israel refuted Iraq's "allegations" and pointed to what it considered to be the "dangers inherent in the strenuous efforts made by Iraq over the last few years to acquire nuclear capability." Israel's reply centered on quoting several reports of how Iraq refused to accept the Caramel-type uranium (impossible to convert to miltary uses) offered it by France because it wanted instead a reactor using enriched uranium of up to 93 percent (*France-Soir*, August 5, 1980; also see *Why Israel Had to Act*, contained in document A/36/610 of October 20, 1981).

On October 24, 1980, another serious event occurred, with Israel deciding to propose its own resolution under the same item of establishing a NWFZ in the Middle East. This came as a serious challenge to the original NWFZ text. Thus, the First Committee of the United Nations had before it two resolutions: an Egyptian one supported by an overwhelming majority, the other Israeli, which seemed destined to stir a great deal of controversy in the committee. In its letter addressed to the Secretary General, (A/C.1/35/8 of October 24, 1980), Israel referred to a statement given by Yitzhak Shamir, then Foreign Minister of Israel, in the general debate of the General Assembly, in which Shamir had stated:

> Israel has consistently supported resolutions of the General Assembly aimed at preventing the spread of nuclear weapons. This global problem, we believe, can best be solved by way of negotiated regional arrangements. Hence, since 1975, Israel has consistently advocated the establishment of a nuclear-weapon-free zone in the Middle East on the Tlatelolco model. Israel believes that an international conference of all the States in the region and adjacent should be held, leading to the conclusion of formal, contractual, multilateral convention between all States of the region. We hope that in the course of this General Assembly, we shall find a suitable opportunity to give concrete expression to our views on this matter. In the meantime, I should like to reiterate my Government's position, which is that Israel will not be the first to introduce nuclear weapons into the Arab-Israel dispute.

Following this letter Israel proposed her own resolution, stipulating the following operative ideas:

> (1) *Calls upon* all States of the Middle East and non-nuclear-weapons States adjacent to the region, which are not signatories to any treaty providing for nuclear-weapon-free zone, to convene at the earliest possible date a conference with a view to negotiating a multilateral treaty establishing a nuclear-weapon-free zone in the Middle East; (2) *Urges* all States of the region to state by 1 May, 1981, their willingness to participate in the Conference; (3) *Requests* the Secretary General to provide the necessary facilities for the convening of such a conference. (A/C.1/ 35/8, October 1980)

As a result of such actions, the situation faced by Egypt revealed the following:

> (1) For the first time since 1974 a competing draft resolution had been tabled under the same item calling for the establishment of a NWFZ in the Middle East. This raised the possibility of an erosion of the support given annually to the Egyptian proposal.

(2) The fact that this situation had originally developed following Israel's repeated threats against Iraq's peaceful nuclear reactor invited a number of disputes to take place under the umbrella of this particular item.

(3) Egypt pursued two parallel objectives. The first was intended to quiet Arab anxieties and lessen any chance of a confrontation taking place under Egypt's item. The second was to persuade Israel, in a manner congruent with the new environment of peace, to reconsider and drop its resolution.

(4) Throughout this process of diplomatic disengagement, Egypt attempted to boost her initiative by getting it approved for the first time ever by consensus, after persuading Israel to withdraw her annual abstention.

Following a great deal of diplomatic bargaining, success was secured. Israel dropped her tabled resolution. The Arabs approved the Egyptian text after deleting a phrase referring to efforts exerted "to create an atmosphere of confidence in the Middle East." (Some Arab states considered such language an insinuation of support for the Egyptian-Israeli accords.) Finally, the resolution submitted by Egypt was adopted for the first time, in December 1980, by consensus as Resolution 35/147. This was considered by many to be a tremendous breakthrough. For the first time ever the initiative to establish a NWFZ in the Middle East was the only one enjoying this kind of intraregional and extraregional support in the General Assembly.

Canada, Finland on behalf of the Nordic countries, the Federal Republic of Germany, Ireland, Italy, the Netherlands, the United Kingdom, and the United States expressed their support and gratitude that the draft resolution was adopted by consensus. The Federal Republic of Germany also stated that it would encourage and assist the parties directly concerned to take the steps required to set up a properly conceived nuclear-weapon-free zone. Finland, the Netherlands, and the United Kingdom advocated that the states of the region should, as one step, adhere to the NPT. Egypt, as sponsor, expressed its appreciation, and it regarded the consensus endorsement of its proposal as a significant development and the beginning of a new phase. It noted particularly the call for the states concerned to deposit appropriate declarations of their support for the zone with the Security Council (United Nations, 1981a:194).

A pause at this juncture is warranted in order to assess the question, why did Israel join the consensus? Several speculations are presented here. First is a view offered by Paul F. Power of the University of Cincinnati, who argues that the Israeli action could be viewed as a diplomatic camouflage aimed at concealing an Israeli intention to militarily destroy the Iraqi reactor in June 1981. By joining the consensus, it is hypothesized, Israel gave the impression that a new atmosphere of confidence and goodwill had just emerged. For the first time since 1974 the only obstacle facing a unanimous vote on this NWFZ was Israel's abstention. By withdrawing her usual recorded abstention and agreeing to have the resolution approved without a vote, unconditional, comprehensive intraregional support for the initiative seemed to have developed. The impression given by Israel's support was that the region was on the brink of a diplomatic breakthrough favorable to the actual implementation of this NWFZ initiative.

A careful study of the dates is necessary at this juncture. It is known that the resolution was approved in the First Committee of the General Assembly on November 20, 1980, and by the General Assembly itself on December 12 (United Nations, 1980a:194). Power, an expert on this subject, has suggested that the decision to destroy the Iraqi nuclear reactor was taken on October 1980. He posited, therefore, that Israel's joining the consensus was nothing but a "diplomatic ploy" to hide the Israeli Cabinet decision to destroy the Iraqi reactor.[12] Power (1983b:619) observed that joining the consensus on the Egyptian text and delaying the raid against the Iraqi reactor were also done for the purpose of lessening Israel's isolation within the United Nations. On the other hand, the view could be considered that Israel saw in its support of the Egyptian position an opportunity to expand its relationship with Egypt and enhance the prospects for a wider extension of peace.

Following the 1979 peace treaty with Egypt, Israel began to feel a new sense of isolation within the United States. The growing closeness between Egypt and the United States was looked upon cautiously.[13] The Israeli decision to join the consensus could be interpreted as an attempt to enhance Israel's image in the United States. Joining the consensus may have been designed to make Israel look good and smell sweet within the United States. It could have been done also to prevent any further isolation of Israel as a non-NPT state in the Middle East at a time when Egypt, Israel's Camp David partner, was moving towards full accession to and ratification of the Non-Proliferation Treaty.

Another possible explanation for Israel joining the consensus might have been Israel's accurate assessment of the voting situation in the First Committee of the General Assembly. It was probably known to Israel that its resolution could not have secured the necessary majority in the General Assembly. Also, it was known that the tide was in favor of the Egyptian draft, which had enjoyed wide support since 1974. Hence, approving and acceding to the Egyptian text could be explained as a face-saving tactic following Israel's withdrawal of its own resolution from the agenda of the First Committee.

An additional explanation for the Israeli change might have been Israel's dissatisfaction over the study being conducted by the Secretary General's appointed expert group on "Israeli Nuclear Armament." Israel could have joined the consensus that year because the study was still in progress, an opportune time to demonstrate Israel's commitment to nonproliferation. This naturally entailed a prediction on the part of Israel concerning the findings and the conclusion of that study. Israel's support of the consensus could therefore be construed as a way to discredit and nullify the study. Support of the General Assembly's consensus on the Egyptian resolution would give Israel the opportunity to assert that one year before the report was issued, Israel had joined efforts to prevent nuclear-weapon proliferation in the Middle East.

Israel's shift also may have been part of a carefully articulated campaign aimed at the U.S. Congress and media to pressure them into taking action against France and Italy. The purpose here would be to dissuade France and Italy from supplying Iraq with a research reactor—to replace the one destroyed in 1981— and associated equipment such as the highly enriched uranium, the technical training center in Tuwaitha, and the "hot cell" laboratories (Power, 1983b:619).

On February 22, 1981, Egypt ratified the Non-Proliferation Treaty. This was an important development, since Egypt demonstrated her commitment to the establishment of a NWFZ in the Middle East by acceding to the treaty, even though Israel had not yet done so. The thrust of this move was, *inter alia*, intended to encourage Israel to join the NPT and thus move closer towards the objective of establishing a NWFZ in the region.

Towards this end Egypt dispatched two letters to the UN Secretary General. The first (S/14387) of February 27, 1981 (see appendix B), contained a statement from Egypt's Ministry of Foreign Affairs on the occasion of Egypt's deposit of the instruments of ratification. The second of April 24, 1981, was a letter dispatched by Egypt's Deputy Permanent Representative Ambassador, Nabil Elaraby. This second letter clarified Egypt's obligation towards the NPT:

> The Treaty, in Article VII, recognizes the right of any group of States to conclude regional treaties in order to assure the total absence of nuclear weapons in their respective territories. The importance of this article is that it took into account the realities of the various regions of the world. The Treaty, therefore, while establishing a general and comprehensive regime, makes provisions for the characteristics of each particular region. Therefore the Treaty, and in particular Article VII, clearly accommodate the conditions inherent in the Middle East.
>
> As a manifestation of Egypt's commitment to the objectives of the Treaty on the Non-Proliferation of Nuclear Weapons, Egypt has, since the twenty-ninth session of the General Assembly in 1974, advocated the establishment of a nuclear-weapon-free zone in the Middle East. It is also important to recall in this connexion that Egypt has consistently maintained that the adherence to the Non-Proliferation Treaty would strengthen the nuclear-weapon-free regime. Therefore, all Assembly resolutions calling for the establishment of such a zone, including Resolution 35/147, urged all parties concerned as a means of promoting this objective (i.e. the nuclear-weapon-free zone in the Middle East) to adhere to the Treaty on the Non-Proliferation of Nuclear Weapons. It is pertinent to recall in this respect that the latter resolution was adopted without objection. Thus, for the first time since the adoption of Assembly resolution 3263 (XXIX), all concerned parties supported the establishment of a nuclear-weapon-free zone in the Middle East. (A/36/220 of April 24, 1981)

Notwithstanding these various speculations on the reasons behind Israel's joining the consensus, everything until this stage seemed to be working in favor of the NWFZ proposal. The resolution, for the first time, was adopted by consensus; it remained the only text discussed under the item; it enjoyed intraregional as well as extraregional support; the five nuclear-weapon states supported it; and Egypt had finally ratified the NPT. Understandably, a great deal of expectations emerged. The next move, as envisioned by the sponsor of the resolution, was to translate these positive achievements into practical measures.

Instead of capitalizing on these achievements, however, a serious setback occurred. One June 7, 1981, Israel attacked the nonmilitary nuclear facility in Iraq, which resulted in its total destruction. Urgent sessions of the Security Council, the European Economic Community, and the IAEA were convened in response to this act. The Security Council adopted Resolution 487, on June 19, in which it condemned the Israeli raid.

Three days after the attack, Israel presented a letter to the UN Secretary General (A/36/315) addressing the item "Establishment of a NWFZ in the region of the Middle East." This letter called for convening at the earliest date a conference to negotiate a multilateral treaty establishing a NWFZ in the Middle East.

However, it is difficult to account for the rationale behind the contents of this letter and the timing of its dispatch. Several observations, nonetheless, can be offered. First, Israel's mention of the establishment of a NWFZ in the Middle East three days after its military attack on an energy-generating nuclear reactor could not help but stir additional insecurity and apprehension at a time of high emotions. Second, this act in essence led some parties to believe in the "futility" of a General Assembly initiative with regard to establishing a NWFZ in the region. Finally, the praise accorded Egypt in Israel's letter at that specific time could have been motivated by the desire to discredit and ostracize Egypt within the Arab world. The same point in fact could be argued concerning the Begin-Sadat meeting in Sinai a few days before the destruction of Ozirak, the Iraqi peaceful nuclear complex.

The fact remains that the Israeli raid was never discussed with President Sadat, and had it been, Egypt without doubt would have been expected to emphatically oppose it and would have sought to prevent it.[14] As a result of Israel's armed destruction of the Iraqi facilities, the item bearing the title "Establishment of a NWFZ in the Region of the Middle East" became fertile territory for deliberations on this serious event. Three draft resolutions in connection with this item were presented during the 1981 General Assembly. The first one was the conventional text once again presented by Egypt. In essence the 1981 text was similar to the previous resolutions except for one innovative idea. This new element was aimed at translating the theoretical concept of a NWFZ into a practical one. The resolution requested the Secretary General to appoint a special representative who would contact all "parties" concerned in order to ascertain their attitudes as to the procedures, scope, and modalities of establishing such a zone (United Nations, 1981e:171).

Egypt's position at that delicate stage was governed by three factors:

(1) The reaffirmation of the consensus reached the previous year and the necessity of strengthening it

(2) Promoting the initiative from an abstract to a practical level by dispatching to the Middle East a Special Representative of the Secretary General[15]

(3) The necessity of developing the role of the Security Council in implementing the zone.

Eventually, throughout the delicate process of informal consultations, additional problems arose. For example, the United States insisted on incorporating a reference to arrangements or agreements freely arrived at among the states of the zone. The phrase *freely arrived at* was in essence a diplomatic wording of Israel's long-standing calls for direct negotiation. The United States also requested reference to the notion that the zone could become a reality only after the achievement of a stable peace in the region. This was in fact a recalcitrant position since it denoted American insistence on an a priori linkage between such a disarmament initiative and a comprehensive peace settlement in the Middle East. Additionally, the United States refused any reference to a role of the Security Council.

However, the situation proved to be both extremely problematic and tense in light of Israel's raid against the Iraqi nuclear reactor. As a result, and despite Egypt's endeavors, Qatar submitted—from the floor of the First Committee— amendments to the Egyptian draft pertaining to Israel's attack on the Iraqi nuclear installations, amendments that deleted reference to the idea of a Special Representative of the Secretary General. Accordingly, Egypt perceived itself as having no alternative but to withdraw its own text. In its place Egypt offered a procedural resolution, whereby the Secretary General would merely transmit the previous year's resolution (35/147) to the General Assembly at its second special session devoted to disarmament. On December 9, 1981, the procedural draft was approved by the General Assembly without a vote. Several delegations went on record expressing regret that the resolution was not dealt with in a substantive way. The United Kingdom, for example, voiced a similar concern, pointing out that the Israeli raid should have spurred international endeavors to establish this zone and prevent the occurrence of such acts in the future (United Nations, 1982a:170–75).

Consequently, the General Assembly approved two different draft resolutions dealing with the June attack against the Iraqi nuclear installation. Both resolutions basically condemned Israel. The United States observed that the resolutions were "disruptive" and "improper," since the issue already had been dealt with in the Security Council (United Nations, 1982a:172). The recorded vote for the first resolution was 107 for to 2 against (United States and Israel), with 31 abstentions, and 109 for to 2 against (United States and Israel), with 34 abstentions, for the second resolution. A new reality was imposed, notwithstanding the fact that one year earlier a single consensus resolution was approved, and the implementation of this NWFZ initiative seemed within reach.

In 1982 and 1983 (the thirty-seventh and thirty-eighth General Assemblies), no breakthroughs occurred. Again, three additional resolutions were presented under the item, all relating to Israel's nuclear armament and its armed attack on the Iraqi nuclear installations.

Egypt for its part presented a substantive resolution that was similar in spirit and substance to the one approved by consensus in 1980. It became evident that any mention of dispatching a Special Representative of the Secretary General to the region would still be faced with difficulties. Again, the political climate was not conducive to such actions, especially following Israel's military invasion of Lebanon. The Egyptian resolutions were approved by consensus and tabled as Resolution 37/75 in 1982 and Resolution 38/64 in 1983.

During the thirty-ninth and fortieth sessions of the General Assembly, Egypt decided to introduce some new concepts into its resolutions. The thrust of these additions was twofold: first, to inject new ideas in order to facilitate the process of the implementation of its initiative and second, to word them carefully so as not to compromise the annual consensus accorded to the resolution in the General Assembly.

The resolution before the thirty-ninth (1985) General Assembly revived the idea of entrusting the UN Secretary General with the responsibility of seeking the views of all concerned parties regarding the establishment of this zone and requested him to submit a report to the General Assembly at its fortieth session. Egypt's original proposal was aimed at requesting the Secretary General to follow practical steps to implement the annual resolution either by designating a special representative or by ascertaining the views of countries in the region. In the wake of Syrian opposition to the concept of direct or indirect negotiations with Israel through a UN representative, language was deleted. The Secretary General was therefore requested only to seek the views of the countries of the region as well as, preferably, the nuclear-weapon states on the issue of establishing a NWFZ in the Middle East.

In the fortieth session Resolution 40/82 was adopted without a vote. In substance, this resolution was similar to the resolution of the thirty-ninth session. A few states responded to the previous call by the Secretary General, and only two nuclear-weapon states (France and China) responded. This resolution, therefore, reiterated the General Assembly's call to all countries of the region to communicate their views as soon as possible. It evidently became clear that little progress had been achieved and that Egypt's efforts were geared towards keeping its initiative alive.

THE UNITED NATIONS AND THE MIDDLE EAST NWFZ PROPOSAL: A CRITICAL ASSESSMENT[16]

As has been discerned, the establishment of a NWFZ in the Middle East has been the subject of active consideration by the UN General Assembly every year since 1974. The resolution calling for the establishment of this zone in the Middle East is the only one that has provoked positive developments within the framework of the United Nations, ultimately reaching the degree of a consensus resolution.

In the General Assembly the situation in the region was assessed in relation to two main factors: (1) the prevailing political situation and (2) the probability of introducing nuclear weapons in the area and their eventual impact. On the basis of such an assessment the General Assembly appears to have reached a number of conclusions:

(a) that the prevailing political situation and the potential danger emanating therefrom made the area extremely sensitive and prone to explosion;

(b) that there was global apprehension over possible proliferation of nuclear weapons in the area;

(c) that the situation in the area would be further aggravated by the introduction of nuclear weapons;

(d) that in such a case, the efforts to create an atmosphere of confidence in the region, and thus a just and lasting peace, would be severely damaged;

(e) and therefore, there was an urgent need to keep the countries of the region from becoming involved in a ruinous nuclear-arms race.

The members of the General Assembly overwhelmingly commended the application of a NWFZ in this particular region, and with time recognized that the establishment of such a zone enjoyed wide support in the region, which in turn evolved into a consensus. Hence, the first prerequisite (intraregional support) for establishing the zone was assured. The General Assembly did not limit itself to an endorsement of the initiative nor to sanctioning its necessity or acceptability by the states of the region. On the contrary, the General Assembly, mindful of the tremendous dangers inherent in the situation, both for the region and the world at large, remained constantly aware of and concerned about this matter.

The General Assembly was conscious of the fact that the establishment of a NWFZ in the area was problematic. But the General Assembly was also aware that lack of progress in the present complex and volatile situation would further confound and inhibit progress towards international peace and world security.

Two series of practical measures intended to promote the realization of this objective emerged. The first was devised to maintain the present nuclear-weapon-free status of the area and to keep open the option of establishing a NWFZ. These measures were aimed at avoiding any action by the states of the region, or by nuclear-weapon states, that might be detrimental to the realization of a NWFZ objective. The second set of measures attempted to generate momentum towards the realization of this objective.

Among the first set of measures were the following:

(1) A recommendation to the states of the region to refrain, on a reciprocal basis, from producing, acquiring, or in any other way possessing nuclear weapons and nuclear explosives; or from permitting the stationing of nuclear weapons or nuclear ex-

plosive devices on their territory, or territories under their control, by any third party.

(2) A recommendation that these states refrain, on a reciprocal basis, from any other action that would facilitate the acquisition, testing, or use of such weapons, or that would be detrimental to the objective of establishing a NWFZ in the area.

(3) Calls upon all countries of the region that have not done so, to agree to place all their nuclear activities under IAEA safeguards. Within the first set of measures were recommendations addressed to the nuclear-weapon states to refrain from any action contrary to the objective of establishing a NWFZ in the area.

Among the second set of measures aimed at generating momentum towards the establishment of such a NWFZ were the following: (a) an invitation to the countries concerned to adhere to the NPT; (b) an invitation to the countries of the region to declare their support for the establishment of such a zone in the region, consistent with the relevant paragraphs of the final document of the Tenth Special Session Devoted to Disarmament, and to deposit these declarations with the Security Council for consideration as appropriate.

From all these measures recommended by the General Assembly, we can assert that the accumulated experience presents a coherent strategy aimed at maintaining a nuclear-weapon-free status quo while recommending a series of measures aimed at generating momentum towards the establishment of such a zone in the Middle East.

However, two opposing strategies to the NWFZ approach need to be clarified. The first, offered by Steven Rosen (1977) of the Australian National University, is diametrically opposed to the NWFZ approach. Rosen called for the introduction of "mutual nuclear deterrence in the Arab-Israeli conflict." One other approach is that of Saadallah Hallaba (1982:32) political scientist of the University of South Carolina, who in discussing the effects of Israel's 1981 raid against the Iraqi nuclear facilities, labeled the NWFZ approach as "insufficient" and called for the application of chapter 7 of the United Nations Charter and approval of sanctions against Israel.

There are flaws with both approaches. Rosen's call for an overt introduction of nuclear weapons into the Arab-Israeli conflict is fraught with dangers of a nuclear calamity. Rosen assumes that transplanting a system of deterrence in the Middle East will maintain peace similar to the way deterrence operates in Central Europe.

He neglects, however, to underscore the differences between both settings. Specific to the Central European case is the fact that both the Soviet Union and the United States have devised channels of communications and signed several agreements,[17] a factor missing in the Middle East.[18] Ole Holsti (1972) political scientist of the University of British Columbia has shown how Soviet-American communications helped contain the 1962 crisis, whereas lack of communication in the 1914 crisis led to war. In the Middle East there are no structured channels of communications between the Arabs and the Israelis. Rosen also failed to show

how deterrence that supposedly rests on the notion of rationality can function on that same basic principle in the Middle East. Rationality, argues Professor Charles Osgood (1963:3) a specialist on deterrence theory, breaks down with emotional stress: "Faced with an overwhelming threat over which he feels he has no control, the human individual typically denies the reality of danger rather than keeping it in mind and trying to cope with it." (Nazli Choukri and Robert North [1975], Richard Smoke [1977], and Ole Holsti [1972] have all confirmed the same findings).

There is no guarantee, then, that since deterrence succeeded in Europe, it could succeed in the Middle East, which is torn by numerous conventional wars, an unresolved Arab-Israeli conflict, tension, misperception, and delicate religious issues. International relations specialist Raymond Aron has demonstrated that even if deterrence succeeded in one geographical-cultural context, it might fail in another region. Aron (1969:9) argues, "There is no deterrence in general or abstract terms; it is the case of knowing who can deter whom, from what, in what circumstances, and by what means."

On the other hand, treating Israel as an outcast in the international community is undesirable, since it is better to maintain Israel within rather than without the international system of the UN. Applying sanctions against Israel might lead only to further obstinance and rigidity and a possible United States withdrawal from the international body. Hence, the NWFZ solution offers a moderate approach that is accepted by all the parties concerned. It excludes measures characterized by extremism and immoderation and builds upon already established agreement and success.

CONCLUSION

In this chapter an attempt has been made to trace historically the evolution of the item on the establishment of a NWFZ in the Middle East from 1974 until today. Efforts were exerted not only to explain what had happened but also why. According to this analysis progress on the issue was steady and sure before and shortly after the 1980 consensus, until Israel destroyed Iraq's nuclear complex in June 1981. Paul Power, for instance, blames Israel's action on a decision taken by Menachem Begin's Cabinet in October 1980. Since then the initiative was hindered, slowed down, and the momentum was partially lost.

In the following chapter the emphasis will be on ways and means to invigorate the proposal. Action-oriented policy suggestions will be advanced using lessons offered by other NWFZs surveyed in chapters 2 and 3. The question to be raised at this stage is, where do we go from here? What are the modalities, scope, and mechanisms necessary to implement this NWFZ initiative to rid this region— and the world—once and for all, from the dangers of a nuclear holocaust?

NOTES

1. For the text of all resolutions on the issue of a Middle East NWFZ from 1974–1985, see appendix A.

2. The countries invited were Bahrain, Democratic Yemen, Egypt, Iran, Iraq, Israel, Jordan, Kuwait, Lebanon, Oman, Qatar, Saudi Arabia, Syria, United Arab Emirates, and Yemen.

3. Egypt, Iran, Iraq, Kuwait, Oman, Qatar, and the Syrian Arab Republic.

4. The first disengagement agreement was signed between Egypt and Israel in January 1974; Syria and Israel signed their disengagement agreement in May 1974; Egypt signed a second agreement with Israel on September 1, 1975. It should be noted that the second disengagement agreement, in particular, evoked criticism from some Arab States, including Syria.

5. It is known that the Soviets expressed, in their 1974 and 1975 explanations of vote, their doubts and reservations about the use of language, in a resolution, describing Tlatelolco as a notable achievement applicable to another region. The reasons behind the Soviets' reservations pertaining to Tlatelolco have been discussed earlier. In 1976 the Soviets had not yet signed or ratified Additional Protocol 2 of Tlatelolco. The USSR signed Additional Protocol 2 on May 18, 1978, and ratified it on January 8, 1979 (United Nations, 1983b:63).

6. In an effort to increase the platform of support for its initiatives, Egypt for the first time introduced a resolution in the Seventh Islamic Conference of Foreign Ministers, held at Istanbul May 12–15, 1976. The conference supported the Egyptian draft and called for the implementation of a NWFZ in the Middle East (Resolution 10/7–p of A/ 31/237 of October 4, 1976). Annually the same support was sought for and presented by the same Islamic Conference (Eight, Ninth, Tenth, Eleventh, and Twelfth Islamic Conferences held, respectively, in Tripoli (1977: Resolution P-12/8. A/32/235 Annex); Dakar (1978: Resolution P-6/9. A/33/151 Annex); Fez (1979: Resolution P-16/10. A/ 34/389 and Corr. 1); Islamabad (1980: Resolution P/25/11. A/35/419); and Baghdad (1981; Resolution P/33/12. A/36/421 and Corr. 1). Later on, in 1982 the Ministerial Meeting of the Co-ordinating Bureau of the Non-Aligned Countries, held in Havana from May 31 to June 5, included in their Final Communiqué a declaration of support for the efforts to establish a NWFZ in the Middle East (Report A/37/657).

7. The result of the vote was 98 to none, with 14 abstentions coming mainly from non-NPT countries (Algeria, Argentina, Bhutan, Brazil, Burma, Cuba, France, Guyana, India, Israel, Portugal, Spain, Uganda, and Tanzania.

8. This paragraph received 103 votes to none, with 12 abstentions (Argentina, Bhutan, Brazil, Burma, Cuba, France, Guyana, India, Israel, Spain, Uganda, and Tanzania) (United Nations, 1978b:176).

9. Following President Sadat's trip, the Cairo Preparatory Meetings for the Geneva Conference convened in Mena House, Cairo, in December 1977. Egypt named its Ambassador to the United Nations, Ahmed Esmat Abdel Meguid, as its chief spokesman to this conference. The conference was followed by the Ismalia Talks; the meetings of the joint Egyptian Israeli Political Committee in Jerusalem; the July 17, 1978, London trilateral meetings between Egypt, Israel, and the United States; and the September 1978 Camp David meetings.

10. Algeria, Angola, Bhutan, Bolivia, Brazil, Burma, Cape Verde, Cuba, France, Guyana, India, Israel, Mozambique, Spain and Tanzania for paragraph 1, and paragraph 3 was adopted by 114 votes to none, with 7 abstentions (Angola, Bhutan, Brazil, India, Israel, Turkey, and Tanzania.)

11. The Rejectionist Front was formed at Tripoli, Libya, on December 5, 1977, following the Sadat journey to Jerusalem. It was then called the Front for Resistance and

Confrontation. It should not be forgotten that the Arabs had convened a conference in Baghdad, Iraq, at which they agreed to seek Egypt's expulsion from the Islamic Conference, the Non-Aligned movement and the Organization of African Unity as well as the removal of all UN regional offices from Egypt. The only substantive action achieved was the temporary removal of Egypt from the Islamic Conference. All other attempts failed, in the face of Egypt's stature and prestige. (By 1984 the Chairman of the PLO visited Egypt, and the Islamic Conference by an overwhelming majority decided to invite Egypt back into the organization. A formal delegation from the Islamic Conference met with Egypt's President Hosni Mubarak, who agreed to return provided there were no attached conditions. Egypt stated that it would continue to honor its commitments and obligations envisaged in the Camp David accord and the Egyptian-Israeli peace treaty.)

12. Power elaborated on this particular point in a lengthy meeting he and the author held during the Silver Anniversary Convention of the International Studies Association in Atlanta, Ga., March 30, 1984.

13. An interesting case in this regard was Israel's disclosure of the departure of four C-130s from Cairo West airport to join the U.S. rescue mission of the fifty-two American hostages held in Iran in 1980. The disclosure, which was attributed to a ham radio operator in Israel, was made public even before the mission ended. Thus, not only did the disclosure appear to be aimed at embarrassing Egypt but also risked exposing the whole military operation. No explanation has been given for how a private individual ham-radio operator could detect the departure of four U.S. C-130s from Cairo, intercept their communications, decode them, and leak the message to the press before the complete withdrawal of U.S. ground, air, and naval forces from the vicinity of Iran.

14. This point has been strongly presented by Ambassador Osama el-Baz, Director of the Political Bureau for Egyptian President M. Hosni Mubarak. Dr. el-Baz had also been a confidant of President Sadat. However, Begin's urgent request to see President Sadat could be viewed as an attempt to depict Egypt as an accomplice in such an attack. This strategy eventually levied its toll on the support given to the original text for the establishment of a NWFZ in the region in 1981.

15. Several names were under consideration at this stage to fill this post. These included Ambassador Keijo Korhonen from Finland, who presided in 1975 over the working group on NWFZs in all its aspects; Ambassador J. Hepburn, Permanent Representative of the Bahamas; and J. Martenson, Under Secretary General of the United Nations, Head of the UN Disarmament Department.

16. The views in this section are largely based on the views presented by Egypt's expert Ambassador, Ahmed Osman, to the UN Secretary General's expert-group meetings on the Nuclear Weapon Free Zone in All Its Aspects (1984).

17. The Bilateral Arms Control agreements between the United States and the Soviet Union are the Hot Line Agreement (1963); Hot Line Improvement and Modernization (1971); Agreement on Measures to Reduce the Risk of Outbreak of Nuclear War (1971); Agreement on Prevention of Incidents on and over the High Seas (1972); ABM Treaty (1972); Interim Agreement on the Limitation of Strategic Offensive Arms (1972, expired 1977); Memorandum of Understanding Regarding Establishment of a Standing Consultative Commission (1972); Protocol to the ABM (1976); Threshold Test Ban Treaty (signed only, 1974); Treaty on the Limitations of Underground Nuclear Explosions for Peaceful Purposes (signed only, 1976); Treaty on the Limitation of Strategic Offensive Arms (signed only, 1979) (Arms Control and Disarmament Agency, 1984:141).

18. Except for the peace treaty between Egypt and Israel.

6

TOWARDS THE ESTABLISHMENT OF A NWFZ IN THE MIDDLE EAST: CONCLUDING OBSERVATIONS ABOUT PROBLEMS AND PROSPECTS

This study has sought to demonstrate the applicability of a NWFZ regime in the Middle East, based on the proved effectiveness of this approach in primarily four different regions. The attempt to link such an approach to the Middle East is especially inviting, since this region remains one of the most sensitive and turbulent regions of the world. The Middle East remains vulnerable to pressures exerted by strong political commitments, an unresolved and historic Arab-Israeli conflict, superpower involvement, and continuous military confrontation between diverse sets of adversaries and rivals.

The rationale for a NWFZ in the Middle East is complicated because of the unique obstacles confronting it. But its advocacy can be defended because the prevention of the explicit integration of nuclear weapons into the overall military capabilities and national security policies of the Middle Eastern countries would constitute a grave threat to global peace. As shown throughout this study, a nuclear Middle East could have devastating global effects. It should be remembered that it was because of the turmoil emergent in the Middle East that the world in 1973 came close to the brink of a nuclear exchange. Since the 1962 Cuban missile crisis, no other region but this explosive area has yet to force both superpowers into a worldwide nuclear mobilization. This fact alone gives credence and impetus to efforts for the establishment of a regional NWFZ, and justifies scrutiny of the approach investigated in this study. That fact underscores the topicality of implementing a NWFZ in the Middle East, which would yield positive regional and global effects by enhancing international peace and security.

Throughout this study two principal threats to nuclear-weapon proliferation have received emphasis. First, extraregional dangers have been given special attention. These emanate from powers that may include the Middle East in their overall nuclear-security umbrella by using, threatening to use, or placing nuclear weapons in the Middle East. The lessons offered by other NWFZ proposals in other insecure regions such as Central Europe, the Nordic region, and the Baltic have all shown how such dangers and localized attributes may inhibit the translation of many NWFZ proposals into successful outcomes. These lessons summarized in previous chapters serve as a reminder and operate as catalysts that inform discussion of the challenges presented by potential obstacles to the creation of a NWFZ in the Middle East. Second, intraregional changes have been emphasized, and these have been underscored by the lessons offered by the Israeli case. This case study attempted to isolate the unique aspects of these dangers, to analyze the particular barriers they introduce to the creation of a NWFZ in the Middle East.

Three sets of objectives identified in the introduction to the study have therefore been addressed. First, this study has put into perspective the dangers posed by the possible proliferation of nuclear weapons into the Middle East and their possible linkage to the volatile configuration of the Arab-Israeli conflict. Second, it has sought to show that the NWFZ alternative is the most viable approach to arms control and would serve countries both in the Middle East and beyond it (especially the five nuclear-weapon states that constitute the permanent members of the UN Security Council). Finally (primarily in this chapter), this study has and will present alternatives and policy recommendations on how this objective might be achieved using the historical and diplomatic analysis offered in the previous chapters. Analyses of the twists and turns of efforts and initiatives as they have unfolded in the United Nations since 1974 will be used as an empirical foundation for such recommendations.

At this juncture a retrospective look is warranted. Some lessons can be drawn from the foregoing analysis that are applicable to the establishment of a NWFZ in the Middle East. The following review of such lessons, however, is neither exhaustive nor comprehensive. The purpose of the following discussion is to identify some of the options that have proved successful in other regional settings and to assess their applicability in the Middle East.[1]

Within the Antarctic regime a successful multilateral verification mechanism has been established and enforced. The United States, for instance, invoked the right of inspection of Soviet stations in 1964, 1971, 1975, 1977, and 1980 (Arms Control and Disarmament Agency, 1982:21). Since 1959 two elements have been conducive to the success of this regime: the mutual consent of both superpowers and the absence from the zone of military balance structures.

Whether today in the Middle East a successful multilateral verification mechanism can be enforced remains problematic. An essential first step would be the strengthening of existing relationships between member states in the Middle East and the International Atomic Energy Agency. Such a step presumably would serve to increase the confidence of member states in the agency's international safeguard regime. This would seem to constitute the cornerstone of any effort to establish a NWFZ in the region. It is known that a role for the IAEA was devised during the initial process of setting up the treaty of Tlatelolco (Article 16).

Equally important, based on the experience of previously established NWFZ regimes, would be the request of those Middle Eastern states to place their nuclear activities under IAEA safeguards. However, because of the difficulty associated with individual right of inspections (Arab states' rejection of the Israeli right of inspection of their nuclear facilities, and vice versa), it appears to be more feasible to entrust an international body such as the IAEA with such a mission. Since the 1960s this body has developed worldwide experience in administering safeguards, verification activities, and on-site inspections.

If the political will exists, the establishment of such a role for the IAEA in a Middle East NWFZ would appear to be within reach. Israel has gone on record voicing support for allowing the IAEA to monitor the safeguard functions of its Nahal Soreq reactor, thus seemingly removing a barrier to the initiative. Since 1965 such functions have been delegated to IAEA inspectors (Shaker, 1980:836). Hence, the IAEA seems to be a viable alternative for implementing the resolution and establishment of a NWFZ in the Middle East.

In addition, the two elements that aided the establishment of the Antarctic regime—namely, superpower consent and absence of military structure—are important considerations for our attention. As far as superpower consent is concerned, both the United States and the Soviet Union have publicly voiced their support for the establishment of a NWFZ in the Middle East. Both have voted in favor of the Egyptian resolution on the issue consistently from 1974 to the present. In 1980 both again joined the consensual support for the Egyptian proposal. As of 1984 no superpower alliances resulting in military bases or the establishment of contractual agreements for the military presence of any such superpowers in the Middle East were extant.

This superpower concurrence could be translated into tangible actions that might facilitate a Middle Eastern NWFZ. As Shai Feldman, an Israeli scholar, observed:

A more comprehensive Soviet-American agreement to ban nuclear weapons from the entire Middle East may be considered. The agreement may be aimed at forcing the region's state to join the NPT and to place their nuclear installations under IAEA inspections and safeguards. Finally, the United States and the Soviet Union might instead, arrive at a common position expressed in the form of a joint declaration stating that they would act in concert against any of the states in the region that dared to use nuclear weapons first. Any of the above arguments could be achieved within the framework of a SALT III and SALT IV agreement covering the Middle East. (Feldman, 1982a:233)

Hence, it can be asserted that as a matter of principle both these elements seem to apply and to have relevance to the Middle East—a conclusion that future deliberations must take into account.

The Outer Space Treaty also offers valuable lessons. Like the Antarctic regime, the Outer Space Treaty provided for reciprocal verification by both the United States and the Soviet Union. This provision reflected in essence the fact that both countries agreed to yield to inspection measures on the moon by the other party. Such an agreement required the presence of political will of both parties. From this it may be deduced that for any NWFZ proposal, such as the one in the Middle East, it is essential that not only the agreement of both superpowers be secured but also their cooperation, for in the absence of superpower support, any NWFZ initiative—including the one in the Middle East—is unlikely to prove successful.

The Outer Space Treaty also reflected a quid pro quo period of cooperation and negotiation between both superpowers in the United Nations, it is useful to recall. This experience demonstrates, as well, the utility and successful use of the United Nations as a viable negotiation forum. This point is particularly important, since it explains the dual role that the United Nations can play as peacemaker and peacekeeper. Therefore, if the United Nations can assist in bridging gaps between both superpowers (prior to the period of detente between them) the possibility that this same forum can assist in implementing a NWFZ proposal for the Middle East seems compelling. It should be remembered that the proposal to establish a NWFZ in the Middle East was originally a UN-sponsored proposal and remains an agenda item within the United Nations today (a fact that is auspicious for the prospects of a NWFZ in this troubled region).

The discussion of the Central European NWFZ proposal yields some applicable lessons for the Middle East as well. At the outset it should be noted that the confrontational nuclear posture that governs the military relationship between the two competing military alliances in the region is markedly dissimilar to the situation that exists in the Middle East. No delicate balance of theater nuclear forces exists in the Middle East. In fact, the Middle East NWFZ proposal seeks to maintain such a status quo by preventing the acquisition, deployment, or stationing of nuclear weapons by intraregional or extraregional members of the zone. This is an asset members of the Middle East region may productively build upon before any adverse development takes place that erodes the opportunities presently available. This asset coupled with intraregional support given to the UN resolutions on the proposal since 1974 and support given by the five nuclear-weapon states, a unique situation clearly exists in the Middle East. A "window of opportunity" exists and is available for pursuit under the prevailing (if potentially transient) circumstances.

A similar observation may be made with respect to the Nordic NWFZ proposal. Although the President of Finland stated in 1963 that the Nordic region enjoyed an "existing *de facto* situation of absence of nuclear weapons" (United Nations, 1976b:25), there are structural differences between this situation and the one existing in the Middle East. First, such a delineation applies only to times of peace. In times of war two Nordic members of NATO—Norway and Denmark— would allow the use of their territories for the transport and stationing of nuclear weapons. Second, the entire Nordic region is integrated in the nuclear defense plans of both NATO and the Warsaw Treaty Organization. Also, the presence of Soviet nuclear weapons in the Kola Peninsula bordering Finland and Norway should not be forgotten.

The Middle East is presently free from such complications. Currently, no nuclear military pacts in the region are operative. Countries of the Middle East have not offered contractual agreements allowing for the use of their territories to station, deploy, or to transport nuclear weapons belonging to any military bloc in times of peace or war. The Middle East, unlike the Nordic region, is not directly integrated into the overall nuclear-weapon security balance between NATO and Warsaw. Also, the Middle East is not part of a contractual defense agreement such as the ones that govern NATO and Warsaw Pact members. Hence, it can be argued that the Middle East is not directly integrated in the nuclear-weapon plans of such camps, and Middle Eastern states are not directly covered by the nuclear umbrella provided by either pact. This is a condition that presents considerable possibilities for maneuver in the creation of a NWFZ in the Middle East.

Studies of NWFZ proposals with respect to the Balkans, Adriatic, and the Mediterranean suggest three relevant issues. First, agreement between and among the countries of those zones with respect to declaring their regions nuclear-weapon-free does not exist. Second, one or both superpowers, unilaterally or in combination, oppose these initiatives. Third, initiatives in these regions remain in the embryonic stage of concepts or general statements. They also remain absent from the agenda of the UN General Assembly.[2] Since the three regions lie in close geographic proximity to Central Europe, criticisms have been leveled against these proposals. The proposals have been characterized as having been presented for tactical political reasons, such as lessening the chance of deployment of new types of missiles in Europe, or as being a propagandistic ploy directed at European peace movements.

Such conditions do not pertain to the Middle East. To reiterate, there is superpower concurrence over the Middle East NWFZ proposal. Additionally, unlike the three aforementioned proposals, the Middle East initiative enjoys the agreement and support of members of its own region. The Middle East proposal has long surpassed the stage of general concept and has achieved the status of an official UN proposal that has been overwhelmingly supported since 1974.

The discussion of the African NWFZ proposal also elicits several observations and lessons. First, collective efforts, it is suggested, appear to assume extreme importance, especially if they are backed by countries enjoying a privileged relationship with the country under consideration. The unified efforts of the Western European countries to prevent South Africa from conducting a nuclear test after 1977 is a case in point. It was reported that these Western countries not only sought assurances from South Africa but also threatened to sever diplomatic relations if South Africa detonated a nuclear device (*The New York Times*, August 21, 1977). Can the same commitment be transplanted in the Middle East? One answer, using the South African example as an explication, would be to propose the adoption by the Security Council of a specific resolution applicable to the Middle East case. The most important measure, it would seem, in such an alternative would be to secure a priori approval of the five permanent members of the Security Council. Such a resolution might incorporate several important ideas.

First, certain assurances should be given by nuclear-weapon states to the non–nuclear-weapon states of the Middle East as to measures to safeguard their security. Such assurances are not new and could be based on an elaborated version of Security Council Resolution 255 of 1968. In that resolution it was considered that an aggression accompanied by the use of nuclear weapons against a non–nuclear-weapon state would endanger international peace and security, and thus would invite the nuclear-weapon states (permanent members) to uphold their obligations stipulated by the Charter of the United Nations. Since some states consider such assurances as insufficient, the Council could approach the issue from two directions. Using the text of declarations by the five nuclear-weapon states on unilateral security assurances as a base, a common text could be constructed (see appendix C). In all such primary draft declarations the five permanent members have been asked to state that they would not use nuclear weapons against non–nuclear-weapon states, their dependent territories, armed forces, or allies.

In addition, an arrangement could be worked out for the Middle East, modeled after paragraph 62 of the Final Document of the Tenth Special Session of the General Assembly Devoted to Disarmament (A/S-10/4). This document, approved by consensus, states that nuclear-weapon countries are called upon to respect the status of a NWFZ and to refrain from the use or threat of use of nuclear weapons against the states of such a zone.

Second, the nuclear-weapon states could collectively declare that because of the primary responsibilities in upholding the principles and provision of the charter of the United Nations, they would oppose any regional attempt to station, develop, deploy, or test any nuclear weapon or nuclear device in the Middle East. Such a commitment is obviously extremely important, since it is congruent with the special responsibilities the five permanent members of the Security Council have articulated as appropriate posture towards maintaining international peace and security. It also would serve as a strong reminder to any threshold country in the Middle East that any attempt to proliferate nuclear weapons in the Middle East would be met with a firm, unified, and collective action by the five permanent members of the Security Council. As stated earlier, perhaps a declaration by the five permament members to that effect would be the most fungible parallel mechanism for this purpose.

Third, the African NWFZ proposal provides another useful lesson. At least two space satellites have been responsible for detecting nuclear developments in the region of South Africa. The first satellite, which was Soviet, detected the presence of an underground nuclear-weapon test site in the Kalahari desert in 1977. The second satellite, an American device, detected a possible nuclear explosion in 1979.[3] Thus, satellite monitoring would appear to be a very helpful capability for verifying compliance with the letter and spirit of any NWFZ agreement.

Earlier the formation of a scientific committee working under the auspices of the United Nations was proposed in order to report any possible violations that could endanger the regime of a NWFZ in the Middle East. A relationship could also be established with the International Satellite Monitoring Agency (ISMA) (Study A/AC 206/14 of August 16, 1981). This agency, because of its international character, could become more appropriate and acceptable to a larger number of countries in the Middle East. It is pertinent to recall here Article 303 of the ISMA study (A/AC 206/14), which states, "There are no provisions in general international law, including space law, that would entail a prohibition for an international governmental organization to carry out monitoring activities by satellite."

One additional suggestion, related to the African NWFZ proposal, is that the countries of the Middle East might adopt a declaration modeled after the 1964 African Declaration on the Denuclearization of Africa. This declaration could incorporate a commitment by the Middle Eastern countries not to manufacture any nuclear weapons or nuclear devices, and could call on all nuclear-weapon states to respect the status of the zone and the principles and provisions of the declaration. If needed, reference could be made to the right of the countries in the Middle East to develop and utilize nuclear energy for peaceful purposes under effective international control. In order to ensure the success of the declaration in the General Assembly, the reference to both the Non-Proliferation Treaty and IAEA safeguards might be phrased in accordance with the 1980 consensus resolution on the establishment of a NWFZ in the Middle East. This resolution uses moderate language that

> invites the countries concerned to adhere to the Treaty on the Non-Proliferation of Nuclear Weapons [and] calls upon those countries to refrain, on a reciprocal basis, from permitting the stationing of nuclear weapons on their territories by any third party and to agree to place all their nuclear activities under International Atomic Energy Agency safeguards. (35/147 of December 12, 1980)

The advantage of having such a declaration approved by the General Assembly would be that such a development would elevate the initiative from the status of a resolution to that of a comprehensive declaration enjoying the total support and favorable vote of all members of the General Assembly.

The South Asian NWFZ proposal also offers valuable insights. Unlike the Middle East NWFZ initiative, the resolution calling for a NWFZ in South Asia does not enjoy the regional support of all countries in the region. India, unlike Israel, has already detonated a nuclear device. Annually, India has voted against the South Asian NWFZ resolution. In addition, there is disagreement among the five nuclear-weapon states on this particular proposal. While all voted in favor of the Egyptian draft on the establishment of a NWFZ in the Middle East, the Soviet Union and France have abstained on the Pakistani proposal to establish a NWFZ in South Asia (United Nations, 1982e:279).

Several scholars (Power, 1983a and b) and policymakers (especially in Israel and the United States) have advanced the idea of applying the Tlatelolco model to the Middle East.[4] The reasoning behind such logic is that Tlatelolco represents both a *de facto* and *de jure* case of success in establishing a NWFZ in a densely populated region similar to the Middle East.

Such a view is attractive as long as the process of applying Tlatelolco to the Middle East remains selective and discriminate, this study would conclude. Transplanting Tlatelolco in its entirety, however, would create serious problems that might well hamper the establishment of a Middle East NWFZ. This region is both functionally and structurally different from Latin America, and it must be concluded that these differences need to be acknowledged.

Tlatelolco was achieved following intraregional cooperation in the form of direct and uninhibited negotiations between and among its members. The Middle East, on the other hand, still suffers from a complex political and military conflict and a host of unresolved issues. All these and other considerations make the possibilities, at this stage, of direct contact between the Arabs and the Israelis extremely difficult. Hence, what should be applied is a selective approach—extracting what is suitable from the Tlatelolco situation and applying it to the Middle East, bearing in mind the different characteristics of each region. What then are some of the lessons that can be drawn from the Tlatelolco model?

One desirable and possibly transferable feature is the agreement among the contracting parties to Tlatelolco never to test, use, manufacture, produce, or possess either directly or indirectly or on behalf of anyone else any nuclear weapons (Article 1 of Tlatelolco). The parties in the Middle East NWFZ could be asked to pledge never to receive, store, install, deploy, encourage, or authorize the testing, use, manufacture, production, possession, or control of any nuclear weapon. This in essence stipulates the legal underpinnings of the zonal states towards the treaty itself, by presenting *de jure* assurances regarding the objective of preventing nuclear proliferation into the Middle East.

Israel is already on record as stating that it will not be the first to introduce nuclear weapons into the Middle East. Efforts could be directed to the cause of convincing Israel to issue a unilateral, legally binding declaration along the same line of what it has already expressed.

One further obligation would be to request members of the zone to agree to prohibit—on a reciprocal basis—the transport of nuclear weapons in territories under their jurisdiction (since such an act could be interpreted to imply possession). Additionally, it would seem to be advisable to ban the transit of nuclear weapons altogether in the territories falling under national jurisdiction of zonal members. Vehicles, ships, or airplanes carrying nuclear weapons could become targets for attacks from extraregional powers, thereby endangering the denuclearized status of the zone. This view is held by many Third World countries, including Argentina (which claimed that the United Kingdom, which ratified Protocol 2 of Tlatelolco, had violated the denuclearized sanctity of the zone during the Malvinas/Falkland war in 1982, by allowing for the transit of nuclear weapons into the Tlatelolco zone).

Furthermore, Tlatelolco also provides for obligations from extraregional nuclear-weapon states. Protocol 2 in particular stipulated that such nuclear-weapon states will not only respect the obligations of regional Latin American contracting parties, in accordance with Article 1, but added that such nuclear-weapon states "undertake not to use, or threaten to use nuclear weapons against the contracting parties," of Tlatelolco (Article 3 of Protocol 2, in United Nations, 1983b:61). These contractual assurances from the nuclear-weapon states could be emulated in the Middle East NWFZ model.

One additional possible transferable feature of the Tlatelolco model is that accession to the Non-Proliferation Treaty was not stipulated as a rigid, a priori condition for the establishment of such a Latin American NWFZ.

Two views emerge from this NWFZ episode. One strategy would be to refer to the NPT in the same manner reflected in the consensus resolution of 1980 (35/147; see appendix A). Since the language of that resolution was unanimously accepted by the members of the General Assembly, its repetition should not be expected to create problems. The rationale behind such a strategy would be to offer a conciliatory demarche and then to review the situation after the zone is established, rather than to rigidly insist on a priori accession to the NPT and to risk an all-out rejection of a proposed NWFZ in the Middle East.

It should be borne in mind that Israel would not be the only country objecting to any reference to the NPT. Other non-NPT countries in the Middle East, such as Algeria, for instance, could be expected to find itself bonded in a communion of interest with Israel by opposing reference to the NPT proper. This is an extremely important consideration in trying to ensure the effectiveness of the zone, since the boycott by major states cannot be allowed if its success is to be assured. In a speech before the Council on Foreign Relations in New York on May 20, 1983, Hans Blix, Director General of IAEA, observed:

Unlike Israel, all the Arab States are now building or operating nuclear plants (Egypt, Iraq and Libya) are parties to the Non-Proliferation Treaty and their installations are under IAEA safeguards. This may not be enough. To be credible to all countries concerned, the verification system of a NWFZ in the Middle East might have to be reinforced and perhaps backed up by commitments from outside Powers. This is obviously a political matter in which IAEA cannot take initiatives but its services or experiences might be helpful (United Nations, 1983c:2–8).

An alternative strategy that could prove problematic and hamper the zone's establishment would be to insist on the accession of all countries of the region to the NPT before the establishment of the zone. The majority of countries in the Middle East have adhered to the NPT, including all those bordering on Israel. Hence, calling on Israel to accede to the treaty would be consonant with the obligations carried out by other members of the zone. It also could be stated that the definition of the zone desired is in full compliance with Article 7 of the NPT, which states, "Nothing in this Treaty affects the right of any group of States to conclude regional treaties in order to assure the total absence of nuclear weapons in their respective territories." Additionally, Article 17 of Tlatelolco ensures the right of contracting members to develop and use nuclear energy for peaceful purposes, in particular for their economic development and social progress. This is a valuable asset, given the aspiration of several countries in the Middle East for the peaceful uses of nuclear energy. Parallel to this point is the fact that Iraq, Iran, Egypt, and Libya (the countries with nuclear facilities) have all signed safeguard agreements with the IAEA (see table 5.1). Other bilateral safeguard agreements have been signed, as well—such as the French-Iraqi agreement placing 100 French inspectors to monitor the spent fuel in Iraq, and the agreement between Egypt and the United States, reported to be stringent.

One additional desirable component for a decision in a NWFZ regime for the Middle East would be Tlatelolco's provision for the use of special inspections in the event any party suspects "that some activity prohibited by the Treaty has been carried out or is about to be carried out" (Article 16). This article gives its members the right to prevent the possibilities of weapon-grade material diversion, thus ensuring that the use of nuclear energy is exclusively for peaceful purposes. The system envisaged in this article is tightly knit. It allows for a cooperative role between the IAEA and Tlatelolco's Agency for the Prohibition of Nuclear Weapons in Latin America (OPANAL) in carrying out these special inspections. The costs of these inspections are to be carried by the requesting party or parties; or if such inspections prove positive, then the expenses are to be borne by the agency (Article 16[2]). Accordingly, the contracting parties agree to allow for such inspection connected with suspicion of violation of the treaty but have the right to designate their own representatives. The article also calls for dispatching a report of the findings of such an investigation to the General Assembly, the Security Council, and to the Organization of American States (OAS), in addition to the right of convening a special session of the General Conference established by Tlatelolco in the case of any violations.

What could be applicable to the Middle East model is inclusion of a bonded link between such a NWFZ and the establishment of IAEA-safeguarded boundaries. Since the possibility of establishing an OPANAL in the Middle East seems dim, owing to a variety of political reasons, it would seem more appropriate to designate the role of inspection and verification to an independent agency—such as the IAEA—that would host all countries of the Middle East. This in essence would entrust the IAEA, for example, not only with the duty of periodic inspection but also with the ad hoc duty of carrying out unscheduled challenge inspections. Again, few problems would be envisaged from the side of Arab countries bordering Israel, since all of them have signed inspection agreements with the IAEA. Israel might refuse such a stipulation; however, in light of her constant support of and insistence on the application of the Tlatelolco model to the Middle East NWFZ, this difficulty could be overcome.

In this respect contracting parties could be urged to negotiate either multilateral or bilateral agreements with the IAEA for the application of its safeguards to their nuclear facilities. This could possibly entail an enlargement of the verification responsibilities entrusted to the IAEA. A proposed change in the agency's statute could therefore allow for additional inspection rights for the "Core of Inspectors" to verify the nonpresence of nuclear weapons in the territories of the proposed denuclearized zone. The same core might also acquire new privileges to verify party members' compliance with the objectives of the zone.

Article 24 of Tlatelolco offers, as well, a valuable idea concerning settlement of disputes. The mechanism envisaged to settle different interpretations and/or application of this treaty would be to refer them to the International Court of Justice. This, in fact, would be in full compliance with the Charter of the United Nations (Chapter 6, Article 33), which underscores the solution of such disputes through "negotiations, enquiry, mediation, conciliation, arbitration, judicial settlement, resort to regional agencies or arrangement," and also Article 36 (3), which stipulates that as a general rule, disputes should be referred by the parties to the International Court of Justice.

Additionally, Articles 27 and 30 of Tlatelolco provide for two usable criteria: first, that the treaty shall not be subject to reservations; second, that it shall be of a permanent nature and shall remain in force indefinitely. Applied to the Middle East, this would mean that countries in the region would cultivate an interest in the indefinite application of the nonproliferation objectives, and that these objectives would remain, irrespective of any possible political changes within the region. This, if accomplished, would underscore the importance accorded by member states to the urgency of the issue.

On the other hand, there are several principles that are applicable only to the Latin American model. These should not be emulated in developing the Middle East NWFZ, since they would only complicate the process of implementing the resolutions.

First, calling for an OPANAL, multilateral-type agency in the Middle East would not appear to be realistic. What is recommended instead is widening the role entrusted to the United Nations, since it is an international organization enjoying comprehensive membership, encompassing both Arabs and Israelis.

The relationship between the United Nations and such a NWFZ in the Middle East in actuality encompasses many aspects. A sharing of common objectives exists because the establishment of a Middle East would ultimately reduce international tension and thereby strengthen the role of the United Nations in the field of disarmament, international peace, and security. And as demonstrated earlier throughout chapters 2 and 3, the United Nations can play a cardinal role as a forum where the states of the Middle East can present proposals, can deliberate, and can negotiate their contents. That the proposal to establish a NWFZ in the Middle East has been successfully debated in the UN forum from 1974 to the present should not be forgotten. Without the United Nations this progress can be deemed to have been impossible. Also, the United Nations offers the Security Council as the primary political organ responsible for the maintenance of international peace and security. The United Nations may hence assist the parties in the Middle East in their consulations for the implementation of such a zone. Additionally, the United Nations can serve as a guarantor of the zone by devising an international regime that applies certain control measures of verification, inspections, and safeguards to ensure the compliance of NWFZ obligations.

Another deficiency that should be avoided is Tlatelolco's textual ambiguity concerning the vital issue of Peaceful Nuclear Explosions (PNEs). Article 18 of Tlatelolco did not altogether prevent nuclear explosions; it only regulated them. The authors of the treaty were circumscribed as well as ambiguous in their measures to limit the possibilities of nuclear-weapon horizontal proliferation in Latin America. The Soviet reservation, centering on the technical difficulty of distinguishing nuclear explosive devices for peaceful uses from those for military purposes is, within this context, relevant. This ambiguity can and should be avoided during the course of negotiating the implementation of a Middle East NWFZ.

But the main preoccupation of the Middle East NWFZ proposal should be to ban any type of nuclear explosion in the Middle East. Any such explosion, for whatever alleged purposes, would spur a ruinous nuclear-arms race, invite superpower rivalry in the region, and further polarize members of the zone. The explosion of any type of nuclear device in the Middle East would, in addition, be automatically once again tied by concerned parties to the complexities of the Arab-Israeli conflict. If this were to happen, other actors within the region would find incentives to search for parity in an unstable system of mutual nuclear deterrence, thereby defeating the objectives of a NWFZ. The language of any article dealing with such an issue in a denuclearized Middle East proposal should therefore be resolute and unambiguous in its effort to deter any nuclear-aspiring member from conducting any nuclear test.

An alternate, conciliatory course or strategy would be to resolve the entire issue of PNEs in accordance with Article 5 of the Non-Proliferation Treaty, which states:

> Each Party to the Treaty undertakes to take appropriate measures to ensure that, in accordance with this Treaty, under appropriate international observation and through appropriate international procedures, potential benefits from any peaceful applications of nuclear explosions will be made available to non-nuclear-weapon States Party to the Treaty on a non-discriminatory basis and that the charge to such Parties for the explosive devices used will be as low as possible and exclude any charge for research and development. Non-nuclear-weapon States Party to the Treaty shall be able to obtain such benefits, pursuant to a special international agreement or agreements, through an appropriate international body with adequate representation of non-nuclear-weapon States. Negotiations on this subject shall commence as soon as possible after the Treaty enters into force. Non-nuclear weapon States Party to the Treaty so desiring may also obtain such benefits pursuant to bilateral agreements.

Moreover, it should be noted that Tlatelolco does not account for, nor does it possess, the machinery to deal in a multilateral form with the problem of spent-fuel disposal, reprocessing, and plutonium recycling. Power (1983b:633) explains: "These and related matters having proliferation implications should be addressed by Mideast Free-zone architects when the free-zone Treaty is being drafted. An immediate concern: the disposition of separated plutonium that may be present in Israel when the zone begins."

In addition, one of the issues succinctly and efficaciously dealt with in the Tlatelolco regime has been the geographic definition of the zone of Latin America (Article 4 [1] and [2]). This is a problematic issue when addressed to the Middle East. Exactly what is meant by "the Middle East," and how can its geographic scope and the members composing it be defined?[5] Before an attempt to present a definition is offered, some of the countries that can be excluded from that definition can be identified. For instance, Turkey would not be included in the political definition of the Middle East applicable to the establishment of a NWFZ in that region. Turkey is already a full-fledged NATO member with contractual defense agreements and obligations. Whether there are nuclear weapons in Turkey's territory or not remains outside the framework of this treatment. What is certain, nevertheless, is that any inclusion of Turkey into such a zone would revive conflicting arguments concerning treaty obligations of state members to extraregional powers. A UN study asserts:

> For those states that are parties to one or more security alliances and who are potential parties to a NWFZ treaty, special questions will arise, especially if they belong to alliances which have nuclear weapon states in their membership. In these cases there is often an obligation, whether explicit or implicit, for the nuclear weapon states to come to the aid of their allies with all sufficient means if the latter are attacked. This aid need not, of course, involve nuclear weapons, but the

possibility exists. Matters can be complicated in some cases by the issue of deployment, as mutual alliance treaties of this nature can, and sometimes do, involve agreement for the deployment of nuclear weapons in the territory of a non-nuclear weapon ally, or for special facilities involving nuclear weapon delivery systems. (United Nations, 1976b:33)

This fact was envisaged by the cosponsors of the original resolution on the establishment of a NWFZ in the Middle East. Cognizant of Turkey's situation and its integration into the East-West nuclear umbrella, the sponsors did not request Turkey to become a cosponsor of the resolution.

The exclusion, as well, of Afghanistan and Pakistan from a definition of what might constitute the region for such a NWFZ seems justifiable, since Pakistan has presented its own initiative to the General Assembly to establish yet another NWFZ in South Asia. Afghanistan would appropriately fall geographically under that classification.

One possible alternative would be to define the region of the Middle East "as wide as possible," consonant with the definition advanced by Iran (A/9693 of July 15, 1974) and Israel (A/36/315 of June 10, 1981). Such a definition could encompass all the Arab members[6]—including Mauritania, since it cosponsored the 1976 resolution—in addition to Iran and Israel.

One other possible alternative would be to start with a narrow definition of such a region, possibly with Egypt and Israel (both governed by a peace treaty), and allow for the region to widen as the regime proves successful. This limited definition of a NWFZ region in the Middle East is compatible with a similar definition of what constitutes a "region" offered by a group of experts who prepared a UN study on "all aspects of regional disarmament." Paragraphs 152 and 153 of that study observed:

In relation to regional disarmament, a flexible approach to the concept of a "region" must be adopted. It is not possible to define in advance and in general what might constitute a suitable "region," as this will depend both on the initiative of the States concerned, and in many cases, on the type of measure envisaged. Thus, two or more neighbouring States can constitute a "region" for disarmament purposes. So can, in fact, contiguous parts of the territories of States, as in the case of a demilitarized border zone. In other cases an entire continent or other known geographical entity may be the most appropriate framework for disarmament measures. It is clear, however, that in all cases the area of application of the measure must be precisely defined, including, where appropriate, definition of the maritime and air spaces covered.

In fact, the area of application of a regional disarmament measure need not be fixed once and for all. Also in this respect a flexible approach is sometimes preferable. In some cases, for example, it may be desirable or necessary to aim from the outset for a wide coverage, such as an entire continent or sub-continent. Even so, it may be that the only practicable approach is for some States of the region to adopt and implement the measure in question, in the expectation that the remaining States of the region will eventually accede to it as well. In other cases one could envisage a process in which a disarmament measure is first negotiated among a nucleus of States where the need for relaxation of tension, reduction of force levels or pre-emption of further military expansion is particularly great. From that nucleus the "region" may then be gradually extended by the accession of neighbouring States to the measure in question, without it being necessary to define from the outset the exact boundaries of the region to which the measure in question will ultimately apply. (United Nations, 1981c:36)

Another study (United Nations, 1976b:34) has observed, "Although the creation of large zones would provide greater progress towards nuclear disarmaments than small ones, the establishment of medium or small zones could play a significant part in enhancing regional security."

SUMMARY

If progress towards the establishment of a NWFZ in the Middle East is to commence, it is imperative at this stage to build on the success of previous initiatives to establish a NWFZ in the Middle East. Otherwise, the risks are high that the item will be left unenforced and ultimately discarded into oblivion. One of the purposes of this chapter has been to demonstrate that despite all the difficulties associated with the region, the proposal to denuclearize the Middle East remains viable and requires wide support for the proposal's realization. Two fundamental measures must be maintained if progress is to commence, this study concludes.

First, a clear-cut distinction must be drawn between the Arab-Israeli conflict and this disarmament proposal. Efforts should be directed towards separating the military and political conflict from the disarmament proposal for the establishment of a NWFZ in order to save the region from a ruinous nuclear-arms race. To protect the indigenous population from the scourge of costly military investments, an initiative must be undertaken to establish a direly needed atmosphere of confidence, which eventually could spill over into other sectors. This commands more hope than does the strategy of a defeatist approach, which would destine the Middle East to sinking into a multilateral nuclear-weapons race. Former Assistant Secretary of State Harold K. Saunders explained how issues involving nuclear dangers and threats of proliferation in the Middle East should be dealt with at a separate level of priority and should not be tied to the Arab-Israeli dispute by noting:

The question of agreements concerning nuclear weapons belongs on a separate agenda because there may be opportunities for discussions of this issue apart from the peace negotiations and any related discussion of limitations on conventional arms. Evidence of this possibility lies in the fact that a proposal for a nuclear-free zone in the Middle East at least formally supported by Israel, is already being discussed at the United Nations. Whether or not a serious effort will be made to achieve progress, the opening is there to pursue the nuclear dialogue even in the absence of a comprehensive Arab-Israeli peace. (Saunders, 1981:60)

Had this approach been pursued and if a clear-cut distinction had been maintained between the urgent necessities of averting nuclear dangers in the Middle East (through a UN initiative) and the intricacies of the Arab-Israeli conflict, the prospects for containing conflict and proliferation could have been enhanced and perhaps avoided and even solved in the first half of the 1970s.

Second, an amelioration in the position of the Arab states is also required. As a matter of fact, the establishment of a NWFZ in the Middle East is not possible without the participation of Israel. This is a basic reality that cannot be ignored. Hence, instead of indulging in procedural difficulties by holding the NWFZ proposal "hostage," through refusal to consult directly or indirectly with Israel, efforts should be exerted to take the course Egypt has followed: to allow for conciliation and for compromise.

Equally, if this study is requesting that the Arab world change posture vis-à-vis Israel, this study is also requesting that Israel take more conciliatory steps towards the establishment of a NWFZ in the Middle East. Some observers raise the question, Why should Israel relinquish its undeclared nuclear posture and risk a conventional war facing twenty-one Arab entities? The answer could be summed up in the following. First, the establishment of a NWFZ in the Middle East would prevent any Arab country from resorting to the nuclear option, either by developing nuclear capabilities or by drawing on the nuclear umbrella of an extraregional power. Second, and in the context of a comprehensive peaceful settlement of the Arab-Israeli conflict, the Arabs may insist that settlement is not possible as long as a nuclear menace hovers over the region. In that case the solution of the conflict would be contingent on the presentation by Israel of concrete and tangible assurances. Consequently, the establishment of a NWFZ in the Middle East could be a facilitative factor towards the realization of peace in the region.   The UN Secretary General should be encouraged to appoint a special representative to discuss with the countries in the Middle East the modalities of implementing this NWFZ proposal in the region. This potentially could lead to a dialogue between and among all the parties concerned and a breakthrough in communication and negotiation, which would permit the interaction of ideas and concepts, enabling all to ponder the next advisable move.

The General Assembly shall once again discuss the same NWFZ proposal. The question then will be: How should discussion proceed on the issue? Two strategies emerge. One is to retain the initiative intact by introducing minor substantive amendments in order not to undermine the consensus vote until more favorable circumstances can be allowed to develop. A second strategy is to introduce new concepts. Examples of such dramatic changes would include the following actions:

(1) Request the General Assembly to adopt a Declaration on the Denuclearization of the Middle East, modeled after the African example, or to add an operative paragraph

to the text of the resolution that would "declare the establishment of a Middle East NWFZ."

(2) Reinvigorate the idea of dispatching a special representative of the UN Secretary General to discuss, with the parties in the region, the scope and modalities of implementing the zone—and here effort should be exerted to convince certain Arab states such as Syria to accept this notion.

(3) Request the Secretary General to carry out, with the assistance of a group of experts, a study on the "modalities of establishing a NWFZ in the Middle East."

(4) Request Egypt to table a resolution before the Security Council calling on members to deposit, with the Council their declarations to respect such a zone, refrain from use or threat of use of nuclear weapons against members of the zone, and carry out a commitment never to produce, acquire, or station any kind of nuclear weapon or nuclear device in the Middle East in accordance with paragraph 60–63 of the Final Document of the First Special Session of the General Assembly on Disarmament, which was approved by consensus.

In conclusion, the problematic nature of this NWFZ proposal's implementation, discussed earlier in this chapter, is understandable. However, this challenge must be addressed. The resolution on a NWFZ in the Middle East, adopted by overwhelming majorities since 1974 and by consensus since 1980, attests to the fact that the international community agrees on two important requirements: the first is cognizance of the need to put an end to the danger that would threaten the Middle East and the world as a whole as a result of the introduction into that region of nuclear weapons and weapons of mass destruction. The second is awareness of the need for an effective step forward towards the limitation of the proliferation of nuclear weapons, which again is a principle supported and long expressed by the international community.

The region of the Middle East differs from other regions of the world. First of all, it is a region that is strategically sensitive and economically unique; and, therefore, any escalation in the armament systems of the states of the region would have far-reaching repercussions for peace and security throughout the world. Second, the region has been and continues to be the arena of one of the world's most prolonged, embittered, and tragic conflicts, which has lasted for more than thirty years and which still continues, despite all the serious efforts made to find a solution to it and abate it.

The suffering in the Middle East as a result of the bitter conflict and of the wars that have employed the most sophisticated kinds of conventional weapons make that region most deserving of international efforts to ensure that nuclear weapons will not be introduced into the arsenals of the region. The difficulties and threats inherent in the region can serve as a catalyst to preventive action by the international community at large.

The proposal outlined in this study has been designed to facilitate the generation and broadening of peace. Political will is needed in order to advance these proposals and recommendations. Such efforts must be collective rather than unilateral. Because there may be no more urgent task facing humankind today than the prevention of a nuclear exchange or nuclear-weapon proliferation, policymakers must respond to the challenge posed. A NWFZ in the Middle East offers, indeed, the "only solution," to quote S. Flapan, an Israeli scholar. Whether such political will materialize depends on the response of world leaders, who alone possess the political resources necessary to mobilize action for peace. By outlining the challenge confronting these leaders, by drawing on the lessons of experience to inform those leaders of obstacles and options, this study has sought to provide policy prescriptions that could lead to the creation of a Middle East free of the fear of nuclear war.

The world awaits a response. If one is not forthcoming, apocalyptic demise could result. But it is hoped that by identifying the dangers and the opportunities, policymakers will be moved to seize the problem and work in concert for a solution.

NOTES

1. A word of caution is needed here. The purpose of this survey is not to present rigid recommendations in a *mise en demeure* form. On the contrary, the purpose of analysis at this stage is to present theoretical alternatives, list options, and enumerate prerogatives.

2. The Mediterranean proposal, tabled in 1983, on the agenda of the First Committee of the General Assembly is a treatment of the issue that involves strengthening security and cooperation in the Mediterranean region rather than pronouncing the Mediterranean a NWFZ (Resolution 39/189).

3. The United States VELA-type satellite was placed in orbit in 1963 to monitor compliance with the provisions of the Partial Test Ban Treaty.

4. See *Prohibition of Nuclear Weapons in Latin America,* Hearing, Committee on Foreign Relations, U.S. Senate, 97th Cong., 1st sess., September 22, 1981:4–13; also, see statement by Eugene V. Rostow, Director of the Arms Control and Disarmament Agency *(The New York Times,* August 14, 1981).

5. Historically, the term *Middle East* was introduced in 1902 by the naval historian Alfred Mahan to describe the region between Arabia and India with its center in the Persian Gulf. This was adopted later by *The Times* and by the British government, and along with the term *Near East,* became generally used. The word *East* meant, for the West, the Orient, the "Eastern question," and territories under the rule of the Ottoman Empire (Bernard Lewis 1964:9–10). According to the U.S. State Department (U.S. Department of State Directory, 1984), the Bureau of Near Eastern Affairs includes Morocco, Algeria, Tunisia, Libya, Lebanon, Jordan, Syria, Israel, Iraq, Iran, Egypt, and the Arabian Peninsula. The definition excludes the Sudan, as it is listed under the Bureau for East African Affairs, and Turkey, which is included in European Affairs.

6. According to membership in the League of Arab States, the Arab world comprises Morocco, Algeria, Tunisia, Libya, Egypt, Sudan, Mauritania, Djibouti, Lebanon, Syria, the PLO, Iraq, Jordan, Kuwait, Bahrain, Qatar, United Arab Emirates, Saudi Arabia, Oman, Democratic Yemen, Yemen Arab Republic, and Somalia.

APPENDIX A

3263 (XXIX). Establishment of a nuclear-weapon-free zone in the region of the Middle East

Date: 9 December 1974
Vote: 128–0–2 (roll call)
Meeting: 2309
Report: A/9909

The General Assembly,

Having considered the question of the establishment of a nuclear-weapon-free zone in the region of the Middle East,

Desiring to contribute to the maintenance of international peace and security by bolstering and expanding the existing regional and global structures for the prohibition and/or prevention of the further spread of nuclear weapons,

Realizing that the establishment of nuclear-weapon-free zones with an adequate system of safeguards could accelerate the process towards nuclear disarmament and the ultimate goal of general and complete disarmament under effective international control,

Recalling the resolution adopted by the Council of the League of Arab States at its sixty-second session, held in Cairo from 1 to 4 September 1974, on this subject,

Recalling the message sent by His Imperial Majesty the Shahanshah of Iran on 16 September 1974 on the establishment of a nuclear-weapon-free zone in the region of the Middle East (A/9693/Add.3),

Considering that the establishment of zones free from nuclear weapons, on the initiative of the States situated within each zone concerned, is one of the measures which can contribute most effectively to halting the proliferation of those instruments of mass destruction and to promoting progress towards nuclear disarmament, with the goal of total destruction of all nuclear weapons and their means of delivery,

Mindful of political conditions particular to the region of the Middle East and of the potential danger emanating therefrom, which would be further aggravated by the introduction of nuclear weapons in the area,

Conscious, therefore, of the need to keep the countries of the region from becoming involved in a ruinous nuclear arms race,

Recalling the Declaration on Denuclearization of Africa issued by the Assembly of Heads of State and Government of the Organization of African Unity in July 1964,

Noting that establishment of a nuclear-weapon-free zone in the region of the Middle East would contribute effectively to the realization of aims enunciated in the above-mentioned Declaration on Denuclearization of Africa,

Recalling the notable achievement of the countries of Latin America in establishing a nuclear-free zone,

Also recalling resolution B of the Conference of Non-Nuclear-Weapon States, convened at Geneva on 29 August 1968, in which the conference recommended that non-nuclear-weapon States not comprised in the Latin American nuclear-free zone should study the possibility and desirability of establishing military denuclearization of their respective zones,

Recalling the aims pursued by the Treaty on the Non-Proliferation of Nuclear Weapons (General Assembly resolution 2373 [XXII], annex) and, in particular, the goal of preventing the further spread of nuclear weapons,

Recalling resolution 2373 (XXII) of 12 June 1968, in which it expressed the hope for the widest possible adherence to the Treaty on the Non-Proliferation of Nuclear Weapons by both nuclear-weapon and non-nuclear-weapon States,

    1. *Commends* the idea of the establishment of a nuclear-weapon-free zone in the region of the Middle East;

    2. *Considers* that, in order to advance the idea of a nuclear-weapon-free zone in the region of the Middle East, it is indispensable that all parties concerned in the area proclaim solemnly and immediately their intention to refrain, on a reciprocal basis, from producing, testing, obtaining, acquiring or in any other way possessing nuclear weapons;

    3. *Calls upon* the parties concerned in the area to accede to the Treaty on the Non-Proliferation of Nuclear Weapons;

    4. *Expresses the hope* that all States and, in particular, the nuclear-weapon States, will lend their full co-operation for the effective realization of the aims of this resolution;

    5. *Requests* the Secretary-General to ascertain the views of the parties concerned with respect to the implementation of the present resolution, in particular, with

regard to its paragraphs 2 and 3, and to report to the Security Council at an early date and, subsequently, to the General Assembly at its thirtieth session;

6. *Decides* to include in the provisional agenda of its thirtieth session the item entitled "Establishment of a nuclear-weapon-free zone in the region of the Middle East."

ROLL-CALL VOTE ON RESOLUTION 3263 (XXIX):

In favour: Afghanistan, Algeria, Argentina, Australia, Austria, Bahamas, Bahrain, Bangladesh, Barbados, Belgium, Bhutan, Bolivia, Botswana, Brazil, Bulgaria, Burundi, Byelorussian SSR, Canada, Central African Republic, Chad, Chile, China, Colombia, Congo, Costa Rica, Cuba, Cyprus, Czechoslovakia, Dahomey, Democratic Yemen, Denmark, Dominican Republic, Ecuador, Egypt, El Salvador, Equatorial Guinea, Ethiopia, Fiji, Finland, France, Gambia, German Democratic Republic, Federal Republic of Germany, Ghana, Greece, Grenada, Guatemala, Guinea, Guinea-Bissau, Guyana, Haiti, Honduras, Hungary, Iceland, India, Indonesia, Iran, Ireland, Italy, Ivory Coast, Jamaica, Japan, Jordan, Kenya, Khmer Republic, Kuwait, Laos, Lebanon, Lesotho, Liberia, Luxembourg, Madagascar, Malaysia, Mali, Malta, Mauritania, Mauritius, Mexico, Mongolia, Morocco, Nepal, Netherlands, New Zealand, Nicaragua, Niger, Nigeria, Norway, Oman, Pakistan, Panama, Paraguay, Peru, Philippines, Poland, Portugal, Qatar, Romania, Rwanda, Senegal, Sierra Leone, Singapore, Somalia, Spain, Sri Lanka, Sudan, Swaziland, Sweden, Syrian Arab Republic, Thailand, Togo, Trinidad and Tobago, Tunisia, Turkey, Uganda, Ukrainian SSR, USSR, United Arab Emirates, United Kingdom, United Republic of Cameroon, United Republic of Tanzania, United States, Upper Volta, Uruguay, Venezuela, Yemen, Yugoslavia, Zaire, Zambia.

Against: None.

Abstaining: Burma, Israel.

Absent: Albania, Gabon, Iraq, Libyan Arab Republic, Malawi, Maldives, Saudi Arabia, South Africa.

3474 (XXX). Establishment of a nuclear-weapon-free zone in the region of the Middle East

Date: 11 December 1975
Vote: 125–0–2 (recorded)
Meeting: 2437
Report: A/10443

The General Assembly,

Recalling resolution 3263 (XXIX) of 9 December 1974, in which the General Assembly overwhelmingly commended the idea of the establishment of a nuclear-weapon-free zone in the region of the Middle East,

Taking note of the report of the Secretary-General to the Security Council and the General Assembly, (S/11778 and Add.1–4; A/10221 and Add.1 and 2) and the responses contained therein, on the question of the establishment of a nuclear-weapon-free zone in the region of the Middle East,

Recognizing, on the basis of the above-mentioned report, that the establishment of a nuclear-weapon-free zone in the Middle East enjoys wide support in the region,

Mindful of the prevailing political situation in the region and of the potential danger emanating therefrom, which would be further aggravated by the introduction of nuclear weapons in the area,

Conscious, therefore, of the need to keep the countries of the region from becoming involved in a ruinous nuclear arms race,

Taking note of the comprehensive study of the question of nuclear-weapon-free zones in all its aspects, (A/10027/Add.1, annex I) prepared by the *Ad Hoc* Group of Qualified Governmental Experts pursuant to General Assembly resolution 3261 F (XXIX) of 9 December 1974,

Recalling its resolution 2373 (XXII) of 12 June 1968, in which it expressed the hope for the widest possible adherence to the Treaty on the Non-Proliferation of Nuclear Weapons (General Assembly resolution 2373 [XXII], annex) by both nuclear-weapon and non-nuclear-weapon States,

1. *Expresses the opinion* that the Member States with which the Secretary-General has consulted through his notes verbales of 10 March 1975 and 13 June 1975 pursuant to General Assembly resolution 3263 (XXIX) should exert efforts towards the realization of the objective of establishing a nuclear-weapon-free zone in the Middle East;

2. *Urges* all parties directly concerned to adhere to the Treaty on the Non-Proliferation of Nuclear Weapons as a means of promoting this objective;

3. *Recommends* that the Member States referred to in paragraph 1 of the present resolution, pending the establishment of the nuclear-weapon-free zone under an effective system of safeguards:

(*a*) Proclaim solemnly and immediately their intention to refrain, on a reciprocal basis, from producing, acquiring or in any other way possessing nuclear weapons and nuclear explosive devices, and from permitting the stationing of nuclear weapons, in their territory or the territory under their control by any third party;

(*b*) Refrain, on a reciprocal basis, from any other action that would facilitate the acquisition, testing or use of such weapons, or would be in any other way detrimental to the objective of the establishment of a nuclear-weapon-free zone in the region under an effective system of safeguards;

4. *Recommends* to the nuclear-weapon States to refrain from any action contrary to the purpose of the present resolution and the objective of establishing in the region of the Middle East, a nuclear-weapon-free zone under an effective system of safeguards and to extend their co-operation to the States of the region in their efforts to promote this objective;

5. *Decides* to include in the provisional agenda of its thirty-first session the item entitled ''Establishment of a nuclear-weapon-free zone in the region of the Middle East.''

RECORDED VOTE ON RESOLUTION 3474 (XXX):

In favour: Afghanistan, Algeria, Argentina, Australia, Austria, Bahrain, Bangladesh, Barbados, Belgium, Benin, Bhutan, Bolivia, Botswana, Brazil, Bulgaria, Burundi, Byelorussian SSR, Canada, Chad, Chile, China, Colombia, Comoros, Congo, Costa Rica, Cuba, Cyprus, Czechoslovakia, Democratic Yemen, Denmark, Dominican Republic, Egypt, El Salvador, Equatorial Guinea, Ethiopia, Fiji, Finland, France, Gabon, German Democratic Republic, Federal Republic of Germany, Ghana, Greece, Grenada, Guatemala, Guinea, Guyana, Haiti, Honduras, Hungary, Iceland, India, Indonesia, Iran, Iraq, Ireland, Italy, Ivory Coast, Jamaica, Japan, Jordan, Kenya, Kuwait, Laos, Lebanon, Lesotho, Liberia, Luxembourg, Madagascar, Malawi, Malaysia, Mali, Mauritania, Mauritius, Mexico, Mongolia, Morocco, Mozambique, Nepal, Netherlands, New Zealand, Nicaragua, Niger, Nigeria, Norway, Oman, Pakistan, Panama, Papua New Guinea, Paraguay, Peru, Philippines, Poland, Portugal, Qatar, Romania, Rwanda, Saudi Arabia, Senegal, Sierra Leone, Singapore, Spain, Sri Lanka, Sudan, Swaziland, Sweden, Syrian Arab Republic, Thailand, Togo, Trinidad and Tobago, Tunisia, Turkey, Uganda, Ukrainian SSR, USSR, United Arab Emirates, United Kingdom, United Republic of Tanzania, United States, Upper Volta, Uruguay, Venezuela, Yugoslavia, Zaire, Zambia.

Against: None.

Abstaining: Israel, United Republic of Cameroon.

Absent: Albania, Bahamas, Burma, Cambodia, Cape Verde, Central African Republic, Ecuador, Gambia, Guinea-Bissau, Libyan Arab Republic, Maldives, Malta, Sao Tome and Principe, Somalia, South Africa, Surinam, Yemen.

31/71. Establishment of a nuclear-weapon-free zone in the region of the Middle East

Date: 10 December 1976
Vote: 130–0–1 (recorded)
Meeting: 96
Report: A/31/381

The General Assembly,

Recalling its resolution 3263 (XXIX) of 9 December 1974, in which it overwhelmingly commended the idea of the establishment of a nuclear-weapon-free zone in the region of the Middle East,

Recalling also its resolution 3474 (XXX) of 11 December 1975, in which it recognized that the establishment of a nuclear-weapon-free zone in the Middle East enjoys wide support in the region,

Mindful of the prevailing political situation in the region and the potential danger emanating therefrom that would be further aggravated by the introduction of nuclear weapons in the area,

Concerned that the lack of any appreciable progress in the direction of the establishment of a nuclear-weapon-free zone, in the present atmosphere in the region, will further complicate the situation,

Convinced that progress towards the establishment of a nuclear-weapon-free zone in the Middle East will greatly enhance the cause of peace both in the region and in the world,

Conscious of the particular nature of the problems involved and the complexities inherent in the situation in the Middle East and the urgency of keeping the region free from involvement in a ruinous nuclear arms race,

1. *Expresses the need* for further action to generate momentum towards realization of the establishment of a nuclear-weapon-free zone in the Middle East;

2. *Urges* all parties directly concerned to adhere to the Treaty on Non-Proliferation of Nuclear Weapons (General Assembly resolution 2373 [XXII], annex) as a means of promoting this objective;

3. *Reiterates* its recommendation that the States Members of the United Nations referred to in paragraph 2 above, pending the establishment of the nuclear-weapon-free zone under an effective system of safeguards, should:

(*a*) Proclaim solemnly and immediately their intention to refrain, on a reciprocal basis, from producing, acquiring or in any other way possessing nuclear weapons and nuclear explosive devices, and from permitting the stationing of nuclear weapons in their territory or the territory under their control by any third party;

(*b*) Refrain, on a reciprocal basis, from any other action that would facilitate the acquisition, testing or use of such weapons, or would be in any other way detrimental to the objective of the establishment of a nuclear-weapon-free zone in the region under an effective system of safeguards;

(*c*) Agree to place all their nuclear activities under the International Atomic Energy Agency safeguards;

4. *Reaffirms* the recommendations to the nuclear-weapon States to refrain from any action contrary to the progress of the present resolution and the objective of establishing in the region of the Middle East a nuclear-weapon-free zone under an effective system of safeguards and to extend their co-operation to the States of the region in their efforts to promote this objective;

5. *Invites* the Secretary-General to explore the possibilities of making progress towards the establishment of a nuclear-weapon-free zone in the area of the Middle East;

6. *Decides* to include in the provisional agenda of its thirty-second session the item entitled ''Establishment of a nuclear-weapon-free zone in the region of the Middle East.''

RECORDED VOTE ON RESOLUTION 31/71:

In favour: Afghanistan, Algeria, Argentina, Australia, Austria, Bahamas, Bahrain, Bangladesh, Barbados, Belgium, Bhutan, Bolivia, Botswana, Brazil, Bulgaria, Burundi, Byelorrussian SSR, Canada, Central African Republic, Chad, Chile, China, Colombia, Comoros, Congo, Costa Rica, Cuba, Cyprus, Czechoslovakia, Democratic Yemen, Denmark, Dominican Republic, Ecuador, Egypt, El Salvador, Equatorial Guinea, Ethiopia,

Fiji, Finland, France, Gabon, Gambia, German Democratic Republic, Federal Republic of Germany, Ghana, Greece, Grenada, Guinea-Bissau, Guyana, Hungary, Iceland, India, Indonesia, Iran, Iraq, Ireland, Italy, Ivory Coast, Jamaica, Japan, Jordan, Kenya, Kuwait, Lao People's Democratic Republic, Lebanon, Lesotho, Liberia, Luxembourg, Madagascar, Malawi, Malaysia, Maldives, Mali, Malta, Mauritania, Mauritius, Mexico, Mongolia, Morocco, Mozambique, Nepal, Netherlands, New Zealand, Niger, Nigeria, Norway, Oman, Pakistan, Panama, Papua New Guinea, Paraguay, Peru, Philippines, Poland, Portugal, Qatar, Romania, Rwanda, Saudi Arabia, Senegal, Sierra Leone, Singapore, Somalia, Spain, Sri Lanka, Sudan, Surinam, Swaziland, Sweden, Syrian Arab Republic, Thailand, Togo, Trinidad and Tobago, Tunisia, Turkey, Uganda, Ukrainian SSR, USSR, United Arab Emirates, United Kingdom, United Republic of Cameroon, United Republic of Tanzania, United States, Upper Volta, Uruguay, Venezuela, Yemen, Yugoslavia, Zaire, Zambia.

Against: None.

Abstaining: Israel.

Absent: Albania, Angola, Benin, Burma, Cape Verde, Democratic Kampuchea, Guatemala, Guinea, Haiti, Honduras, Libyan Arab Republic, Nicaragua, Sao Tome and Principe, Seychelles, South Africa.

32/82. Establishment of a nuclear-weapon-free zone in the region of the Middle East

The General Assembly,

Recalling its resolution 3263 (XXIX) of 9 December 1974, in which it overwhelmingly commended the idea of the establishment of a nuclear-weapon-free zone in the region of the Middle East,

Recalling also its resolution 3474 (XXX) of 11 December 1975, in which it recognized that the establishment of a nuclear-weapon-free zone in the Middle East enjoys wide support in the region,

Further recalling its resolution 31/71 of 10 December 1976, in which it expressed the conviction that progress towards the establishment of a nuclear-weapon-free zone in the Middle East would greatly enhance the cause of peace both in the region and in the world,

Mindful of the growing international desire for establishing a just and lasting peace in the region of the Middle East,

Conscious of the global apprehension over possible proliferation of nuclear weapons, in particular in the sensitive region of the Middle East,

Fully convinced that the possible development of nuclear capability would further complicate the situation and immensely damage the efforts to create an atmosphere of confidence in the Middle East,

Reiterating anew the particular nature of the problems involved and the complexities inherent in the situation in the Middle East, and the urgency of keeping the region free from involvement in a ruinous nuclear-arms race,

Recognizing, as a consequence, the need to create momentum towards the goal of establishing a nuclear-weapon-free zone in the Middle East,

1. *Urges anew* all parties directly concerned to adhere to the Treaty on the Non-Proliferation of Nuclear Weapons (Resolution 2373 [XXII], annex.) as a means of promoting this objective;

2. *Reiterates* its recommendation that the Member States referred to in paragraph 1 above, pending the establishment of a nuclear-weapon-free zone under an effective system of safeguards, should:

(*a*) Proclaim solemnly and immediately their intention to refrain, on a reciprocal basis, from producing, acquiring or in any other way possessing nuclear weapons and nuclear explosive devices and from permitting the stationing of nuclear weapons on their territory or the territory under their control by any third party;

(*b*) Refrain, on a reciprocal basis, from any other action that would facilitate the acquisition, testing or use of such weapons, or would be in any other way detrimental to the objective of the establishment of a nuclear-weapon-free zone in the region under an effective system of safeguards;

(*c*) Agree to place all their nuclear activities under the International Atomic Energy Agency safeguards;

3. *Reaffirms* its recommendation to the nuclear-weapon States to refrain from any action contrary to the purpose of the present resolution and the objective of establishing, in the region of the Middle East, a nuclear-weapon-free zone under an effective system of safeguards and to extend their co-operation to the States of the region in their efforts to promote this objective;

4. *Renews* its invitation to the Secretary-General to continue to explore the possibilities of making progress towards the establishment of a nuclear-weapon-free zone in the region of the Middle East;

5. *Decides* to include in the provisional agenda of its thirty-third session the item entitled ''Establishment of a nuclear-weapon-free zone in the region of the Middle East.''

100th plenary meeting
12 December 1977

33/64. Establishment of a nuclear-weapon-free zone in the region of the Middle East

Date: 14 December 1978
*Vote:*138–0–1 (recorded)
Meeting: 84
Report: A/33/430

The General Assembly,

Recalling its resolution 3263 (XXIX) of 9 December 1974, in which it overwhelmingly commended the idea of the establishment of a nuclear-weapon-free zone in the region of the Middle East,

Recalling also its resolution 3474 (XXX) of 11 December 1975, in which it recognized that the establishment of a nuclear-weapon-free zone in the Middle East enjoyed wide support in the region,

Bearing in mind its resolution 31/71 of 10 December 1976, in which it expressed the conviction that progress towards the establishment of a nuclear-weapon-free zone in the Middle East would greatly enhance the cause of peace in the region and in the world,

Considering its resolution 32/82 of 12 December 1977, in which it expressed conviction that the development of nuclear capability would further complicate the situation and immensely damage the efforts to create an atmosphere of confidence in the Middle East,

Guided by its relevant recommendations in the Final Document of the Tenth Special Session, dealing with the establishment of a nuclear-weapon-free zone in the region of the Middle East (Resolution S–10/2, para. 63 *d*),

Recognizing that the establishment of a nuclear-weapon-free zone in the Middle East would greatly enhance international peace and security,

1. *Urges* all parties directly concerned seriously to consider taking the practical and urgent steps required for the implementation of the proposal to establish a nuclear-weapon-free zone in the Middle East in accordance with the relevant resolutions of the General Assembly, and, as a means of promoting this objective, invites the countries concerned to adhere to the Treaty on the Non-Proliferation of Nuclear Weapons (Resolution 2373 [XXII], annex);

2. *Invites* these countries, pending the establishment of such a zone in the Middle East and during the process of its establishment, to declare solemnly that they will refrain on a reciprocal basis from producing, acquiring or in any other way possessing nuclear weapons and nuclear explosive devices;

3. *Calls upon* these countries to refrain, on a reciprocal basis, from permitting the stationing of nuclear weapons on their territory by any third party, and to agree to place all their nuclear activities under International Atomic Energy Agency safeguards;

4. *Further invites* these countries, pending the establishment of a nuclear-weapon-free zone in the Middle East and during the process of its establishment, to declare, consistent with paragraph 63 *d* of the Final Document of the Tenth Special Session, their support for the establishing of such a zone in the region and to deposit these declarations with the Security Council;

5. *Reaffirms again* its recommendation to the nuclear-weapon States to refrain from any action contrary to the spirit and purpose of the present resolution and the objective of establishing in the region of the Middle East a nuclear-weapon-free zone under an effective system of safeguards, and to extend their co-operation to the States of the region in their efforts to promote these objectives;

6. *Renews* its invitation to the Secretary-General to continue to explore the possibilities of making progress towards the establishment of a nuclear-weapon-free zone in the region of the Middle East;

7. *Decides* to include in the provisional agenda of its thirty-fourth session the item entitled "Establishment of a nuclear-weapon-free zone in the region of the Middle East."

RECORDED VOTE ON RESOLUTION 33/64:

In favour: Afghanistan, Algeria, Angola, Australia, Austria, Bahamas, Bahrain, Bangladesh, Barbados, Belgium, Benin, Bhutan, Bolivia, Botswana, Brazil, Bulgaria, Burma,

Burundi, Byelorussian SSR, Canada, Cape Verde, Central African Empire, Chile, China, Colombia, Comoros, Congo, Costa Rica, Cuba, Cyprus, Czechoslovakia, Democratic Yemen, Denmark, Djibouti, Dominican Republic, Ecuador, Egypt, El Salvador, Equatorial Guinea, Ethiopia, Fiji, Finland, France, Gabon, Gambia, German Democratic Republic, Federal Republic of Germany, Ghana, Greece, Guatemala, Guinea, Guinea-Bissau, Guyana, Haiti, Honduras, Hungary, Iceland, India, Indonesia, Iran, Iraq, Ireland, Italy, Ivory Coast, Jamaica, Japan, Jordan, Kenya, Kuwait, Lao Peoples Democratic Republic, Lebanon, Lesotho, Luxembourg, Madagascar, Malawi, Malaysia, Maldives, Mali, Malta, Mauritania, Mexico, Mongolia, Morocco, Mozambique, Nepal, Netherlands, New Zealand, Nicaragua, Niger, Nigeria, Norway, Oman, Pakistan, Panama, Papua New Guinea, Paraguay, Peru, Philippines, Poland, Portugal, Qatar, Romania, Rwanda, Samoa, Sao Tome and Principe, Saudi Arabia, Senegal, Sierra Leone, Singapore, Somalia, Spain, Sri Lanka, Sudan, Suriname, Swaziland, Sweden, Syrian Arab Republic, Thailand, Togo, Trinidad and Tobago, Tunisia, Turkey, Uganda, Ukrainian SSR, USSR, United Arab Emirates, United Kingdom, United Republic of Cameroon, United Republic of Tanzania, United States, Upper Volta, Uruguay, Venezuela, Viet Nam, Yemen, Yugoslavia, Zaire, Zambia.

Against: None.

Abstaining: Israel.

Absent: Albania, Argentina, Chad,* Democratic Kampuchea, Grenada, Liberia, Libyan Arab Republic, Mauritius,* Seychelles, Solomon Islands, South Africa.

*Later advised the Secretariat it had intended to vote in favour.

34/77. Establishment of a nuclear-weapon-free zone in the region of the Middle East

Date: 11 December 1979
Vote: 136–0–1 (recorded)
Meeting: 97
Report: A/34/746

The General Assembly,

Recalling its resolution 3263 (XXIX) of 9 December 1974, in which it overwhelmingly commended the idea of the establishment of a nuclear-weapon-free zone in the region of the Middle East,

Recalling also its resolution 3474 (XXX) of 11 December 1975, in which it recognized that the establishment of a nuclear-weapon-free zone in the Middle East enjoyed wide support in the region,

Bearing in mind its resolution 31/71 of 10 December 1976, in which it expressed the conviction that progress towards the establishment of a nuclear-weapon-free zone in the Middle East would greatly enhance the cause of peace in the region and in the world,

Considering its resolution 32/82 of 12 December 1977, in which it expressed the conviction that the development of nuclear capability would further complicate the situation and immensely damage the efforts to create an atmosphere of confidence in the Middle East,

Guided by its relevant recommendations in the Final Document of the tenth special session of the General Assembly, dealing with the establishment of a nuclear-weapon-free zone in the region of the Middle East (Resolution S-10/2, para. 63 [*d*]),

Recalling also its resolution 33/64 of 14 December 1978,

Recognizing that the establishment of a nuclear-weapon-free zone in the Middle East would greatly enhance international peace and security,

1. *Urges* all parties directly concerned seriously to consider taking the practical and urgent steps required for the implementation of the proposal to establish a nuclear-weapon-free zone in the Middle East in accordance with the relevant resolutions of the General Assembly, and, as a means of promoting this objective, invites the countries concerned to adhere to the Treaty on the Non-Proliferation of Nuclear Weapons (Resolution 2373 [XXII], annex);

2. *Invites* these countries, pending the establishment of such a zone in the Middle East and during the process of its establishment, to declare solemnly that they will refrain on a reciprocal basis from producing, acquiring or in any other way possessing nuclear weapons and nuclear explosive devices;

3. *Calls upon* these countries to refrain, on a reciprocal basis, from permitting the stationing of nuclear weapons on their territory by any third party, and to agree to place all their nuclear activities under International Atomic Energy Agency safeguards;

4. *Further invites* these countries, pending the establishment of a nuclear-weapon-free zone in the Middle East and during the process of its establishment, to declare their support for establishing such a zone in the region consistent with paragraphs 60 to 63, and in particular 63 (*d*), of the Final Document of the tenth special session and to deposit these declarations with the Security Council for consideration as appropriate;

5. *Reaffirms again* its recommendation to the nuclear-weapon States to refrain from any action contrary to the spirit and purpose of the present resolution and the objective of establishing in the region of the Middle East a nuclear-weapon-free zone under an effective system of safeguards, and to extend their co-operation to the States of the region in their efforts to promote these objectives;

6. *Renews its invitation* to the Secretary-General to continue to explore the possibilities of making progress towards the establishment of a nuclear-weapon-free zone in the region of the Middle East;

7. *Decides* to include in the provisional agenda of its thirty-fifth session the item entitled "Establishment of a nuclear-weapon-free zone in the region of the Middle East."

RECORDED VOTE ON RESOLUTION 34/77:

In favour: Afghanistan, Algeria, Angola, Australia, Austria, Bahamas, Bahrain, Bangladesh, Barbados, Belgium, Benin, Bhutan, Bolivia, Botswana, Brazil, Bulgaria, Burma, Burundi, Byelorussia, Canada, Cape Verde, Central African Republic, Chad, Chile, China, Comoros, Costa Rica, Cuba, Cyprus, Czechoslovakia, Democratic Kampuchea,

Democratic Yemen, Denmark, Djibouti, Dominican Republic, Ecuador, Egypt, El Salvador, Ethiopia, Fiji, Finland, France, Gabon, German Democratic Republic, Federal Republic of Germany, Ghana, Greece, Grenada, Guatemala, Guinea, Guinea-Bissau, Guyana, Haiti, Honduras, Hungary, Iceland, India, Indonesia, Iran, Iraq, Ireland, Italy, Ivory Coast, Jamaica, Japan, Jordan, Kenya, Kuwait, Lao People's Democratic Republic, Lebanon, Lesotho, Liberia, Luxembourg, Madagascar, Malaysia, Maldives, Mali, Malta, Mauritania, Mauritius, Mexico, Mongolia, Morocco, Mozambique, Nepal, Netherlands, New Zealand, Niger, Nigeria, Norway, Oman, Pakistan, Panama, Papua New Guinea, Paraguay, Peru, Philippines, Poland, Portugal, Qatar, Romania, Rwanda, Samoa, Sao Tome and Principe, Saudi Arabia, Senegal, Sierra Leone, Singapore, Spain, Sri Lanka, Sudan, Suriname, Swaziland, Sweden, Syria, Thailand, Togo, Trinidad and Tobago, Tunisia, Turkey, Uganda, Ukraine, USSR, United Arab Emirates, United Kingdom, United Republic of Cameroon, United Republic of Tanzania, United States, Upper Volta, Uruguay, Venezuela, Viet Nam, Yemen, Yugoslavia, Zaire, Zambia.

Against: None.

Abstaining: Israel.

Absent: Albania, Argentina, Colombia, Congo, Dominica, Equatorial Guinea, Gambia, Libya, Malawi, Nicaragua, Saint Lucia, Seychelles, Solomon Islands, Somalia.

35/147. Establishment of a nuclear-weapon-free zone in the region of the Middle East

> *Date:* 12 December 1980
> Adopted without a vote
> *Meeting:* 94
> *Report:* A/35/690

The General Assembly,

Recalling its resolution 3263 (XXIX) of 9 December 1974, in which it overwhelmingly commended the idea of the establishment of a nuclear-weapon-free zone in the region of the Middle East,

Recalling also its resolution 3474 (XXX) of 11 December 1975, in which it recognized that the establishment of a nuclear-weapon-free zone in the Middle East enjoyed wide support in the region,

Bearing in mind its resolution 31/71 of 10 December 1976, in which it expressed the conviction that progress towards the establishment of a nuclear-weapon-free zone in the Middle East would greatly enhance the cause of peace in the region and in the world,

Recalling its resolution 32/82 of 12 December 1977, in which it expressed the conviction that the development of nuclear capability would further complicate the situation and immensely damage the efforts to establish a nuclear-weapon-free zone in the Middle East,

Guided by the recommendations in the Final Document of the Tenth Special Session of the General Assembly dealing with the establishment of a nuclear-weapon-free zone in the region of the Middle East,

Recalling also its resolutions 33/64 of 14 December 1978 and 34/77 of 11 December 1979,

Recognizing that the establishment of a nuclear-weapon-free zone in the Middle East would greatly enhance international peace and security,

1. *Urges* all parties directly concerned seriously to consider taking the practical and urgent steps required for the implementation of the proposal to establish a nuclear-weapon-free zone in the Middle East in accordance with the relevant resolutions of the General Assembly and, as a means of promoting this objective, invites the countries concerned to adhere to the Treaty on the Non-Proliferation of Nuclear Weapons (General Assembly resolution 2373 [XXII], annex);

2. *Invites* those countries, pending the establishment of such a zone in the Middle East and during the process of its establishment, to declare solemnly that they will refrain, on a reciprocal basis, from producing, acquiring or in any other way possessing nuclear weapons and nuclear explosive devices;

3. *Calls upon* those countries to refrain, on a reciprocal basis, from permitting the stationing of nuclear weapons on their territory by any third party and to agree to place all their nuclear activities under International Atomic Energy Agency safeguards;

4. *Further invites* those countries, pending the establishment of a nuclear-weapon-free zone in the Middle East and during the process of its establishment, to declare their support for establishing such a zone in the region consistent with paragraphs 60 to 63, in particular paragraph 63 (*d*), of the Final Document of the Tenth Special Session and to deposit those declarations with the Security Council for consideration as appropriate;

5. *Reaffirms again* its recommendation to the nuclear-weapon States to refrain from any action contrary to the spirit and purpose of the present resolution and the objective of establishing in the region of the Middle East a nuclear-weapon-free zone under an effective system of safeguards and to extend their co-operation to the States of the region in their efforts to promote these objectives;

6. *Renews its invitation* to the Secretary-General to continue to explore the possibilities of making progress towards the establishment of a nuclear-weapon-free zone in the region of the Middle East;

7. *Decides* to include in the provisional agenda of its thirty-sixth session the item entitled "Establishment of a nuclear-weapon-free zone in the region of the Middle East."

36/87. Establishment of a nuclear-weapon-free zone in the region of the Middle East

Date: 9 December 1981
Votes: A—Adopted without a vote; B—107–2–31 (recorded)
Meeting: 91
Report: A/36/747
Draft: A/36/L.53

A

The General Assembly,

Recalling its resolutions 3263 (XXIX) of 9 December 1974, 3474 (XXX) of 11 December 1975, 31/71 of 10 December 1976, 32/82 of 12 December 1977, 33/64 of 14 December 1978, 34/77 of 11 December 1979 and 35/147 of 12 December 1980 on the establishment of a nuclear-weapon-free zone in the Middle East,

1. *Requests* the Secretary-General to transmit General Assembly resolution 35/147 to the General Assembly at its second special session devoted to disarmament;

2. *Decides* to include in the provisional agenda of its thirty-seventh session the item entitled "Establishment of a nuclear-weapon-free zone in the region of the Middle East."

B

The General Assembly,

Recalling its resolutions concerning the establishment of a nuclear-weapon-free zone in the Middle East,

Recalling also the recommendations in the Final Document of the Tenth Special Session of the General Assembly (General Assembly resolution S–10/2) for the establishment of such a zone in the Middle East consistent with paragraphs 60 to 63, in particular paragraph 63 (*d*) thereof,

Recalling further Security Council resolution 487 (1981) of 19 June 1981,

Taking into consideration the resolution adopted on 12 June 1981 by the Board of Governors of the International Atomic Energy Agency (see GC[XXV]/643) and resolution GC(XXV)/RES/381 adopted on 26 September 1981 by the General Conference of the Agency.

Recalling further the report of the Secretary-General concerning Israeli nuclear armament (A/36/431),

Realizing that adherence to the Treaty on the Non-Proliferation of Nuclear Weapons by all Parties of the region will be conducive to a speedy establishment of a nuclear-weapon-free zone,

Deeply concerned that the future of the Treaty on the Non-Proliferation of Nuclear Weapons in the region has been gravely endangered by the attack carried out by Israel, which is not a party to the Treaty, on the nuclear installations of Iraq, which is a party to that Treaty,

1. *Considers* that the Israeli military attack on the Iraqi nuclear installations adversely affects the prospects of the establishment of a nuclear-weapon-free zone in the region;

2. *Declares* that it is imperative, in this respect, that Israel place forthwith all its nuclear facilities under International Atomic Energy Agency safeguards;

3. *Requests* the Secretary-General to transmit the present resolution to the General Assembly at its second special session devoted to disarmament.

RECORDED VOTE ON RESOLUTION 36/87 B:

In favour: Afghanistan, Albania, Algeria, Austria, Bahamas, Bahrain, Bangladesh, Barbados, Benin, Brazil, Bulgaria, Burundi, Byelorussia, Cape Verde, Chad, China, Colombia, Comoros, Congo, Cuba, Cyprus, Czechoslovakia, Democratic Kampuchea, Democratic Yemen, Djibouti, Ecuador, Egypt, El Salvador, Equatorial Guinea, Ethiopia, Gabon, Gambia, German Democratic Republic, Ghana, Greece, Grenada, Guinea, Guinea-Bissau, Guyana, Hungary, Indonesia, Iran, Iraq, Ivory Coast, Jamaica, Jordan, Kenya, Kuwait, Lao People's Democratic Republic, Lebanon, Lesotho, Liberia, Libya, Madagascar, Malaysia, Maldives, Mali, Malta, Mauritania, Mauritius, Mexico, Mongolia, Morocco, Mozambique, Nepal, Nicaragua, Niger, Nigeria, Oman, Pakistan, Panama, Philippines, Poland, Portugal, Qatar, Romania, Rwanda, Saint Lucia, Sao Tome and Principe, Saudi Arabia, Senegal, Seychelles, Sierra Leone, Singapore, Somalia, Spain, Sri Lanka, Sudan, Suriname, Syria, Thailand, Togo, Trinidad and Tobago, Tunisia, Turkey, Uganda, Ukraine, USSR, United Arab Emirates, United Republic of Tanzania, Upper Volta, Venezuela, Viet Nam, Yemen, Yugoslavia, Zaire, Zambia.

Against: Israel, United States.

Abstaining: Australia, Belgium, Belize, Canada, Central African Republic, Chile, Costa Rica, Denmark, Dominican Republic, Fiji, Finland, France, Federal Republic of Germany, Guatemala, Haiti, Honduras, Iceland, India, Ireland, Italy, Japan, Luxembourg, Netherlands, New Zealand, Norway, Papua New Guinea, Paraguay, Solomon Islands, Swaziland, Sweden, United Kingdom.

Absent: Angola,* Antigua and Barbuda, Bhutan, Bolivia, Botswana, Burma, Dominica, Malawi,* Peru,* Saint Vincent, Samoa, United Republic of Cameroon,* Uruguay, Vanuatu, Zimbabwe.

Argentina announced that it was not participating in the vote.

*Later advised the Secretariat it had intended to vote in favour.

37/75. Establishment of a nuclear-weapon-free zone in the region of the Middle East

Date: 9 December 1982
Adopted without a vote
Meeting: 98
Report: A/37/657

The General Assembly,

Recalling its resolutions 3263 (XXIX) of 9 December 1974, 3474 (XXX) of 11 December 1975, 31/71 of 10 December 1976, 32/82 of 12 December 1977, 33/64 of 14 December 1978, 34/77 of 11 December 1979, 35/147 of 12 December 1980 and 36/87 of 9 December 1981 on the establishment of a nuclear-weapon-free zone in the Middle East,

Recalling also the recommendations for the establishment of such a zone in the Middle East consistent with paragraphs 60 to 63, in particular paragraph 63 (*d*), of the Final

Document of the Tenth Special Session of the General Assembly, the first special session devoted to disarmament (General Assembly resolution S–10/2, annex),

Emphasizing the basic provisions of the above resolutions, which call upon all parties directly concerned to consider taking the practical and urgent steps required for the implementation of the proposal to establish a nuclear-weapon-free zone in the Middle East and, pending and during the establishment of such a zone, to declare solemnly that they will refrain, on a reciprocal basis, from producing, acquiring or in any other way possessing nuclear weapons and nuclear explosive devices and from permitting the stationing of nuclear weapons on their territory by any third party, and to agree to place all their nuclear facilities under International Atomic Energy Agency safeguards and declare their support for the establishment of the zone and deposit such declaration with the Security Council for consideration, as appropriate,

Reaffirming the inalienable right of all States to acquire and develop nuclear energy for peaceful purposes,

Emphasizing further the need for appropriate measures on the question of the prohibition of military attacks on nuclear facilities,

Bearing in mind the consensus reached by the General Assembly at its thirty-fifth session that the establishment of a nuclear-weapon-free zone in the Middle East would greatly enhance international peace and security,

Desirous to build on that consensus so that substantial progress can be made towards establishing a nuclear-weapon-free zone in the Middle East,

1. *Urges* all parties directly concerned to consider seriously taking the practical and urgent steps required for the implementation of the proposal to establish a nuclear-weapon-free zone in the Middle East in accordance with the relevant resolutions of the General Assembly and, as a means of promoting this objective, invites the countries concerned to adhere to the Treaty on the Non-Proliferation of Nuclear Weapons;

2. *Calls upon* all countries of the region that have not done so, pending the establishment of the zone, to agree to place all their nuclear activities under International Atomic Energy Agency safeguards;

3. *Invites* those countries, pending the establishment of a nuclear-weapon-free zone in the Middle East, to declare their support for establishing such a zone in the region, consistent with the relevant paragraph of the Final Document of the Tenth Special Session of the General Assembly, the first special session devoted to disarmament, and to deposit those declarations with the Security Council;

4. *Invites further* those countries, pending the establishment of the zone, not to develop, produce, test or otherwise acquire nuclear weapons or permit the stationing on their territories, or territories under their control, of nuclear weapons or nuclear explosive devices;

5. *Invites* the nuclear-weapon States and all other States to render their assistance to the establishment of the zone and at the same time to refrain from any action that runs counter to both the letter and spirit of the present resolution;

6. *Requests* the Secretary-General to submit a report to the General Assembly at its thirty-eighth session on the implementation of the present resolution;

7. *Decides* to include in the provisional agenda of its thirty-eighth session the item entitled "Establishment of a nuclear-weapon-free zone in the region of the Middle East."

38/64. Establishment of a nuclear-weapon-free zone in the region of the Middle East

Date: 15 December 1983
Adopted without a vote
Meeting: 97
Report: A/38/625

The General Assembly,

Recalling its resolutions 3263 (XXIX) of 9 December 1974, 3474 (XXX) of 11 December 1975, 31/71 of 10 December 1976, 32/82 of 12 December 1977, 33/64 of 14 December 1978, 34/77 of 11 December 1979, 35/147 of 12 December 1980, 36/87 of 9 December 1981 and 37/75 of 9 December 1982 on the establishment of a nuclear-weapon-free zone in the region of the Middle East,

Recalling also the recommendations for the establishment of such a zone in the Middle East consistent with paragraphs 60 to 63, in particular paragraph 63 (*d*), of the Final Document of the Tenth Special Session of the General Assembly (General Assembly resolution S–10/2),

Emphasizing the basic provisions of the above-mentioned resolutions, which call upon all parties directly concerned to consider taking the practical and urgent steps required for the implementation of the proposal to establish a nuclear-weapon-free zone in the region of the Middle East and, pending and during the establishment of such a zone, to declare solemnly that they will refrain, on a reciprocal basis, from producing, acquiring or in any other way possessing nuclear weapons and nuclear explosive devices and from permitting the stationing of nuclear weapons on their territory by any third party, to agree to place all their nuclear facilities under International Atomic Energy Agency safeguards and to declare their support for the establishment of the zone and deposit such declarations with the Security Council for consideration, as appropriate,

Reaffirming the inalienable right of all States to acquire and develop nuclear energy for peaceful purposes,

Emphasizing further the need for appropriate measures on the question of the prohibition of military attacks on nuclear facilities,

Bearing in mind the consensus reached by the General Assembly at its thirty-fifth session that the establishment of a nuclear-weapon-free zone in the region of the Middle East would greatly enhance international peace and security (See General Assembly resolution 35/147 of 12 December 1980),

Desirous to build on that consensus so that substantial progress can be made towards establishing a nuclear-weapon-free zone in the region of the Middle East,

Taking note of the report of the Secretary-General (A/38/197),

1. *Urges* all parties directly concerned to consider seriously taking the practical and urgent steps required for the implementation of the proposal to establish a nuclear-weapon-free zone in the region of the Middle East in accordance with the relevant resolutions of the General Assembly and, as a means of promoting this objective, invites the countries concerned to adhere to the Treaty on the Non-Proliferation of Nuclear Weapons (General Assembly resolution 2373 [XXII], annex);

2. *Calls upon* all countries of the region that have not done so, pending the establishment of the zone, to agree to place all their nuclear activities under International Atomic Energy Agency safeguards;

3. *Invites* those countries, pending the establishment of a nuclear-weapon-free zone in the region of the Middle East, to declare their support for establishing such a zone, consistent with the relevant paragraph of the Final Document of the Tenth Special Session of the General Assembly (General Assembly resolution S–10/2), and to deposit those declarations with the Security Council;

4. *Invites further* those countries, pending the establishment of the zone, not to develop, produce, test or otherwise acquire nuclear weapons or permit the stationing on their territories, or territories under their control, of nuclear weapons or nuclear explosive devices;

5. *Invites* the nuclear-weapon States and all other States to render their assistance in the establishment of the zone and at the same time to refrain from any action that runs counter to both the letter and spirit of the present resolution;

6. *Requests* the Secretary-General to submit a report to the General Assembly at its thirty-ninth session on the implementation of the present resolution;

7. *Decides* to include in the provisional agenda of its thirty-ninth session the item entitled "Establishment of a nuclear-weapon-free zone in the region of the Middle East."

39/54. Establishment of a nuclear-weapon-free zone in the region of the Middle East

Date: 12 December 1984
Adopted without a vote
Meeting: 97
Report: A/39/738

The General Assembly,

Recalling its resolutions 3263 (XXIX) of 9 December 1974, 3474 (XXX) of 11 December 1975, 31/71 of 10 December 1976, 32/82 of 12 December 1977, 33/64 of 14 December 1978, 34/77 of 11 December 1979, 35/147 of 12 December 1980, 36/87 of 9 December 1981, 37/75 of 9 December 1982 and 38/64 of 15 December 1983 on the establishment of a nuclear-weapon-free zone in the region of the Middle East,

Recalling also the recommendations for the establishment of such a zone in the Middle East consistent with paragraphs 60 to 63, in particular paragraph 63 (*d*), of the Final Document of the Tenth Special Session of the General Assembly (General Assembly resolution S–10/2), the first special session devoted to disarmament,

Emphasizing the basic provisions of the above-mentioned resolutions, which call upon all parties directly concerned to consider taking the practical and urgent steps required for the implementation of the proposal to establish a nuclear-weapon-free zone in the region of the Middle East and, pending and during the establishment of such a zone, to declare solemnly that they will refrain, on a reciprocal basis, from producing, acquiring or in any way possessing nuclear weapons and nuclear explosive devices and from permitting the stationing of nuclear weapons on their territory by any third party, to agree to place all their nuclear facilities under International Atomic Energy Agency safeguards and to declare their support for the establishment of the zone and deposit such declarations with the Security Council for consideration, as appropriate,

Reaffirming the inalienable right of all States to acquire and develop nuclear energy for peaceful purposes,

Emphasizing further the need for appropriate measures on the question of the prohibition of military attacks on nuclear facilities,

Bearing in mind the consensus reached by the General Assembly at its thirty-fifth session that the establishment of a nuclear-weapon-free zone in the region of the Middle East would greatly enhance international peace and security (See General Assembly resolution 35/147),

Desirous to build on that consensus so that substantial progress can be made towards establishing a nuclear-weapon-free zone in the region of the Middle East,

Emphasizing the essential role of the United Nations in the establishment of a nuclear-weapon-free zone in the region of the Middle East,

Taking note of the report of the Secretary-General (A/39/472),

1. *Urges* all parties directly concerned to consider seriously taking the practical and urgent steps required for the implementation of the proposal to establish a nuclear-weapon-free zone in the region of the Middle East in accordance with the relevant resolutions of the General Assembly and, as a means of promoting this objective, invites the countries concerned to adhere to the Treaty on the Non-Proliferation of Nuclear Weapons (General Assembly resolution 2373 [XXII], annex);

2. *Calls upon* all countries of the region that have not done so, pending the establishment of the zone, to agree to place all their nuclear activities under International Atomic Energy Agency safeguards;

3. *Invites* those countries, pending the establishment of a nuclear-weapon-free zone in the region of the Middle East, to declare their support for establishing such a zone, consistent with the relevant paragraph of the Final Document of the Tenth Special Session of the General Assembly (General Assembly resolution S-102), the first special session devoted to disarmament, and to deposit those declarations with the Security Council;

4. *Further invites* those countries, pending the establishment of the zone, not to develop, produce, test or otherwise acquire nuclear weapons or permit the stationing on their territories, or territories under their control, of nuclear weapons or nuclear explosive devices;

5. *Invites* the nuclear-weapon States and all other States to render their assistance

in the establishment of the zone and at the same time to refrain from any action that runs counter to both the letter and spirit of the present resolution;

6. *Requests* the Secretary-General to seek the views of all concerned parties regarding the establishment of a nuclear-weapon-free zone in the region of the Middle East;

7. *Requests* the Secretary-General to submit a report to the General Assembly at its fortieth session on the implementation of the present resolution;

8. *Decides* to include in the provisional agenda of its fortieth session the item entitled "Establishment of a nuclear-weapon-free zone in the region of the Middle East."

40/82. Establishment of a nuclear-weapon-free zone in the region of the Middle East

Date: 12 December 1985
Adopted without a vote
Meeting: 113
Report: A/40/905

The General Assembly,

Recalling its resolutions 3263 (XXIX) of 9 December 1974, 3474 (XXX) of 11 December 1975, 31/71 of 10 December 1976, 32/82 of 12 December 1977, 33/64 of 14 December 1978, 34/77 of 11 December 1979, 35/147 of 12 December 1980, 36/87 of 9 December 1981, 37/75 of 9 December 1982, 38/64 of 15 December 1983 and 39/54 of 12 December 1984 on the establishment of a nuclear-weapon-free zone in the region of the Middle East,

Recalling also the recommendations for the establishment of such a zone in the Middle East consistent with paragraphs 60 to 63, and, in particular, paragraph 63 (*d*), of the Final Document of the Tenth Special Session of the General Assembly (General Assembly resolution S–10/2), the first special session devoted to disarmament,

Emphasizing the basic provisions of the above-mentioned resolutions, which call upon all parties directly concerned to consider taking the practical and urgent steps required for the implementation of the proposal to establish a nuclear-weapon-free zone in the region of the Middle East and, pending and during the establishment of such a zone, to declare solemnly that they will refrain, on a reciprocal basis, from producing, acquiring or in any other way possessing nuclear weapons and nuclear explosive devices and from permitting the stationing of nuclear weapons on their territory by any third party, to agree to place all their nuclear facilities under International Atomic Energy Agency safeguards and to declare their support for the establishment of the zone and deposit such declarations with the Security Council for consideration, as appropriate,

Reaffirming the inalienable right of all States to acquire and develop nuclear energy for peaceful purposes,

Emphasizing further the need for appropriate measures on the question of the prohibition of military attacks on nuclear facilities,

Bearing in mind the consensus reached by the General Assembly at its thirty-fifth session that the establishment of a nuclear-weapon-free zone in the region of the Middle

East would greatly enhance international peace and security (See General Assembly resolution 35/147),

Desirous to build on that consensus so that substantial progress can be made towards establishing a nuclear-weapon-free zone in the region of the Middle East,

Emphasizing the essential role of the United Nations in the establishment of a nuclear-weapon-free zone in the region of the Middle East,

Taking note of the report of the Secretary-General (A/40/442 and Add.1),

1. *Urges* all parties directly concerned to consider seriously taking the practical and urgent steps required for the implementation of the proposal to establish a nuclear-weapon-free zone in the region of the Middle East in accordance with the relevant resolutions of the General Assembly and, as a means of promoting this objective, invites the countries concerned to adhere to the Treaty on the Non-Proliferation of Nuclear Weapons (General Assembly resolution 2373 [XXII], annex);

2. *Calls upon* all countries of the region that have not done so, pending the establishment of the zone, to agree to place all their nuclear activities under International Atomic Energy Agency safeguards;

3. *Invites* those countries, pending the establishment of a nuclear-weapon-free zone in the region of the Middle East, to declare their support for establishing such a zone, consistent with the relevant paragraph of the Final Document of the Tenth Special Session of the General Assembly, the first special session devoted to disarmament, and to deposit those declarations with the Security Council;

4. *Further invites* those countries, pending the establishment of the zone, not to develop, produce, test or otherwise acquire nuclear weapons or permit the stationing on their territories, or territories under their control, of nuclear weapons or nuclear explosive devices;

5. *Invites* the nuclear-weapon States and all other States to render their assistance in the establishment of the zone and at the same time to refrain from any action that runs counter to both the letter and spirit of the present resolution;

6. *Extends its thanks* to the Secretary-General for his report containing the views of parties concerned regarding the establishment of a nuclear-weapon-free zone in the region of the Middle East;

7. *Takes note* of the above-mentioned report;

8. *Requests* those parties that have not yet communicated their views to the Secretary-General to do so;

9. *Welcomes* any further comments from those parties that have already communicated their views to the Secretary-General;

10. *Requests* the Secretary-General to submit a report to the General Assembly at its forty-first session on the implementation of the present resolution;

11. *Decides* to include in the provisional agenda of the forty-first session the item "Establishment of a nuclear-weapon-free zone in the region of the Middle East."

APPENDIX B

**Letter Dated February 26, 1981, from the Permanent Representative of
Egypt to the United Nations Addressed to the Secretary General**

I have the honour to inform you that the Government of Egypt has completed the
process of ratification of the Treaty on the Non-Proliferation of Nuclear Weapons (General
Assembly resolution 2373 [XXII], annex) on 22 February 1981. Further, the instruments
of ratification have been deposited today, 26 February 1981, with the Government of the
United Kingdom of Great Britain and Northern Ireland.

Kindly find attached to this letter a copy of the statement issued by the Ministry of
Foreign Affairs of Egypt on the occasion of depositing the instruments of ratification of
the herein referred to treaty.

I further wish to seize this opportunity to bring the following to your attention:

(a) Egypt signed the non-proliferation Treaty on 1 July 1968 and ratified it on 22
February 1981 as a further expression of its deep commitment to the non-proliferation
of nuclear weapons.

(b) Egypt has, since the twenty-ninth session of the General Assembly, in 1974,
advocated the establishment of a nuclear-weapon-free zone in the Middle East. It was
on the basis of Egypt's initiative that the General Assembly adopted its resolution 3263

(XXIX) of 9 December 1974 on the creation of such a zone. Since that time, the General Assembly has adopted a series of resolutions, upon the initiative of Egypt, the last of which is resolution 35/147 of 12 December 1980.

(c) Egypt's ratification of the non-proliferation Treaty should be seen as a concrete manifestation of its commitment to the non-proliferation of nuclear weapons in general and a tangible contribution to ensuring that a nuclear-weapon-free zone in the Middle East be established in particular.

(d) In acceding to the Treaty, Egypt has fulfilled its obligations under paragraph 1 of General Assembly resolution 35/147 and is, therefore, reiterating its call for the establishment of a nuclear-weapon-free zone in the Middle East.

I kindly request you to circulate this letter, together with the statement attached, as an official document of the General Assembly, under items 46, 51, 53, 55 and 58 of the preliminary list, and of the Security Council.

Signed,

A. Esmat/Abdel Meguid
Ambassador
Permanent Representative

Statement by the Ministry of Foreign Affairs on the Occasion of the Deposit by the Government of the Arab Republic of Egypt of Its Instruments of Ratification of the Treaty on the Non-Proliferation of Nuclear Weapons

Egypt's signing and subsequent ratification of the Treaty on the Non-Proliferation of Nuclear Weapons stems from its conviction that the proliferation of nuclear weapons threatens the security of mankind and therefore must be curbed. It may be pertinent to recall in this respect that Egypt being among the first countries calling for the early conclusion of the Treaty, played an instrumental role in its negotiation. The Treaty was a logical culmination to the earlier efforts that successfully lead to the conclusion of the 1963 Treaty Banning Nuclear Weapon Tests in the Atmosphere, in Outer Space and Under Water.

Egypt's commitment by virtue of the provisions of the Non-Proliferation Treaty, to refrain in any way from acquiring or manufacturing nuclear weapons, should not impair its inalienable right to develop and use nuclear energy for peaceful purposes, in conformity with the provisions of Article IV of the Treaty, which affirms the inalienable right of all the parties to the Treaty to develop research, production and use of nuclear energy for peaceful purposes without discrimination. The stipulation of that right in the Treaty itself is, in fact, a codification of a basic right, which can neither be waived or derogated from.

It is based on this premise that Egypt attaches special attention to the provisions of Article IV of the Treaty calling on the Parties to the Treaty, who are in a position to do so, to co-operate in contributing to the further development of the application of nuclear energy for peaceful purposes, especially in the territories of non-nuclear-weapon States Party to the Treaty, with due consideration for the needs of the developing areas of the world.

Accordingly, as Egypt is embarking on the construction of nuclear power reactors to generate electric power in order to meet its increasing energy needs necessary for the prosperity and welfare of its people, it feels justified to expect the assistance and support, from industrialized nations possessing a developed nuclear industry. This, we emphasize, would be in consonance with the letter and spirit of Article IV of the Treaty. Particularly, since Egypt, in accordance with the provisions of Article III of the Treaty, accepts application of the safeguards system of the International Atomic Energy Agency to peaceful nuclear activities carried out within its territory.

Within the framework of the rights provided for in the Treaty for all Parties thereto insofar as the use of nuclear energy for peaceful purposes is concerned, Egypt wishes to refer to the provisions of Article V of the Treaty, which states that potential benefits from any peaceful applications of nuclear explosions will be made available to non-nuclear-weapon States Party to the Treaty. Though such applications pose at present certain difficulties, particularly in view of their detrimental effects on the environment, Egypt nevertheless, is of the firm view that the nuclear-weapon States Party to the Treaty should not be relieved from their responsibility to promote research and development of these applications, in order to overcome all the difficulties presently involved in such applications.

Egypt wishes to express its strong dissatisfaction with the nuclear-weapon States, in particular the two Super-Powers, because of their failure to take effective measures relating to cessation of the nuclear arms race and to nuclear disarmament. Although it welcomes the 1972 and 1979 Strategic Arms Limitation Treaties, known as SALT I and SALT II, Egypt cannot but underline the fact that the Treaties have not only failed to bring about an effective cessation of the nuclear arms race, quantitatively and qualitatively, but have also permitted the development of a new generation of weapons of mass destruction.

Moreover, and in spite of the fact that more than 17 years have elapsed since the conclusion of the 1963 Treaty Banning Nuclear Weapon Tests in the Atmosphere, in Outer Space and Under Water, the nuclear-weapon States allege that various difficulties still stand in the way of an agreement on a permanent ban on all nuclear weapon tests; what is required, in fact, is the need for a political will to achieve that end.

Consequently, Egypt avails itself of this opportunity, namely the deposit of its instruments of ratification of the Treaty on the Non-Proliferation of Nuclear Weapons, to appeal to the nuclear-weapon States Parties to the Treaty to fulfill their obligation whereby the nuclear arms race will be stopped and nuclear disarmament achieved.

Egypt also calls upon all nuclear-weapon States to exert all possible efforts so as to achieve a permanent ban of all nuclear weapon tests at an early date. This will bring to an end the development and manufacture of new types of weapons of mass destruction, inasmuch as the cut-off of fissionable material for military purposes will curb the quantitative increase of nuclear weapons.

As regards the security of non-nuclear-weapon States, Egypt is of the considered view that Security Council resolution 255 of 19 June 1968 does not provide non-nuclear-weapon States with a genuine guarantee against the use or threat of use of nuclear weapons by nuclear-weapon States. Egypt, therefore, appeals to the nuclear-weapon States to exert their effort with a view to concluding an agreement prohibiting once and for all, the use or threat of use of nuclear weapons against any State.

The undertaking of these steps is consistent with the letter and spirit of the basic guiding principles formulated by the General Assembly of the United Nations for the conclusion of the Non-Proliferation Treaty, in particular the principles of balance of mutual responsibilities and obligations of the nuclear and non-nuclear Powers; and that stipulating that the Treaty should be a step towards the achievement of general and complete disarmament and in particular, nuclear disarmament.

Based on Egypt's firm conviction that the establishment of nuclear-weapon-free zones in different parts of the world shall be instrumental in enabling the Non-Proliferation Treaty to achieve its goal, it has exerted great efforts to establish nuclear-weapon-free zones in the Middle East as well as in Africa.

In this respect, Egypt expresses its satisfaction with the United Nations General Assembly resolution 35/147 adopted by consensus at its 35th session inviting the countries of the Middle East, pending the establishment of nuclear-weapon-free zone in the area, to declare solemnly their support for the achievement of this objective, that they will refrain on a reciprocal basis from producing, acquiring or possessing nuclear weapons, and to deposit such declarations with the United Nations Security Council.

In conclusion, Egypt wishes to point out that it has ratified the Treaty on the Non-Proliferation of Nuclear Weapons, out of the strong belief that this step conforms with its vital national interests, insofar as the Treaty succeeds in curbing the proliferation of nuclear weapons throughout the world, particularly in the Middle East—a region which should remain completely free of nuclear weapons—if the Treaty is to effectively contribute to peace, security and prosperity for it s people as well as for the world at large.

APPENDIX C

The following unilateral security assurances have been made by the nuclear-weapon states.

China: On May 29, 1978 the representative of China stated that all the nuclear countries, particularly those that possess nuclear weapons in large quantities,

should immediately undertake not to resort to the threat or use of nuclear weapons against the non-nuclear countries and nuclear-free zones. China is not only ready to undertake this commitment but wishes to reiterate that at no time and in no circumstances will it be the first to use nuclear weapons. (A/S–10/AC.1/17:3)

On June 12, 1982 the Minister of Foreign Affairs of China stated:

An agreement should be reached by all the nuclear States not to use nuclear weapons. Pending such an agreement, each nuclear State should, without attaching any condition, undertake not to use nuclear weapons against non-nuclear-weapon States and nuclear-weapon-free zones and not to be the first to use such weapons against each other at any time and under any circumstances. (A/S12/PV8:39–40)

France: On June 30, 1978 the Representative of France stated:

As regards paragraph 59 (of the Final Document of the Tenth Special Session) concerning assurances of the non-use of nuclear weapons against non-nuclear States, the delegation of France would recall that France is prepared to give such assurances, in accordance with arrangements to be negotiated, to those States which constituted among themselves non-nuclear zones. (A/S–10/PV.27:68)

On June 11, 1982 the Minister for Foreign Affairs of France stated:

For its part . . . it will not use nuclear arms against a State that does not have them and that has pledged not to seek them, except if an act of aggression is carried out in association or alliance with a nuclear-weapon State against France or against a State with which France has a security commitment. (A/S–12/PV.9:69; CD/417, Annex 1)

Soviet Union: On May 26, 1978 the Foreign Minister of the Soviet Union stated: "From the rostrum of the United Nations special session, our country declares that the Soviet Union will never use nuclear weapons against those States which renounce the production and acquisition of such weapons and do not have them on their territories" (A/S–10/PV.5:28–30). On June 12, 1982 the Foreign Minister of the Soviet Union read a message from the president of the Presidium of the Supreme Soviet of the USSR, according to which the Soviet Union assumed "an obligation not to be the first to use nuclear weapons." This obligation became effective immediately, at the moment it was made public from the rostrum of the General Assembly. In the opinion of the USSR the question of security guarantees to non-nuclear-weapon countries parties to the Non-Proliferation Treaty on the part of the nuclear powers "could be solved by concluding an international convention. The USSR is also prepared to conclude bilateral agreements or guarantees with States which do not possess nuclear weapons and do not have them on their territory" (A/S–12/PV.23:22–27).

United Kingdom: On June 28, 1978 the representative of the United Kingdom declared:

I accordingly give the following assurance, on behalf of my Government, to non-nuclear-weapon States, which are parties to the non-proliferation Treaty or to other international binding commitments not to manufacture or acquire nuclear explosive devices: Britain undertakes not to use nuclear weapons against such states except in the case of an attack on the United Kingdom, its dependent territories, its armed forces or its allies by such a State in association or alliance with a nuclear-weapon State. (A/S–10/PV.26:4)

United States: On June 14, 1978 the Secretary of State of the United States stated:

The United States will not use nuclear weapons against any non-nuclear-weapon State party to the Treaty on the Non-Proliferation of Nuclear Weapons or any comparable international binding commitment not to acquire nuclear explosive devices, except in the case of an attack on the United States, its territories or armed forces, or its allies, by such a State allied to a nuclear-weapon State, or associated with a nuclear-weapon State in carrying out or sustaining the attack. (A/S–10PV.30:1)

REFERENCES

Akehurst, Michael. *A Modern Introduction to International Law*. London: George Allen and Unwin (1982).

Albrecht, Ulrich. "The Proposal for a Nordic Nuclear-Weapon-Free Zone: A German Perspective," pp. 35–38 in Kari Mottola (ed.), *Nuclear Weapons and Northern Europe*. Helsinki: Finnish Institute of International Affairs (1983).

Alley, Roderic. "Nuclear-Weapon-Free Zones: The South Pacific Proposal." Occasional Paper. Muscatine, Iowa: Stanley Foundation (1977).

Apunen, Osmo. "The Freezing of Nuclear Weapons in Northern Europe: An Imaginary Treaty of 1963," pp. 24–28 in Kari Mottola (ed.), *Nuclear Weapons and Northern Europe*. Helsinki: Finnish Institute of International Affairs (1983).

Arms Control and Disarmament Agency. *1983 Annual Report*. Washington, D.C.: Government Printing Office (1984).

———. *Arms Control and Disarmament Agreements*. Washington, D.C.: Government Printing Office (1982).

Aron, Raymond. "The Evolution of Modern Strategic Thought," in *Problems of Modern Strategy: Part One*, Adelphi Papers no. 54. London: Institute for Strategic Studies (1969).

Aronson, Shlomo. *Conflict and Bargaining in the Middle East*. (London, 1978).

———. "Israel's Nuclear Options," *ACIS Working Paper no. 7*. Los Angeles: Center for Arms Control and International Security, University of California (1977).

Bailey, Sydney. "Christian Churches and Nuclear Weapons," pp. 8–18 in *Disarmament Periodic Review by the United Nations*. New York: United Nations (1983).

Bar-Joseph, Uri. "The Hidden Debate: The Formation of Nuclear Doctrines in the Middle East," *The Journal of Strategic Studies* 5 (June):205–27 (1982).

Bell, Bowyer J. "Israel's Nuclear Options," *The Middle East Journal* 26 (Autumn):378–88 (1972).

Blackett, P. M. S. *Studies of War*. London: Oliver and Boyd (1962).

Boczek, Boleslaw. "The Soviet Union and the Antarctic Regime." Paper presented at the annual meeting of the International Studies Association, Atlanta, Ga., March 27–31 (1984).

Bolt, Basil. Statement to the Third Review Conference of the Parties to the Treaty on the Non-Proliferation of Nuclear Weapons. Geneva, (August 29, 1985).

Bull, Hedley. *The Control of the Arms Race*. New York: Praeger (1961).

Burnham, David. "The Case of the Missing Uranium," *The Atlantic* 243 (April):78–82 (1979).

Burns, Richard. "Salt, Nonproliferation, and Nuclear Weapons Free Zones: An Introduction." Occasional Paper no. 6. Los Angeles: California State University Center for the Study of Armaments and Disarmament (1979).

Bustin, Edouard. "South Africa's Foreign Policy Alternatives and Deterrence Needs," pp. 205–27 in Inkar Marwah and Ann Schulz (eds.), *Nuclear Proliferation and the Near-Nuclear Countries*. Cambridge, Mass.: Ballinger Publishing Company (1975).

Bykov, Oleg. "A Nuclear-Weapon-Free Zone in the North of Europe—A Soviet View," pp. 29–32 in Kari Mottola (ed.), *Nuclear Weapons and Northern Europe*. Helsinki: Finnish Institute of International Affairs (1983).

Cantori, Louis J., and Steven L. Spiegel. *The International Politics of Regions: A Comparative Approach*. Englewood Cliffs, N.J.: Prentice-Hall, Inc. (1970).

Carnesale, Albert Etal. *Living with Nuclear Weapons*. New York: Bantam Books (1983).

Centre for Conflict Studies. *No Substitute for Pace*. New Brunswick, Calif.: University of New Brunswick (1983).

Chari, P. R. "The Israeli Nuclear Option: Living Dangerously," *International Studies* 16 (September):343–55 (1977).

Choucri, Nazli, and Robert C. North. *Nations in Conflict: National Growth and International Violence*. San Francisco, Calif.: W. W. Freeman (1975).

Clarke, D. L., and K. Grieco. "The United States and Nuclear Weapon Free Zones," *World Affairs* 138 (Fall):155–61 (1976).

Claude, Inis L. *Swords into Plowshares*. 4th ed. New York: Random House (1984).

Coate, Roger. *Global Issue Regimes*. New York: Praeger (1982).

Coffey, Joseph I. (ed.) "Nuclear Proliferation: Prospects, Problems and Proposals." (Special issue.) *The Annals of the American Academy of Political and Social Science* 430 (March) (1977).

Collins, Edward (ed.) *International Law in a Changing World: Cases, Documents and Readings*. New York: Random House (1970).

Collins, John M. *U.S. Soviet Military Balance Concepts and Capabilities 1960–1980*. New York: McGraw Hill (1980).

Coplin, William, and Charles W. Kegley, Jr. (eds.) *A Multi-Method Introduction to International Politics*. Chicago: Markham Publishing Co. (1971).

Cronin, Richard P. "Prospects for Nuclear Proliferation in South Asia," *The Middle East Journal* 37 (Autumn):594–616 (1983).

Davinic, P. "Nuclear-Free Zones, a Step Towards Averting the Nuclear Threat," *Review of International Affairs* 26 (Fall):28–29 (1975).

Delcoigne, G. "An Overview of Nuclear-Weapon-Free Zones," *International Atomic Energy Agency Bulletin* 24 (June):50–55 (1982).

Deutsch, Karl. *The Nerves of Government*. New York: The Free Press (1964).

Dougherty, James E., and Robert L. Pfaltzgraff, Jr. *Contending Theories of International Relations: A Comprehensive Survey*. New York: Harper and Row Publishers (1981).

Dowty, Alan. "Nuclear Proliferation: The Israeli Case," *International Study Quarterly* 22 (March):79–120 (1978).

———. "Israel and Nuclear Weapons," *Midstream* (November):13–14 (1976).

Dunn, Lewis A. *Controlling the Bomb: Nuclear Proliferation in the 1980's*. New Haven: Yale University Press (1982).

———. "Some Reflections on the Dove's Dilemma," pp. 181–93 in George Quester (ed.), *Nuclear Proliferation: Breaking the Chain*. Madison: University of Wisconsin Press (1981).

———. "Nuclear Proliferation and World Politics," *The Annals of the American Academy of Political and Social Sciences* 430 (March):96–109 (1977).

Eban, Abba. *The New Diplomacy: International Affairs in the Modern Age*. New York: Random House (1983).

Enthoven, Alain C., and K. Wayne Smith. *How Much Is Enough?* New York: Harper and Row (1971).

Epstein, W. "Non-Proliferation and a Mid-East Nuclear-Free Zone," *New Outlook: Middle East Monthly* (May):93–95 (1982).

———. "A Nuclear-Weapon-Free Zone in Africa?" Occasional Paper 14. Muscatine, Iowa: Stanley Foundation (1977a).

———. "Why States Go and Don't Go Nuclear," *Annals of the American Academy of Social and Political Science* 430 (March):22–23 (1977b).

———. "Nuclear Proliferation in the Third World," *Journal of International Affairs* 2 (February):198–99 (1975a).

———. "Nuclear-Free Zones," *Scientific American* 233 (November):25–35 (1975b).

Evron, Yair. "Israel and Nuclear Weapons," pp. 120–34 in Jae Kyu Park (ed.), *Nuclear Proliferation in Developing Countries*. Seoul: Institute for Far Eastern Studies (1979).

———. "The Arab Position in the Nuclear Field: A Study of Policies up to 1967," *Cooperation and Conflict* 1 (January):22–24 (1973).

Fahmy, Ismail. *Negotiations for Peace in the Middle East*. Baltimore: Johns Hopkins University Press (1983).

Falk, Richard. "Toward a Legal Regime for Nuclear Weapons," *McGill Law Journal* 28 (July):519–41 (1983).

———. "How a Nuclear War Can Start," *The Bulletin* 4 (April):21–22 (1979).

———. *Nuclear Policy and World Order: Why Denuclearization*. New York: Institute for World Order (1978).

Feldman, Shai. *Israeli Nuclear Deterrence*. New York: Columbia University Press (1982a).

―――. "The Bombing of Osiraq-Revisited," *International Security* 7 (Fall):114–42 (1982b).

―――. *The Raid on Osiraq.* Tel Aviv: Center for Strategic Studies (1981).

Fialka, John. "How Israel Got the Bomb," *The Washington Monthly* (January):50–58 (1979).

Flapan, Simha. "A Nuclear Weapon Free Zone in the Middle East: The Only Solution," *New Outlook: Middle East Monthly* (May):6–10 (1982).

―――. "Nuclear Power in the Middle East," *New Outlook: Middle East Monthly* (July):39–49 (1974a).

―――. "Nuclear Power in the Middle East: The Critical Years," *New Outlook: Middle East Monthly* (October):23–24, (1974b).

Freedman, Lawrence. "Israel's Nuclear Policy," *Survival* 17, (May–June):114–20 (1975).

Friedman, Todd. "Israel's Nuclear Option," *Bulletin of the Atomic Scientists* 30 (September):30–36 (1974).

Fritzel, Roger N. *Nuclear Testing and National Security.* Washington, D.C.: National Defense University (1981).

Gaines, Matthew. *Atomic Energy.* New York: Grossett and Dunlap (1970).

Galal, E. "Israeli Military and Nuclear Alternatives to Peace," *New Outlook* (special ed.):73–78 (1982).

Gelb, Leslie. "The Future of Arms Control: A Glass Half Full," *Foreign Policy* 36 (Fall):21–32 (1979).

George, Alexander L., and Richard Smoke. *Deterrence in American Foreign Policy: Theory and Practice.* New York: Columbia University Press (1974).

Gillette, Robert. "Uranium Enrichment: Rumors of Israeli Progress with Lasers," *Science* 183 (March) (1974).

Gompert, David. *Nuclear Weapons and World Politics: Alternatives for the Future.* New York: McGraw-Hill (1977).

Green, Stephen. *Taking Sides: America's Secret Relations with a Militant Israel.* New York: William Morrow and Company (1984).

Guilhaudis, J. F. "Nuclear-Free Zones and Zones of Peace: The Regional Approach to Disarmament within the Non-Nuclearized Regions," *Arms Control* 2:198–217 (1981).

Hallaba, Saadallah A. S. "The Daura Raid: Naked Agression or Self-Defense?" Paper presented at the annual meeting of the International Studies Association, Atlanta, Ga., November 4–6 (1982).

Halperin, Morton H. *Contemporary Military Strategy.* Boston, Mass.: Little, Brown & Co. (1967).

Harkavy, Robert E. "Pariah States and Nuclear Proliferation," pp. 135–65 in George Quester (ed.), *Nuclear Proliferation: Breaking the Chain.* Madison: University of Wisconsin Press (1981).

―――. *Spectre of a Middle Eastern Holocaust: The Strategic and Diplomatic Implications of the Israeli Nuclear Weapon Program.* Denver: University of Denver (1977).

Harvard Nuclear Study Group. *Living with Nuclear Weapons.* New York: Bantam Books (1983).

Haselkorn, Avigdor. "Israel from an Option to a Bomb in the Basement," pp. 149–83 in Robert M. Lawrence and Joel Larus (eds.), *Nuclear Proliferation Phase II*. Lawrence: University of Kansas Press (1974).

Hohenemser, Christoph. "Risks of the Nuclear Fuel Cycle and the Developing Countries," pp. 85–111 in Onkar Marwah and Ann Schulz (eds.), *Nuclear Proliferation and the Near-Nuclear Countries*. Cambridge, Mass.: Ballinger Publishing Company (1975).

Holst, Johan Jorgen. "A Nuclear-Weapon-Free Zone in the Nordic Area: Conditions and Options," pp. 5–13 in Kari Mottola (ed.), *Nuclear Weapons and Northern Europe*. Helsinki: Finnish Institute of International Affairs (1983).

———. "The Challenge from Nuclear Weapons and Nuclear-Weapon-Free Zones," *Bulletin of Peace Proposals* 12 (December):239–45 (1981).

Holsti, Ole R. *Crisis Escalation War*. Montreal: McGill University Press (1972).

Hunter, Robert E. "Nuclear Weapons and Northern Europe: The Global Setting," pp. 43–47 in Kari Mottola (ed.), *Nuclear Weapons and Northern Europe*. Helsinki: Finnish Institute of International Affairs (1983).

International Atomic Energy Agency. *The Annual Report for 1981*. Vienna: IAEA (1982).

International Institute for Strategic Studies. *Military Balance*. Washington, D.C.: U.S. Department of Defense (1982–83).

Jabber, Fuad. "Israel's Nuclear Option and the U.S. Arms Control Policies." Research paper no. 9. Los Angeles: Crescent Publications (1972).

———. *Israel and Nuclear Weapons: Present Options and Future Strategies*. London: Chatto and Windus/International Institute for Strategic Studies (1971).

Jabber, Paul. *Not by War Alone*. Berkeley: University of California Press (1981).

Jacobson, Harold K. *Networks of Interdependence*, 2nd ed. New York: Alfred A. Knopf (1984).

Jane's. *All the World's Aircraft 1983–84*. New York: Jane's Publishing (1984).

Jervis, Robert. "Deterrence Theory Revisited," *World Politics* 31 (April):289–324 (1979).

Kalela, Jaakko, and Raimo Vayrynen. "Nuclear-Weapon-Free Zones: Past Experience and New Perspectives," pp. 67–79 in Kari Mottola (ed.), *Nuclear Weapons and Northern Europe*. Helsinki: The Finnish Institute of International Affairs (1983).

Kapur, Ashok. *International Nuclear Proliferation*. New York: Praeger (1979).

Kegley, Charles W., and Eugene Wittkopf (eds.) *The Global Agenda: Issues and Perspectives*. New York: Random House (1984).

———. *American Foreign Policy: Pattern and Process*, 2nd ed. New York: St. Martin's Press (1982).

———. *World Politics: Trend and Transformation*. New York: St. Martin's Press (1981).

Kemp, Geoffrey. *A Nuclear Middle East*. Washington, D.C.: Brookings Institution (1979).

Kennan, George F. *The Nuclear Delusion*. New York: Pantheon Books (1982).

Kimball, Lee. "The Antarctic Treaty Regime: Future Challenges and Creative Response," Paper presented at the annual meeting of the International Studies Association, Atlanta, Ga., March 27–31 (1984).

King, John Kerry (ed.) *International Political Effects of the Spread of Nuclear Weapons*. Washington, D.C.: Government Printing Office (1979).

Kissinger, Henry. *Years of Upheaval*. Boston: Little, Brown & Co. (1982).

———. *The Necessity for Choice*. Garden City, N.J.: Doubleday (1962).

———. *Nuclear Weapons and Foreign Policy*. New York: Harper and Row (1957).

Larson, Joyce E., and William C. Bodie. *The Intelligent Layperson's Guide to the Nuclear Freeze and Peace Debate*. New York: National Strategy Information Center (1983).

Lawrence, Robert M., and Joel Larus (eds.) *Nuclear Proliferation Phase II*. Lawrence: University of Kansas Press (1974).

Lefever, Ernest W. *Nuclear Arms in the Third World: U.S. Policy Dilemma*. Washington, D.C.: Brookings Institution (1979).

Leitenberg, Milton. "The Stranded USSR Submarine in Sweden and the Question of a Nordic Nuclear-Free Zone," *Nordic Journal of International Politics* 17, no. 1:17–28 (1982).

Leventhal, Paul. "International and National Responses to the Spread of Nuclear Energy and Nuclear Weapons," *ECO Journal*. Paper originally presented at the Salzburg Conference for a Non-Nuclear Future, Salzburg, April 29–May 1 (1977).

Lewis, Bernard. *The Middle East and the West*. New York: Harper Torchbooks (1964).

Lewis, Jesse W., Jr. *The Strategic Balance in the Mediterranean*. Washington, D.C.: American Enterprise Institute (1976).

Lifton, Robert Jay, and Richard Falk. *Indefensible Weapons: The Political and Psychological Case against Nuclearism*. New York: Basic Books (1982).

Lodgaard, Sverre. "Nuclear Disengagement in Europe," pp. 38–42 in Kari Mottola (ed.), *Nuclear Weapons and Northern Europe*. Helsinki: Finnish Institute of International Affairs (1983).

Lodgaard, Sverre, and Marek Thee (eds.) *Nuclear Disengagement in Europe*. New York: Taylor and Francis (1983).

Lutenberg, Milton (ed.) *Great Power Intervention in the Middle East*. New York: Pergamon (1979).

McGowan, Patrick J., and Charles W. Kegley, Jr. (eds.) *Threats, Weapons, and Foreign Policy*. Beverly Hills, Calif.: Sage Publications (1980).

Marwah, Onkar. "India and Pakistan: Nuclear Rivals in South Asia," pp. 165–81 in George Quester (ed.), *Nuclear Proliferation: Breaking the Chain*. Madison: University of Wisconsin Press (1980).

Marwah, Onkar, and Ann Schulz (eds.) *Nuclear Proliferation and the Near-Nuclear Countries*. Cambridge, Mass.: Ballinger Publishing Company (1975).

Medlovitz, Saul H. *On the Creation of a Just World Order*. New York: Free Press (1975).

Ministry of Foreign Affairs, Arab Republic of Egypt. *Egypt and the Peaceful Uses of Nuclear Energy*. Cairo: Ministry of Foreign Affairs (1983).

———. *Egypt and the Treaty on the Non-Proliferation of Nuclear Weapons*. Cairo: State Information Service (1981).

Mottola, Kari (ed.) *Nuclear Weapons and Northern Europe*. Helsinki: Finnish Institute of International Affairs (1983).

Namboodiri, P. K. S. "Pakistan's Nuclear Posture," in K. Subrahmanyam (ed.), *Nuclear Myths and Realities: India's Dilemma*. New Delhi: ABC Publishing House (1981).

Newcombe, E. "Approaches to a Nuclear-Free Future," *Peace Research Review* 9, no. 2:73–79 (1982).

Nixon, Richard. *The Real War*. New York: Warner Books (1980).

North Atlantic Treaty Organization. *NATO Handbook*. Brussels: NATO Information Service (1982a).

———. *NATO and the Warsaw Pact: Force Comparisons*. Brussels: NATO Information Service (1982b).

Nyrop, Richard F. (ed.) *Egypt: A Country Study*. Washington, D.C.: American University Foreign Area Studies (1983).

————. *Israel: A Country Study*. Washington, D.C.: American University Foreign Area Studies (1979).

Osgood, Charles E. "Questioning Some Unquestioned Assumptions about National Defense," *Journal of Arms Control* 1 (January):2–17 (1963).

Paasilinna, Reino. *Perspective on Proliferation*, no. 1. Cambridge, Mass.: Proliferation Reform Project (1985).

Pa'il, M. "Nuclear Threat Should Become Part of the Arab-Israeli Conflict," *New Outlook* (1982):54–62.

Pajak, Roger F. *Nuclear Proliferation in the Middle East: Implications for the Superpowers*. Washington, D.C.: National Defense University Press (1982).

Pearlmitter, Amos. "The Israeli Raid on Iraq: A New Proliferation Landscape," *Strategic Review* 1 (Winter):34–43 (1982).

Peking Review. "Proposals for Establishing Nuclear Weapon Free Zones," *Peking Review* 50 (December 13):15–17 (1974).

Power, Paul F. "The Latin American Nuclear-Weapon-Free-Zone as a Military Denuclearization Model for the Middle East," Paper presented at the annual meeting of the International Studies Association, Mexico City, April 5–9 (1983a).

————. "Preventing Nuclear Conflict in the Middle East: The Free Zone Strategy," *The Middle East Journal* 37 (Autumn):617–35 (1983b).

Pranger, Robert J., and Dale K. Tahtinen. *Nuclear Threat in the Middle East*. Washington, D.C.: American Enterprise Institute (1975).

Pry, Peter. *Israel's Nuclear Threat in the Middle East*. Boulder, Colo.: Westview Press (1984).

Puchala, Donald I. *Issue before the 37th General Assembly of the United Nations (1982–1983)*. New York: United Nations Association of the United States of America (1983).

Quandt, William B. *Decades of Decisions*. Berkeley: University of California Press (1977).

Quester, George H. "Nuclear Weapons and Israel," *The Middle East Journal* 37 (Autumn):547–64 (1983).

———— (ed.). *Nuclear Proliferation: Breaking the Chain*. Madison: University of Wisconsin Press (1981).

————. "Preventing Proliferation: The Impact on International Politics," pp. 213–41 in George Quester (ed.), *Nuclear Proliferation: Breaking The Chain*. Madison: University of Wisconsin Press (1981).

————. *The Politics of Nuclear Proliferation*. Baltimore: Johns Hopkins University Press (1973).

————. "Israel and the Nuclear Non-Proliferation Treaty," *Bulletin of the Atomic Scientists* 25 (June):44–45 (1969).

Rabinowich, Eugene. "Defenders and Avengers," *Bulletin of the Atomic Scientists* 16 (November):350–72 (1960).

Record, Jeffrey. *U.S. Nuclear Weapons in Europe*. Washington, D.C.: Brookings Institute (1974).

Redich, John R. "The Tlatelolco Regime and Non-Proliferation in Latin America," pp. 103–35 in George Quester (ed.), *Nuclear Proliferation: Breaking the Chain*. Madison: University of Wisconsin Press (1981).

Reed, Jean. *NATO's Theater Nuclear Forces: A Coherent Strategy for the 1980's*. Washington, D.C.: National Defense University Press (1983).

Robles, Alfonso Garcia. *The Latin American Nuclear Weapon Free Zone*. Muscatine, Iowa: Stanley Foundation (1979).

Roehm, John F., Jr. "Congressional Participation in U.S.-Middle East Policy, October 1973–1976: Congressional Activism vs. Policy Coherence," pp. 22–44 in John Spanier and Joseph Nogee, (eds.), *Congress, the Presidency and American Foreign Policy*. New York: Pergamon Press (1981).

Rosen, Steven. "A Stable System of Mutual Nuclear Deterrence in the Arab-Israeli Conflict," *American Political Science Review* 6 (December):1367–83 (1977).

———. "Nuclearization and Stability in the Middle East," pp. 157–79 in Onkar Marwah and Ann Schulz (eds.), *Nuclear Proliferation and the Near-Nuclear Countries*. Cambridge, Mass.: Ballinger Publishing Company (1975).

———. *Testing the Treaty of the Military Industrial Complex*. Lexington, Mass.: Heath (1973).

Round Table. "The Case for Nuclear Free Zones," *The Commonwealth Journal for International Affairs* 284 (October): 302–5 (1981).

Rowen, Henry S., and R. Richard Brody. "The Middle East," pp. 204–9 in Joseph A. Yager (ed.), *Non Proliferation and U.S. Foreign Policy*. Washington, D.C.: Brookings Institution (1980).

Russett, Bruce. "Defense Expenditure and National Well-Being," Paper presented at the annual meeting of the International Studies Association, Cincinnati, Ohio, March 24–31 (1982).

———. "The Calculus of Deterrence," pp. 260–76 in William D. Coplin and Charles W. Kegley, Jr. (eds.), *A Multi-Method Introduction to International Politics*. Chicago: Markham Publishing Company (1971).

Sadat, Anwar. *In Search of Identity*. New York: Harper and Row (1978).

Saunders, Harold H. *The Middle East Problem in the 1980's*. Washington, D.C.: American Enterprise Institute (1981).

Schell, Jonathan. "The Abolitions: Defining the Great Predicament," *New Yorker* (January 2):26–75 (1984).

———. *The Fate of the Earth*. New York: Avon Books, (1982).

Schelling, Thomas. "Who Will Have the Bomb?" *International Security* 4, (Summer):75–83 (1976).

———. *Arms and Influence*. New Haven: Yale University Press (1966).

Schmidt, Helmut. *Defense or Relation*. New York: Praeger (1962).

Seven, Steven J. "Nuclearization and Stability in the Middle East," pp. 157–85 in Onkar Marwah and Ann Schulz (eds.), *Nuclear Proliferation and the Near-Nuclear Countries*. Cambridge, Mass.: Ballinger Publishing Company (1975).

Shaker, Mohamed I. *The Nuclear Non-Proliferation Treaty: Origins and Implementations 1959–1979*, vol 2. New York: Oceana Publications (1980).

Al-Shazli, M. F. "Denuclearization of the Middle East and Latin America," *Al-Siyassa Al-Daouliya* 57:42–63 (1983).

Shchyolokova, I. "Nuclear Free Zones: Goal and Content," *International Affairs* (Moscow) 11 (November):104–10 (1981).

Sicherman, Harvey. *The Yom Kippur War: End of Illusion?* Beverly Hills, Calif.: SAGE Publications (1976).

Sivard, Ruth Leger. *World Military and Social Expenditures 1982*. Leesburg, Va.: World Priorities (1982).
———. *World Military and Social Expenditures 1981*. Leesburg, Va.: World Priorities (1981).
———. *World Military and Social Expenditures 1980*. Leesburg, Va.: World Priorities (1980).
Smoke, Richard. *War: Controlling Escalation*. Cambridge, Mass.: Harvard University Press (1977).
Snyder, Glen. "The Balance of Power and the Balance of Terror," pp. 114–26 in Dean G. Pruitt and Richard C. Snyder (eds.), *Theory and Research on the Causes of War*. Englewood Cliffs, N.J.: Prentice-Hall (1969).
Snyder, Jed C. "The Road to Osiraq: Baghdad's Quest for the Bomb," *The Middle East Journal* 37 (Autumn):565–93 (1983).
Spanier, John. *Games Nations Play*. New York: Praeger (1975).
Spanier, John, and Joseph Nogee (eds.). *Congress, the Presidency and American Foreign Policy*. New York: Pergamon Press (1981).
———. *The Politics of Disarmament*. New York: Praeger (1962).
Spence, J. E. "The Republic of South Africa: Proliferation and the Politics of Outward Movement," pp. 209–39 in Robert M. Lawrence and Joel Larus (eds.), *Nuclear Proliferation Phase II*. Lawrence: University of Kansas Press (1974).
Stanford Arms Control Group. *International Arms Control: Issues and Agreement*. Stanford, Calif.: Stanford University Press (1976).
Stanley Foundation. *Non-Proliferation: The 1980's*. Muscatine, Iowa: The Stanley Foundation (1980).
———. *Nuclear Weapon Free Zones*. Muscatine, Iowa: Stanley Foundation (1975).
Stegenga, James A. "The Immortality of Nuclear Deterrency," *International Studies Notes*. Bemidji, Minn.: Bemidji State University (1983).
Stockholm International Peace Research Institute. *SIPRI Yearbook 1983: World Armament and Disarmament*. New York: Taylor and Francis (1983).
———. "Nuclear-Weapon-Free Zones," pp. 297–306 in *SIPRI Yearbook 1976: World Armaments and Disarmament* (1976).
Strange, Susan. "Regime Analysis in the Study of International Political Economy: A Critique," in Charles Kegley and Eugene R. Wittkopf (eds.), *The Global Agenda: Issues and Perspectives*. New York: Random House (1984).
Subrahmanyam, K. "India's Nuclear Policy," pp. 125–49 in Onkar Marwah and Ann Schulz (eds.), *Nuclear Proliferation and the Near-Nuclear Countries*. Cambridge, Mass.: Ballinger Publishing Company (1975).
———. "India: Keeping the Option Open," pp. 112–49 in Robert M. Lawrence and Joel Larus (eds.), *Nuclear Proliferation Phase II*. Lawrence: University of Kansas Press (1974).
Tahtinen, Dale R. *The Arab-Israeli Military Balance since October 1973*. Washington, D.C.: American Enterprise Institute (1974).
Taylor, Theodore B. "Commercial Nuclear Technology and Nuclear Weapon Proliferation," pp. 111–25 in Onkar Marwah and Ann Schulz (eds.), *Nuclear Proliferation and the Near-Nuclear Countries*. Cambridge, Mass.: Ballinger Publishing Company (1975).
Treverton, Gregory F. "The Issue of a Nordic Nuclear Weapon Free Zone: An East-

West Perspective,'' pp. 32–35 in Kari Mottola (ed.), *Nuclear Weapons and Northern Europe*. Helsinki: Finnish Institute of International Affairs (1983).

United Nations. *Common Security: A Blueprint for Survival*. New York: United Nations (1983a).

———. *Status of Multilateral Arms Regulations and Disarmament Agreements*. New York: United Nations (1983b).

———. "Disarmament," *A Periodic Review by the United Nations*. New York: United Nations (1983c).

———. *The United Nations Disarmament Yearbook: Volume 6: 1981*. New York: United Nations (1982a).

———. *Study on Israeli Nuclear Armament, Study Series 6*. New York: United Nations (1982b).

———. *Comprehensive Study on Confidence-Building Measures, Study Series 7*. New York: United Nations (1982c).

———. *Relationship between Disarmament and International Security, Study Series 8*. New York: United Nations (1982d).

———. *The United Nations Disarmament Yearbook, Volume 7: 1982*. New York: United Nations (1982e).

———. *The United Nations Disarmament Yearbook, Volume 5: 1980*. New York: United Nations (1981a).

———. *South Africa's Plan and Capability in the Nuclear Field. Study Series 2*. New York: United Nations (1981b).

———. *Study on All the Aspects of Regional Disarmament, Study Series 3*. New York: United Nations (1981c).

———. *Comprehensive Study on Nuclear Weapons, Study Series 1*. New York: United Nations (1981d).

———. *The United Nations Disarmament Yearbook, Volume 4: 1979*. New York: United Nations (1980).

———. *The United Nations Disarmament Yearbook, Volume 3: 1978*. New York: United Nations (1979).

———. *The United Nations Disarmament Yearbook, Volume 2: 1977*. New York: United Nations (1978).

———. *The United Nations Disarmament Yearbook, Volume 1: 1976*. New York: United Nations (1977).

———. *The United Nations and Disarmament, 1970–1975*. New York: United Nations (1976a).

———. *Comprehensive Study of the Question of Nuclear-Weapon-Free Zones in All Its Aspects*. Special Report of the Conference of the Committee on Disarmament. New York: United Nations (1976b).

———. *The United Nations and Disarmament, 1945–1970*. New York: United Nations (1970a).

U.S. Department of State. *Security and Arms Control: The Search for a More Stable Peace*. Washington, D.C.: Bureau of Public Affairs (1983).

Vaahtoranta, Tapani. "Nuclear Weapons and the Nordic Countries: Nuclear Status and Policies," pp. 53–67 in Kari Mottola (ed.), *Nuclear Weapons and Northern Europe*. Helsinki: Finnish Institute of International Affairs (1983).

Valery, Nicholas. "Israel's Silent Gamble with the Bomb," *New Scientist* 64 (December, 12):809 (1974).

Van Doren, Charles N. "Iraq, Israel and the Middle East Proliferation Problem." Report prepared for the Arms Control Association, Theories of Nuclear Non-Proliferation Policy, Hearing. First Session (June 24):123–67 (1981).

Vayrynen, Raimo. "Military Alliances, Nuclear Deterrence and Nuclear-Weapon-Free Zones," pp. 47–53 in Kari Mottola (ed.), *Nuclear Weapons and Northern Europe*. Helsinki: Finnish Institute of International Affairs (1983).

Vesa, U. "The Revival of Proposals for Nuclear-Free Zones," *Instant Research on Peace and Violence* 5 (January):42–51 (1975).

Von Glahn, Gerhard. *Law among Nations: An Introduction to Public International Law*. New York: Macmillan Company (1965).

Wallace, Michael D. "Arms Races and Escalation," *Journal of Conflict Resolution* 23 (March):3–16 (1979).

Weissman, Steve, and Herbert Krosney. *The Islamic Bomb*. New York: Times Books (1981).

Wiberg, Hakan. "Nuclear-Weapon-Free Zones as a Process: The Nordic Case," pp. 14–23 in Kari Mottola (ed.), *Nuclear Weapons and Northern Europe*. Helsinki: Finnish Institute of International Affairs (1983).

Winkler, Theodor. *Christian Science Monitor* (December 3):17 (1981).

Wittman, George. "Intelligence Forecast: The Persian Gulf in a Nuclear Proliferated World," pp. 50–65 in Lewis Dunn (ed.), *U.S. Defense Planning for a More Proliferated World*. Croton-on-Hudson, N.Y.: Hudson Institute (1979).

Yager, Joseph A., with Ralph T. Mabry, Jr. *International Cooperation in Nuclear Energy*. Washington, D.C.: Brookings Institution (1981).

Yager, Joseph A. (ed.) *Non Proliferation and U.S. Foreign Policy*. Washington, D.C.: Brookings Institution (1980).

Zeigler, David. *War, Peace, and International Politics*. Boston: Little, Brown (1977).

INDEX

116-17 n.11, 117 nn.13–14, 134;
French relations with, 65, 67-71, 72,
80, 83, 87-88 n.1; and heavy water
production, 66, 67, 80; importance to
Middle East NWFZ proposal of, 58,
64-66, 115, 134; influence in US of,
94; inspections of nuclear facilities in,
69, 74, 75, 86; and the International
Atomic Energy Agency, 65, 72, 73-75,
86, 121, 129; makes a Middle East
NWFZ proposal (1980-81), 106-7,
108, 110; missile development in, 83-
85; and the Non-Proliferation Treaty,
27, 65, 71-74, 75, 76, 97-98, 108,
109, 127-28; nuclear capabilities of,
10-11, 104, 108; nuclear policy of, 65,
73, 75-76, 86-87; and the Outer Space
Treaty, 72; and psychological deterrence, 76, 86, 95; regional veto of, 65,
85-86, 87; scientific infrastructure of,
65, 80-81; and South Africa, 70-71;
support for Middle East NWFZ proposal by, 100, 107-9, 110; and Syria,
116 n.4; and the Tlatelolco Treaty,
106; UN condemnation of, 111, 114;
UN studies of, 70, 71, 81, 104, 105,
108; and the United States, 65, 67-74,
78-79, 81-84, 108-9, 111; uranium ac-
quisitions of, 65, 66, 67, 71, 76-80;
use of nuclear weapons by, 93, 106,
126-27. *See also* Arab-Israeli conflict
Israel Atomic Energy Commission, 66-68
Israeli Nuclear Armament (United Nations). *See* United Nations studies
Israeli–South African–Taiwanese consortium, 71
Italy, 46, 77, 107, 109

Jabber, Fuad, 66-67, 77-78, 80-81
Jericho missiles, 71, 81, 83-84
Jervis, Robert, 60-61 n.2
Johnson, Lyndon, 72, 78-79
Jordan, 87, 98, 99, 116 n.2

Kapur, Ashok, 54
Kegley, Charles, 6, 60 n.1
Kekkonen, Urho, 41
Kennan, George, 60-61 n.2

Kennedy, John F., 16
Kfir fighters (Israel), 71, 81, 83
Kiribati, 28 n.1, 51
Kissinger, Henry A., 18, 93
Kodjo, Adam, 49
Korea, 58
Korhonen, Keijo, 117 n.15
Kuwait, 98, 99, 100, 116 nn.2–3

Lahav, Ephraim, 78
Lance missiles, 83-84
Latin America, definition of, 131. *See
also* Tlatelolco, Treaty of; *names of
specific nations*
LAVI (Young Lion) fighters, 82-83
Lebanon, 85, 87, 112, 116 n.2
Leitenberg, Milton, 42, 44
Leventhal, Paul, 77
Libya, 69, 80, 87, 103, 127-28

McNamara, Robert, 78-79
Malaysia, 15
Malvinas/Falkland war (1982), 127
Martenson, J., 117 n.15
Martinique, 22
Mashad, Yehia el-, 104
Mauritania, 99, 132
Mediterranean NWFZ proposal, 45-47,
123, 136 n.2
Meguid, Ahmed Esmat Abdel, 116 n.9
Meir, Golda, 93
Mexico, 21, 26, 27. *See also* Tlatelolco,
Treaty of
Middle East: balance of power in the, 44,
135; definition of, 92, 99, 131-33, 136
n.5; superpowers' views of the, 9
Middle East NWFZ proposal: and the
Arab-Israeli conflicts, 104, 115, 120,
126, 130, 133-34, 135; and arms con-
trol/race, 9, 120, 133-34; and the balance of power, 122, 123; and the
benefits of a NWFZ in the Middle
East, 9-10; Central Europe compared
with, 114; changes needed in, 134-35;
conditions for a, 10-11, 98-99, 113-14,
124- 25, 126-31; critical assessment of,
112-15; and deterrence, 114-15; and
the direct negotiations proposal, 95,

About the Author

MAHMOUD KAREM is Counsellor with the Ministry of Foreign Affairs of Egypt and a member of the Cabinet of the Deputy Prime Minister and Minister of Foreign Affairs. He has served as Egypt's representative to the U.N. Disarmament Committee since 1977 and has represented his country in numerous international conferences on disarmament and nonproliferation. Dr. Karem is also Assistant Professor of Political Science at the American University in Cairo. His articles have appeared in publications in the United States and abroad.